Finding Love That Lasts

Finding Love That Lasts

Breaking the Pattern of Dead End Relationships

Vera Sonja Maass

ROWMAN & LITTLEFIELD PUBLISHERS, INC.
Lanham • Boulder • New York • Toronto • Plymouth, UK

Published by Rowman & Littlefield Publishers, Inc.
A wholly owned subsidiary of The Rowman & Littlefield Publishing Group, Inc.
4501 Forbes Boulevard, Suite 200, Lanham, Maryland 20706
http://www.rowmanlittlefield.com

10 Thornbury Road, Plymouth PL6 7PP, United Kingdom

Copyright © 2012 by Rowman & Littlefield Publishers, Inc.

All rights reserved. No part of this book may be reproduced in any form or by any electronic or mechanical means, including information storage and retrieval systems, without written permission from the publisher, except by a reviewer who may quote passages in a review.

British Library Cataloguing in Publication Information Available

Library of Congress Cataloging-in-Publication Data

Maass, Vera Sonja.
  Finding love that lasts : breaking the pattern of dead end relationships / Vera Sonja Maass.
    p. cm.
  Includes bibliographical references and index.
  ISBN 978-1-4422-1278-7 (cloth : alk. paper) — ISBN 978-1-4422-1280-0 (electronic)
  1. Love. 2. Interpersonal relations. I. Title.
  BF575.L8M223 2011
  158.2—dc23   2011043770

∞™ The paper used in this publication meets the minimum requirements of American National Standard for Information Sciences—Permanence of Paper for Printed Library Materials, ANSI/NISO Z39.48-1992. Printed in the United States of America

Contents

Preface		vii
Acknowledgments		ix
1	The Path of the Repeatedly Single	1
2	Journeys Following Old Road Maps	27
3	If Honesty Is an Issue	53
4	In the Name of Love	75
5	Know Thyself	99
6	Know the Other	125
7	New Horizons—New Commitments	151
Notes		175
Bibliography		185
Index		191
About the Author		195

Preface

The idea for this book came from conducting personal growth workshops for the general public with the title "Single Again"—a topic that has intrigued people for a long time. Why is it that so many people find themselves repeatedly single when they long for the perfect soul mate with whom to share their lives?

Male and female participants in the workshops were of different ages and came from a variety of backgrounds, with one characteristic in common: to find a life companion for a meaningful, intimate, and satisfying relationship, someone to share the journey of their lives.

Psychological and sociopsychological theories lend the framework within which the various topics of this book are discussed. When appropriate, relevant research findings are incorporated into the general text. The participants of the Single Again groups are not the only ones whose stories are told in these pages; they are joined by individuals engaged in counseling or therapy, people from the community at large, and in a few instances individuals known from the public domain.

This book is not primarily about saving or improving ongoing relationships, although it can be helpful there, too; rather it is a book about preventing the often unfortunate combinations of partners deciding to commit to each other for significant parts of their lives. Determined to find the perfect partner, individuals' vision or perception is less than accurate when blinded by emotions, expectations, or wishful thinking. As a result of making decisions based on incomplete information about themselves and about the significant other, people may find themselves once again at the end of what seemed to be a promising relationship.

Finding Love That Lasts explores the various ways people tend to repeat past mistakes, perhaps due to certain personality traits or because they are controlled by forces from the past and engage in actions that exert negative influences on current and future partnerships. The book will highlight some of the pitfalls inherent in blindly and steadfastly believing in the magical forces of love for explaining, curing, and blessing everything, even while behind the smiling façade of love lurk disappointment and pain. Maintaining awareness of one's wishes, desires, habits, attitudes, and many other characteristics, such as the signals one sends out to others that impact interactions in romantic relationships, provides the basis for learning to navigate future relationships. But the learning experience would not be complete without exploring as much as possible the personality characteristics, thoughts and beliefs, and behaviors of a prospective partner before making a serious commitment to that person.

Finally, what form should that commitment take? There are many different types of commitment and often two partners may not even know if they are agreeing to the same commitment; they just assume they do because that is what they expect.

The time has come to dispel the notion that "love is blind" or that it presents this mysterious force that suddenly strikes some innocent individuals and robs them of the power of judgment. The ingredients for a happy ending include the wisdom of knowing oneself, the willingness to face any prospective partner with open eyes, and an inquiring mind about the other person—as illustrated by some of the book's case histories, which have come from clients engaged in therapy, from the participants in the Single Again group, from volunteers in the community at large, and from advice seekers in newspaper columns. To protect their privacy their names and other details have been changed.

Acknowledgments

My special thanks are deserved by the brave members of the Single Again groups for their willingness to share their experiences with the general public. Similarly, to clients from therapeutic settings and those individuals from the community at large who graciously consented to disclose their past experiences as well as their hopes for the future goes my sincere gratitude. Although their true identities remain hidden, their voices speak openly from the pages of this book.

Finally, I want to express my appreciation to all those courageous people who turn to advice-seeking columns in the newspapers for help with their individual relationship-related struggles. By exposing their difficulties to the public eye, they are presenting the rest of us with a real-life picture of our society—thank you all and please continue with your communication efforts.

Last but certainly not least, my thanks go to senior acquisitions editor Suzanne I. Staszak-Silva for supporting the message of this book and to Melissa McNitt, associate editor, production, for her careful attention to all the details during the production phase of the book.

· 1 ·

The Path of the Repeatedly Single

She's been here before; the feeling is familiar, and so are the words. "I like being with you, but I am not ready to make a commitment at this time," Bob said as he turned toward the door—or was it Ted about a year ago? Her eyes were burning from unwept tears when the words registered in her mind. The sound of the door falling shut released a cry from her chest. "No, no, not again!" she sobbed as she let herself fall onto the sofa.

This scenario could be taken from a television soap opera, yet it sounds familiar to many single people. It is becoming one of the big contradictions of our time. Books and media sources proclaim that enjoying healthy, long lives depends on developing and strengthening bonds with others and connecting to them in meaningful ways. Studies consistently report that a happy marriage is the strongest buffer against illness. Married persons not only live longer lives, they appear to be in better physical and mental condition than those who are unmarried.

With those benefits reportedly inherent in the institution of marriage, it would be expected that everyone would want to get married and stay married. But statistics show that the marriage rate in 2005 was 3.6 (per 1,000 people), the lowest since 1990, and 46 percent of all marriages in 2008 involved remarriage for one or both spouses, pointing to an estimate that as of 2008, 40 percent of all marriages have ended in divorce. On the average, first marriages that end in divorce seem to last for a period of about eight years. According to *The State of Our Unions 2005*, a report issued by the National Marriage Project at Rutgers University, 8.1 percent of coupled households consist of unmarried heterosexual partners, further stipulating that only 63 percent of American children grow up with both biological parents. This is the lowest figure in the Western world.[1]

It seems that the number of people living alone now is higher than in the past and not only because there are more people living now. The important distinction to make here is that it is not the marital status per se but rather the quality of the marriage that represents the link to longer and healthier lives. The degree of *happiness* seems to be the determining factor. Presumably, the understanding and support that the partners extend toward each other function as balancing factors that defuse stresses experienced outside the marriage. "It's not marriage that makes you happy; it's happy marriage that makes you happy," a Harvard psychology researcher confirmed at the 2010 American Psychological Association convention. The quality of social relationships is the best predictor of human happiness. "Marriage seems to buy people a decade or more of happiness."[2]

Without those important ingredients, American society becomes what Barbara Dafoe Whitehead called *The Divorce Culture*: "Divorce is now part of everyday American life. . . . As a consequence of the sharp and sustained rise, divorce moved from the margins to the mainstream of American life in the space of three decades." It was not until the first sixty years of the twentieth century that divorce became a more common occurrence in American social history. After 1960 the divorce rate accelerated; it doubled in a decade's time, and stabilized at the highest level among advanced Western societies.[3]

The divorce rate, usually cited as about 50 percent, was in decline in the United States in 2009, but so was the marriage rate. Furthermore, there has been a dramatic increase in the proportion of cohabiting couples, people deciding to live together without being legally married. Cohabitation has been shown to be associated with higher divorce rates and as a study indicated, divorce-prone couples tend to first cohabit and a number of them do not proceed to marriage. This finding leads to the conclusion that without cohabitation, the divorce rate would be higher.[4]

Canadian researchers, focusing on the aspect of repartnering, have found that at five years after first union disruption about 42 percent of women and 54 percent of men had formed new partnerships. The most prevalent choice for repartnering was cohabitation. In addition it was found that second union formation occurred more rapidly for previously cohabiting than for divorced individuals. Not surprisingly, men have a higher rate than women in second union formation. Canadian statistics reported that cohabiting union disruption was twice as high as the divorce rate among young Canadians. Considering the high nonmarital and marital union dissolution rates, repartnering can be expected to become a regular life experience for many.[5]

While it is possible to obtain statistics regarding the number of marriages and divorces, as well as selected data about people who cohabit and either get married or break up at a future point, information about the number of "unofficial" breakups people go through before getting married, forming a cohabiting union, or deciding to fly solo for the remainder of their lives is harder to obtain. Although less talked about, these unofficial breakups can be just as painful to experience as are divorces or separations after having shared bed and living space with a significant other for a period of time. For the purpose of this book, equal attention will be given to the experiences and trauma of relationship dissolution regardless of whether they had been legally sanctioned unions, privately agreed-upon living arrangements, or serious dating relationships.

DOUBLE STANDARD: CELEBRITIES AND THE GENERAL POPULATION

No movie cameras were rolling when movie star Adam X kissed leading lady Barbara Y in a passionate embrace. Only one lucky paparazzo caught the scene on film to be sold to the highest-bidding tabloid press and to be read a little later by movie star Eve Z, Adam's wife, who did not accompany her husband on location and instead stayed in their beautiful home at the ocean, tending to their adorable infant twin daughters.

Stories like the above can be found almost daily in the tabloid media. Fans of some movie stars have a difficult time keeping up with the list of past, present, and future spouses or companions of their idols. Some names may come to mind, for example, when reading about a movie star like Mia Farrow a few decades ago—names like André Previn, Frank Sinatra, and Woody Allen—but were there others? Current movie stars seem to assemble lists of ex-spouses just as long or longer than those older ones but in a shorter period of time. Spouse exchanges of the rich and famous—from Mia Farrow to Tiger Woods—are frequently reported in popular magazines.

The "man who funded the movement that made 'family values' a watchword of the right and badly damaged the Clinton presidency" was suspected by his then wife, Margaret Ritchie Rhea Battle Scaife, to be committing adultery, according to a story in *Vanity Fair* magazine. Apparently it would not have been the first time because Margaret and Richard Mellon Scaife had started their relationship while both were still married to other spouses. The private investigator hired by Margaret confirmed her suspicion as "he took pictures showing the reclusive 75-year-old billionaire with a woman named Tammy Vasco, a tall, blonde 43-year-old whose criminal history includes two arrests for prostitution. The pair was photographed at Doug's Motel, a roadside establishment near Pittsburgh, where rooms rent for $49 a night, or $31 for three hours." Perhaps the setting was not something we normally expect to find the rich and famous in, but saving money may just be one of many roads to becoming a billionaire.[6]

In our Western culture, we seem to operate under a double standard. With the rich and famous we expect to hear about frequent divorces and relationship dissolutions, but in personal lives individuals still maintain the idea of sharing all with one special person. It is not callousness that makes people read in the tabloids without great emotional reaction—or even surprise—that Star X and Star Y who have been married less than a year were seen in romantic or even compromising situations with third, fourth, or fifth persons of celebrity status. It is understood and even expected that those admired and often envied celebrities not only lead glamorous lives, they encounter frequent temptations that most other people do not have to face.

When our friends or relatives mention the word *divorce*, we may respond with "I didn't know you and your spouse were experiencing trouble; have you considered marriage counseling? How are your children responding to your breaking up?" Upon hearing about movie stars breaking up and forming new relationships we understand that those passionate kisses and embraces with the current leading lady or leading man—all in the line of work—are just too tempting for anyone to resist. And when we read that the financial giant is trading his spouse for younger and younger versions as he gets older and older, we are not surprised. We don't wonder whether the rich and famous have considered marriage counseling to keep the family together or how their children will be affected. Opportunities and financial resources that make switching partners trouble-free exchanges are usually less plentiful for members of the general population. And, overall, people appreciate this difference because divorces are costly emotionally and financially. Furthermore, for those fortunate enough to have found the person with whom to spend the rest of their lives in blissful harmony, life is less complicated.

"It's a dream," you say? Perhaps so, especially for those who do not know themselves well enough and therefore are at a loss when it comes to recognizing the persons they would be compatible with. In fact, many people who are facing the condition of being single for the first time, or repeatedly, are not well prepared for living in a coupled situation before they make the next, often hasty, commitment. Consequently, there are men and women who face the trauma of divorce or breakup of an intimate relationship several times in their lives. New unions that started with great expectations of happiness disintegrate into separation or divorce after a few years only to be followed by the search for another, hopefully better match full of new promises that will fade into yet another divorce or separation. But does it have to be this way?

Are people doomed to make the same mistakes over and over again or can they learn from their experiences?

REASONS FOR STAYING TOGETHER—REWARDS OR BARRIERS?

Over several decades researchers have focused on the constructs of rewards, barriers, and alternatives to study marital cohesion. Rewards include the positive consequences connected with being in a given relationship, such as companionship, assistance in task completion, sex, and many other positive experiences. Barriers involve psychological, moral, societal, and legal forces that restrain people from leaving a relationship. Alternatives are generally seen as the temptations associated with desirable potential partners outside the marriage or permanent relationship. The wish to be by oneself rather than remaining in the relationship can also be included in the construct alternatives.

The construct of rewards is also a main ingredient in social exchange theory approaches to relationships. Making a relationship attractive or rewarding is a function of the positive consequences one receives in that relationship minus the costs of maintaining the relationship. It basically goes back to an equation of gains and losses. A proposed model of courtship relationships where decisions to enter into marriage are largely determined by the perceived costs and benefits of the marriage remains equally relevant for decisions on whether to remain in the marriage.[7]

To answer the question "What are the most important factors keeping your marriage together?" two researchers in the field of sociology used national, longitudinal data to obtain people's open-ended responses to that question. As a next step in the study, the researchers coded the responses into categories reflecting the constructs rewards, barriers, and alternatives and looked for links between them and the odds of divorcing in subsequent years.

The responses indicated that most people (74 percent) thought in terms of rewards when discussing their marriages. A very small percentage (about 1 percent) fell into the alternatives category. In addition to rewards some individuals mentioned barriers as factors that kept their marriages together. Overall, the most frequently mentioned barriers to divorce were children and religion.

The study showed that the most common factors that people see as keeping their marriages together are in the rewards category, such as love, respect, friendship, and communication; barriers to divorce were less often mentioned as keeping the marriage intact. Thus, significantly more people evaluated their marriages in terms of rewards than in terms of barriers to divorce.[8]

SEARCHING FOR FACTORS CONTRIBUTING TO RELATIONSHIP DISSOLUTION

Attempting to determine why some relationships last a lifetime and others are terminated because one or both partners become disenchanted and dissatisfied, researchers in the field of marital and family relationships have looked at various factors that are associated with relationship satisfaction. Determinants of relationship separation and divorce, in addition to those factors relevant to durability of relationships, have been investigated from different aspects.

An impressive amount of research is available on the topic of cohabitation and the effects of premarital cohabitation on marital satisfaction and marital stability. Cohabitation has become a common phenomenon in many parts of the world, including the United States. In the two decades between 1977 and 1997, cohabitation in the United States had increased by more than 3.5 million couples and the 2000 Census revealed that 5.5 million couples were cohabiting.[9]

A study investigating the links between premarital cohabitation and marital quality and stability and exploring whether the associations between cohabitation and marital quality and stability have changed across generations used a sample of 1,425 spouses in two U.S. marriage cohorts: those married between 1964 and 1980 (cohabitation was less common then) and those married between 1981 and 1997. It was found that spouses in both cohorts who cohabited prior to marriage reported poorer marital quality and greater marital instability than those who did not cohabit. The researchers concluded that their findings were consistent with the experience of cohabitation perspective, which indicates little evidence that the negative consequences of cohabitation dissipated over time as cohabitation became more prevalent in U.S. society.[10]

The list of stated reasons for cohabiting is long; some see it as a trial period for marriage, others stress the economic advantages when exchanging the costs and maintenance for two residences to just one, and still others consider the reduced complications of breaking up a cohabiting relationship instead of a legal marriage. And many of those reasons have the ring of logic to them. But whatever the stated reason for deciding to cohabit, some research has shown that live-in partners who marry within one to two years of moving in together amount to a relatively small percentage of cohabitors.[11]

In cohabitation, probably more so than in marriage, people do not always express their expectations clearly because their expectations may not be well formulated yet or they may be afraid that an open expression of what they want will scare away their partners. Or they might take it for granted that everyone's expectations are similar to their own and therefore detailed discussions are not needed. However, cohabiting situations may present more space and occasions for unexpressed expectations than marriages.[12]

Different conceptual models regarding the path from the beginning of the relationship to the development of relationship distress have evolved. For instance, the enduring dynamics model explains marital distress as the result of problems that existed from the beginning of the marriage. These problems may derive from different sources, such as personality traits or problematic interaction styles, but whatever their source, they were in existence from the start, even during the courtship phase.

On the other hand, both the disillusionment model, focusing on decrease of positive aspects, and the emergent distress model, emphasizing increasing negative aspects, propose that marital distress is the result of changes in marital functioning. Usually, at the beginning of their relationship, spouses have idealized pictures of their partners and the relationship. At this time of their union they express affection freely and frequently and seem to agree on most important decisions. Over time, their view of each other and the relationship becomes more realistic. Differences in attitudes and limitations in the partner are not overlooked as easily as they were at the start of the relationship.[13]

The applicability of the three models was tested in a study with 146 newlywed couples in first marriages. The couples provided information at the beginning of their marriage and in at least one of two follow-up assessments over the first two years of marriage. The outcome variables were determined as marital stability, timing of divorce, and level of marital satisfaction at thirteen years. It was found that marital stability was consistent with the disillusionment model. Changes in love, responsiveness, affectionate acts, and ambivalence distinguished couples in the still married group from couples in the divorced group more clearly at the two-year point in marriage than at the beginning of marriage.

Considering the timing of the divorce, couples with early divorces (at between two and seven years of marriage) were different from those with late divorces (between seven and thirteen years of marriage) by values of love and responsiveness more so after two years of marriage than at the beginning, thus being congruent with the enduring dynamics model. Regarding the variable of marital satisfaction, the findings again were consistent with the enduring dynamics model as spouses from happily married couples were better distinguished from unhappily married couples by values of love, responsiveness, and ambivalence at the beginning of the marriage than by changes in these values over the first two years of marriage.[14]

Determination of the factors that facilitate the prediction of the timing of separation and those of marital satisfaction had been the goal of an eight-year prospective longitudinal study. Beginning with a sample of 522 couples at one year after marriage and followed by eight annual assessments, the investigator reported that only 130 couples were left over the course of the study to provide complete sets of data; 111 couples had withdrawn, 154 couples were dropped from the study due to insufficient participation, and 127 couples had separated.

Over the course of the study various categories of measures were used. Demographic variables for year one included personal characteristics, divorce history, and child-related status. For years one through four, variables of individual differences included factors such as love for partner, liking of partner, trust, and psychological distress. Measures of marital satisfaction were assessed for year eight.

The results of this study indicated that psychological distress might have predictive value with regard to the timing of the spouses' separation but not for the existence of long-term marital satisfaction. Neither could long-term satisfaction be predicted on the initial level of the affection factors love, liking, and trust alone. It turned out that *both* initial level and rate of change of these factors were needed to account for variability in spouses' later marital satisfaction. These findings are not consistent with the enduring dynamics model, which would suggest that the initial level of these variables is important in predicting long-term marital happiness. As suggested by the investigator, for the factors of love, liking, and trust, the enduring dynamics model and the disillusionment model may operate in complementary rather than mutually exclusive ways.[15]

The disillusionment model seems relevant to the findings of another study. Although it is widely believed that one of the primary reasons for people to get married is to raise children, it is not a guarantee for happiness. As a meta-analysis of longitudinal data revealed, parents report lower marital satisfaction than married nonparents, and there is a significant negative correlation between marital satisfaction and number of children. In other words, marital satisfaction drops as the number of children grows. Furthermore, the greatest difference in marital dissatisfaction has been found in mothers of infants when compared to childless married women. The age levels of the children did not seem to make a difference to the married men in the study. Another finding was that stronger negative effects of parenthood on marital satisfaction were reported among high socioeconomic groups and younger birth cohorts. The researchers interpreted the data to suggest that marital satisfaction decreases after the birth of a child due to role conflicts and restriction of freedom, which would qualify as a decrease in positive aspects as described in the disillusionment model above.[16]

Attempts to fit situations as complex as marital relationships into one or another conceptual model automatically lead to oversimplification and even trivialization because of the multitude of factors that cannot be known and controlled in actual life situations. Although officially the spouses' wedding day marks the beginning of their marriage, influences from experiences prior to the wedding, such as interactions during the couple's courtship phase, impact the state of affairs at the "official" initial level of the marriage.

THE SLEEPING BEAUTY PATTERN

Vickie and Larry became friends in medical school. They met in several of their classes and were equally exposed to the pressures and demands that rule the lives of most medical students. At the time they both had different dating partners. And over a quick cup of coffee they would confide in each other about the difficulties of dating partners who did not have an understanding for the high stress placed on successful medical students. Perhaps the lack of understanding in their dating partners created a common bond between Vickie and Larry. They decided to date each other, which proved much more convenient than their previous dating patterns. Marriage seemed a logical step considering their similar goals and they became engaged. However, Larry held strong religious beliefs and insisted on maintaining his technically virginal state until their wedding night. Vickie would have preferred a more complete sexual relationship but Larry was steadfast in his beliefs.

Shortly after their engagement their relationship seemed to become less romantic; they blamed the stress of completing medical school for the deterioration of their feelings. Both Vickie and Larry considered themselves determined to finish what they had started; they successfully completed their studies and got married. The wedding night and the ensuing honeymoon period were a disaster. Instead of being pleasurable, sexual intercourse proved to be a challenge Larry could not master. His anxiety over the expected performance was so high that his first attempt resulted in premature ejaculation. Vickie could not hide her disappointment, which increased Larry's level of anxiety. In retrospect, Vickie thought that, combined with Larry's earlier reluctance to engage in sexual intercourse before marriage, his current impairment of premature ejaculation were signs of either his lack of sexual desire or a lack of desire for her.

Vickie and Larry did not know how to handle the situation. During the time of their dating and engagement, they had been more concerned with the completion of their studies and the likelihood that their residency requirements would keep them in the same general geographical area so that they would not have to embark on a long-distance relationship. Precious little, if any, time was spent in discussion regarding their future as a married couple. What did they expect to give and to get in this union? How would the mundane daily maintenance chores be divided? They had no idea. Both sets of parents were married; that should be sufficient for a model. The two young people could be compared to the heroine in the fairy tale *Sleeping Beauty*. They were in a deep sleep in regard to everyday marital life with their concerns about their professional life functioning like the growing hedge around the castle in the fairy tale. Putting this case history in context with the conceptual models of relationship development discussed earlier, Vickie and Larry would fall into the enduring dynamics model—even though they did not think much about any of their individual dynamics.

Larry achieved the more prestigious residency placement, so Vickie had to find something suitable in the same general area. She did not like the geographical distance to her parents and the friends of her childhood and she was not excited about her own residency placement. But they decided it was more important for them to be together than for both to be individually satisfied with the situation. It did not take long for negative feelings to develop, especially in Vickie but a little later also in Larry. They embarked upon a style of arguing from which it was difficult to recover their originally positive feelings for each other.

Under those circumstances their sexual relationship did not improve and Vickie announced she had no desire for sex anymore. Six years later when they finally sought professional help, they were unable to modify their style of arguing to the point where they could actually listen to each other. Most of their verbal interactions transpired in an atmosphere of defense and accusation or one of them—usually Vickie—left the argument by remaining silent. Her silence, however, spoke louder than any words.

It is expected in our culture that people spend years in study and preparation for a given profession or a trade that will enable them to make enough money to support a family, but precious little is learned about the functioning of families. The dearth of education given to such a significant part of peoples' lives is scary. Although some churches provide education on the topic of married life to their young parishioners planning marriage, it is but a tiny drop in the big bucket of need. Today there is probably more information and education available about the sexual aspects of married life than there is about other, equally important, parts.

How do people learn about intimate relationships? Parents can serve as models to follow, or examples of what not to do. Some believe that insight into coupled life will come "naturally." People often spend more time and effort finding somebody to pair up with than on investigating what type of person they would be compatible with. Of course, before they can look for compatibility with others, individuals would have to know themselves intimately. Many, however, accept themselves as a "given," something that exists and does not require further exploration.

This book is not primarily about relationships and how to improve them. Books with recipes for relationship enhancement are available on the market. This book is about individuals—men and women—who have experienced the pain that accompanies the dissolution of intimate relationships. Their situations are past the point of fixing, affairs that have reached the point of no return. While confronted with the pain of lost dreams and hopes, these individuals do not function in a vacuum; their lives have been and most likely will be again spent in relationships, in meaningful or intimate interactions with others. For those courageous individuals who are willing to dry their tears and start living and searching again, this book is meant to help them apply the lessons learned from past imperfect choices to the challenges of the future. An inward focus on individuals, their wishes, goals, and desires, their skills, talents, and abilities, will provide them with important knowledge of themselves as persons and will enhance their facility for recognizing compatibility between themselves and any prospective partners.

A MATTER OF CHEMISTRY

Gregory looked back on a history of brief romances following his divorce from Lynn, his first wife. Gregory's collection of photographs of these ladies seemed to indicate that Gregory had dated several sisters of the same family. Like his ex-wife, Lynn, they all had straight blond hair and blue or gray eyes. Some of them smiled, others looked more serious, but overall, they bore a strong resemblance to one another. Gregory's explanation was that he had felt this strong chemistry between each of them and himself. "What's the use in dating someone when the 'chemistry' isn't there," he added.

When people think about what they call the chemistry in relationships, their thoughts may reveal that they tend to be attracted to partners who are similar in personality and behavior; that is, present partners may have characteristics similar to previous partners. Generally, people don't question the basic foundations of that chemistry and they don't recognize the risks of giving in to that chemistry again after it blew away in the previous relationship. If the same "fatal attraction" seems to be operating, individuals might want to find out why they feel drawn to this particular type of lover and how they can become cognizant of the messages and signals emanating from this individual. Unless they are exploring the meaning of those signals, they may find themselves repeatedly attracted to the charming, hard-to-catch, and even harder-to-keep lover, hoping that they are the person with the magic touch that will make the difference in turning this elusive individual into a devoted and committed permanent partner. Wishful thinking may cloud people's view and cause them to miss the hazard signs, while at the same time their lover is studying the road map for the next exit. It is good to remember that awareness of the hazards along the road makes for a safer journey.

The reasons for repeating similar relationships and their terminations are many and varied, but the knowledge of the dynamics that lead to those repetitions is basic information that every individual is entitled to obtain. Men and women are not always aware of how much they are controlled by societal expectations about the roles they fulfill and the changes these roles will undergo with the passage of time. As discussed earlier, a strong belief in the necessity of a certain "chemistry" between two people might turn out to be a prominent ingredient in the formula for repeated singlehood.

Although the prevailing opinion is that in general it is easier for men to adapt to the single life, our couple-oriented society still subjects both men and women to the myth that one can only have a complete life as part of a couple. While succumbing to the myth, eagerly searching for the other half, there are ways in which individuals blind themselves. Expecting the search to produce the other half in record time, individuals may neglect or explain away signals that could warn them that they are about to become involved in a relationship that is not going to last as long as they expect. Devoting time in open-eyed pursuit of this important goal would seem an appropriate approach that could save individuals from emotional and financial losses from yet another relationship termination.

THE COSTS AND REWARDS OF RELATIONSHIPS

Additional reasons for the conditions of repeated "singlehood" might be found in the backgrounds and personalities of the participants. Those factors very likely usher in the breakup of the next relationship and the next . . . The end of a relationship may well signal the need for change, not only in the lifestyle of the individual and the current partner, but also in those variables that were instrumental in the breakup. Many individuals consider relationships in terms of costs and rewards, a fluctuating system that impacts the quality of relationships in various ways. If not satisfied, individuals tend to compare in a hypothetical way the rewards received in the current relationship with those possibly—or even probably—available in relationships with other partners. A lack of satisfaction can easily lead to comparisons of the costs involved and rewards gained in relationships with other available lovers. In making or maintaining commitments, "individuals compare the rewards coming from the partner with the expenditures made by the individuals themselves. 'Do I get my fair share for my investment?' is the comparison in commitment."[17]

As giving and taking are expressions of character traits, what personality traits would be compatible in different individuals for the prediction of a harmonious relationship? It takes courage to ask oneself, "What behaviors might have alienated my partner to the point of no return?" "Were these behaviors one-time occurrences or did any one of them take on the status of a habit, an annoying habit?" Questioning oneself in this way and applying the answers to future behaviors would turn the recent relationship dissolution into a learning experience.

WHO IS TO BLAME?

Questioning oneself in this way is painful; it would be so much easier to focus on the annoying habits and shortcomings of the other person, especially when still in the powerful grip of anger. In her book *Mindfulness*, psychologist Ellen Langer discusses research on divorce that she and a colleague had conducted. They found that divorced people who blamed their ex-spouses for the failure of their marriages suffered for longer periods of time than those divorced people who explored within themselves possible reasons that might have contributed to their situation. Langer explained that by looking at just one set of criteria as the source of our troubles, we narrow our focus and limit our own choices. "Such mindless attributions narrowly limit the range of solutions we might seek." In such a state of mindlessness our control is limited insofar as we are preventing ourselves from making intelligent choices.[18]

Achieving awareness or mindfulness about personality characteristics that might be detrimental to the development and maintenance of satisfying companionship provides individuals with an opportunity for change as well as for redesigning themselves. As the range of solutions expands in our mind, we improve our ability to make sensible choices. If the establishment of meaningful relationships is the goal, why persist in maintaining personality patterns that promise repeated failures? The effects of personality factors will be explored in greater detail later in this book.

A different conception of divorce, one that considers divorce an individual right as well as a psychological resource, has been suggested. The dissolution of marriage can be seen as an opportunity to make oneself over from the inside out. The acquisition of certain valuable psychological competencies would allow individuals to express themselves in a different light.[19] This idea of divorce—or any other relationship dissolution for that matter—is a tempting one, but one that too few people entertain seriously. Perhaps it appears overwhelmingly complicated. People may ask, "With every relationship breakup do I need to become a completely different person? Wouldn't it be much easier to just find a different partner for a while?"

Of course, that sounds like a good recipe for another go-around on the repeatedly single path—finding another partner for a while until incompatible personality traits become disturbing to the harmony of the new romantic partnership. The impact of various personality traits on relationships is such a significant aspect in the development and maintenance of repeatedly single lifestyles that it will be discussed in greater detail in chapters 5 and 6.

THE DON JUAN SYNDROME

When thinking about individuals who enter and exit romantic relationships frequently, most people automatically link this phenomenon to historical accounts they have heard about the innumerable sexual conquests of Don Juan or the eighteenth-century Italian adventurer Giovanni Casanova, who were determined to spread joy and happiness (and sometimes diseases too) among the female population. Generally, men are expected to be interested in a variety of sexual partners without deep emotional investment—just for the thrill of having different experiences. And it is said that women are supposedly monogamous by nature, while men are not. Some women may fail to accept this notion as a law of nature and terminate their relationship with philandering men and look for at least one more man who is less intent on sharing with many others.

The topic of infidelity has received widespread interest but research on this issue has been hampered by the general lack of agreement as to what constitutes infidelity; is it applied to married couples only or does it include dating partners? Does it only involve sexual intercourse outside two primary partners or does it include kissing, fondling, or oral sex with a person outside a particular dyadic relationship, and is engaging in flirting behaviors or romantic thoughts about someone else regarded as being unfaithful? And what about cybersex and romantic Internet involvements? Although clear and well-defined agreement on the issue is difficult to obtain, most people seem to regard betrayal of sexual exclusivity in marriage as a more serious transgression than dating infidelity.

Reviews of the sex research literature have revealed some interesting observations, although most of the studies involved college students and therefore caution is advised in applying the findings to the general public. An interesting but expected difference was found between individuals who had actually engaged in infidelity and those who were asked to imagine their reactions to doing so. Higher levels of anticipated distress and remorse were reported by those who had only imagined their own betrayal of a dating partner than by the individuals who *had actually* been unfaithful to their partners. The actual unfaithful persons apparently had responded to the need to justify their deeds or reduce their level of cognitive dissonance by minimizing the impact of their actions.

The search to identify one aspect of dating infidelity that would be of great interest to many—the question about potential predictors of unfaithfulness and betrayal—has not revealed promising results so far. Variables studied in connection with prediction of infidelity have included religiosity, personality type, love style, and sexuality-related attitudes. As would be expected, sexually permissive attitudes in a person might serve a predictive function, but less clear has been the association with individuals' religious beliefs and practices. Self-rated importance of religion and frequency of church attendance were negatively linked to prediction of infidelity for women, but not for men. Overall, accepting attitudes toward sexual permissiveness and earlier initiation of sexual intercourse are predictive of infidelity and men were more likely to express an interest in extra-dyadic involvement than were women.[20]

Explorations of various personality traits in connection with infidelity showed that persons who admitted having been unfaithful scored higher on the characteristics of extroversion and openness but lower on conscientiousness than those who reportedly had not betrayed their primary partners. Other researchers found that individuals admitting to having been unfaithful scored higher on measures of neuroticism and lower on agreeableness than their more faithful counterparts. Additionally, personality factors may have an impact on the types of motives ascribed to acts of infidelity. For instance, relationship dissatisfaction as a reason for infidelity was likely to be used by extroverted individuals and by women. Neuroticism, on the other hand, was linked to neglect as the stated reason for unfaithfulness. Furthermore, insecure attachment styles, personality styles associated with erratic behavior, and tolerant attitudes toward sexual permissiveness seem to interact in influencing a person's likelihood of being unfaithful to a dating partner.

In general, philandering individuals can be quite charming and why wouldn't they? They usually get what they want and enjoy it. They may remind us of curious children, always looking for new adventures, exploring the world around them, and freely sharing their excitement with those they meet more or less fleetingly. On a deeper level, however, the charming curiosity may hide a basic insecurity, a fear of disclosing oneself emotionally, or—equally likely—a mental and emotional laziness. Involvement in a long-term relationship requires a certain amount of ingenuity from both partners to keep the relationship meaningful and interesting. With frequent partner change, the need for investing much effort or creativity into holding the other's attention is reduced because the same old routine behaviors impress the new partner, who has not been exposed to them yet, as novel and exciting. Even supplemental items of courtship, such as flowers, perfume, wine, or chocolates can be the same for each new partner, thereby eliminating the stress of selection and decision making.

Matthew, a married man representing his employer to companies in different towns, knew the value of organizing the delivery of those courtship items. He had standing orders with florists in the towns his business took him to. Similar services from candy stores or wine merchants were easily arranged.

It would be incorrect, however, to ascribe the Don Juan syndrome exclusively to men. There are sufficient female variations that suggest it as a phenomenon found in both sexes, particularly with the arrival of the female chauvinist pig (FCP) movement. These are postfeminist women who are not disturbed by cartoon-like stereotypes of female sexuality. They portray something that traditionally appealed exclusively to men and in the past was offensive to women, but is now embraced and flaunted by those women who want to be different—not like other women, but more like men.[21]

A relationship with a Don Juan type can be likened to a journey that may have a loving, meaningful, permanent connection as the goal for one partner. But while traveling along that path the other one becomes distracted by a landmark or billboard that promises excitement along with highly charged levels of desire and fulfillment. The message on the billboard changes Don Juan's path—as if directed by a malfunctioning compass—and persuades him to leave the highway to the goal he once shared with his partner. Instead, the Don Juan traveler takes the next exit to seek the advertised adventure. And, unbeknownst to the traveler, the exit may have been one of those points in the road without an entry back onto the highway and it may take quite a detour to return to the originally planned route.

THE CASE OF SERIAL MONOGAMY

Serial monogamy, a term that originated in the 1970s, describes a sort of commitment or exclusivity that is generally linked with monogamy. However, this representation of a romantic relationship is usually maintained for a limited time only. In this increasingly popular romantic pattern, people still believe in some moderate form of ideal love, but give up the basic pretense that it should last forever. The relationship can be quite intense and passionate and the beloved may be regarded as unique, but not necessarily for the rest of one's life.[22]

While people hope and behave as if their current romantic relationship will last forever, it often may not amount to more than a dream or wishful thinking. In this case most of them will search for another ideal love and some may even find it; however, this again may be for a limited time. People are taking their monogamous relationship seriously, but some do not necessarily believe that it must also be forever. Those who consider themselves serial monogamists may consider this lifestyle as the ideal one. However, the comments of those who have been associated with lovers who practice the serial monogamy lifestyle reflect the deep emotional pain and disappointment experienced by the "temporary lovers."

A note of caution is advised here: individuals who have difficulty finding compatible partners perhaps don't quite know what to look for; they may enter and leave several relationships during their search. Their situation may be falsely interpreted as that of a serial monogamist and they may even believe it for themselves. As described in the pages of this book, the list of reasons for finding oneself among the repeatedly single is long and complicated because several of the reasons may combine to form an intricate manifestation of the overall situation.

INTIMACY AND HURT FEELINGS

Behaviors are the outward expressions of people's wishes and wants as well as reflections of their personality, their unique character or trait constellation. Behaviors are also the window through which people get to know each other and determine whether they want to enter into an intimate relationship with someone. Thus, there is a benefit to knowing the effects of one's behaviors on those around. Without that awareness, behaviors lose much of the goal-directedness necessary for the fulfillment of individuals' wishes, and their actions take on the characteristics of uncertainty and randomness. Individuals who display vagueness or ambiguity in their interactions with others may find that others avoid them because it evokes discomfort in them. Especially in romantic relationships, people expect a more committed stance from those they consider as partners.

As much as most people want to be part of an intimate relationship, the wish to avoid emotional pain is even stronger. Some theorists consider hurt feelings and the fear of experiencing them to be at the root of our socialization. Often the impetus of friendly outreach behaviors toward others is tempered by a tendency to avoid hurt feelings. And even though the emotional isolation created through this avoidance of personal contact is painful too, by suppressing these feelings, repressing them, or denying them, one can continue on the lonely path without admitting any losses.[23]

Intimate relationships are the arena where hurt feelings can cause the deepest pain. Although hurt feelings can be experienced in response to words or actions of others, such as neighbors, colleagues, or even strangers, individuals are most vulnerable when the hurt comes from the words or behaviors of those they love. The fear of feeling that pain often leads individuals to hide their vulnerability by refusing to disclose their emotional state to the other. They hide behind a façade in order to protect themselves from being hurt. As they remain emotionally closed or distant, they deprive the other person of the opportunity to really know them, and, similarly, the other person may be equally afraid of being emotionally hurt and likely engages in similar hiding maneuvers.

Individuals who are painfully shy may decide that emotional distance and isolation are less difficult to handle than the risk of experiencing emotional pain. Shy people generally feel inferior to others in some way. Shy people's level of anxiety in the presence of others is so high that it seems to overwhelm them. Their attention is focused on the turmoil within themselves and this leaves them unable to concentrate on the interests of those around them. Their self-consciousness keeps them mentally and emotionally isolated in the company of others.

At first it may be difficult to distinguish between a person who appears emotionally distant because he or she chooses this stance out of a need for control or because of suspicion toward others, or because he or she is tormented by anxiety and self-consciousness. Whatever the reason for the apparent aloofness, the damage to an intimate relationship is similar because it leads to a deterioration of contact between the partners, which, in the opinion of one clinical psychologist, is the single most common marital problem. "The painfully common story of modern marriage is of the wasting away of genuine contact until the relationship is only a hollow shell of what it once was, brittle and subject to fracture at the slightest pressure."[24]

SEXUAL INCOMPATIBILITY

Jay, a handsome, intelligent young man, thought he had a normal sex drive when he married Sarah, a highly sexual woman. Frequent physical contact during the dating period seemed natural to him. From his Italian family background Jay was used to ample physical expression of affection. He was used to hugging family members and close friends. However, not every hug resulted in an erection nor was it meant to. What he did not know was that Sarah expected to have sex on a daily basis once they were married. At first it was exciting as well as flattering to him that she couldn't keep her hands off of him, but in time, the excitement took on the characteristics of an obligation and pressure to perform.

In the second year of his marriage he became concerned about the expected frequency of their sexual activities. As a young account executive with a large chemical company he was expected to be available for entertaining out-of-town customers. On those occasions his days were long and stressful and sex was not necessarily foremost on his mind at the end of them. Sarah's high sex drive appeared to be connected to a fear of abandonment. Decreased frequency of sex increased her level of anxiety. She accused Jay of having lost interest in her and not finding her attractive anymore. Jay felt even more pressured and—as can be expected—his sex drive did not improve. Their arguments increased in frequency and degree of animosity. Sarah's pregnancy ended in a miscarriage.

One day Sarah ran into a male coworker from her previous job. The two had been dating briefly but broke off the relationship when Sarah became seriously interested in Jay. Now sparks developed again and Sarah became involved in an affair with Brent. The divorce was quick and uncontested. Although Jay had loved Sarah deeply, he felt frightened by what he believed was the consequence of not being able to match Sarah's sex drive. He had considered his sex drive healthy and normal but now doubts raised their ugly heads. The few friends he confided in thought that Jay had been in an enviable position when he was married to Sarah. To their dismay, their wives were less interested in sex.

Adjustment to being single again was painful. Divorce was a rare occurrence in his family. In addition, Jay's mother was still grieving over the loss of her first grandchild. Now her son was suffering the loss of his love and the disappointment of a failed marriage. Jay felt he had let his parents down. His self-esteem took a beating and he had mixed feelings about entering the dating scene again. He missed the closeness with a female companion but he feared the possibility of another rejection. And most of all, he didn't trust his own judgment. He had interpreted Sarah's readiness for physical intimacy at the beginning of their dating period as love for him, but how could it die so soon? And if it was not love, what was it? Unfortunately, he did not find the answer to the second question.

Eventually, Jay started dating again. Some of his friends arranged blind dates for him. Remembering his disappointment with Sarah, Jay turned to young women with a more reserved attitude about physical intimacy. The eager-to-hug-and-kiss females represented a threat in his mind. In Angela, a tall, blue-eyed brunette, Jay believed he had found an interesting and emotionally stable and compatible companion. Angela did not invite his caresses, but neither did she reject his touches. She had her own way of slowing down his advances, even though he would have liked a bit more passion. After more than half a year of dating, they entered into a sexual relationship and got married.

Jay's friends did not have a reason to envy him; Angela's interest in sex was not greater than that of their wives. Sex was not a frequent item on the menu in Jay's second marriage. After the threat and pressure over not being able to fulfill Sarah's sexual desire, Jay had turned his focus to the opposite, a woman with little interest in sex. He felt safe for a while until his sex drive returned to its previous level. Being uncomfortable with someone at one extreme of the continuum and moving to find someone at the opposite extreme does not guarantee compatibility was the lesson Jay learned.

There are various aspects of sexuality that give rise to incompatible attitudes and behaviors between partners. One of the most frequently encountered is that of sexual desire, the motivation to engage in sexual activities, which may be present to different degrees in partnered individuals. It is generally accepted that women's lower sex drive is biologically determined. However, that does not mean that all women have a sex drive that is significantly lower than that of men. Some women experience hypersexual desire. Furthermore, sexual interest varies not only from individual to individual, but within the same individual as a function of physical conditions, age, as well as physiological or emotional factors.

In the beginning of relationships when people are still infatuated with each other, differences in the levels of sexual desire are not as pronounced; but as time goes on, some of the passion calms down and sexual desire does not remain at its original high level. This is the time when differences in sex drive become more apparent and can lead to conflict, as many marriage and sex therapists can attest to.

SEXUAL CHOICES

"People are happiest when they're having sex and talking, or otherwise investing in social relationships" was the finding in a recent study done by Harvard graduate students. Statements like that would indicate the importance of making good choices when selecting sexual partners.[25]

According to the literature on assortative mating, partners tend to select each other on the basis of similarity along various dimensions. Prior sexual experience constitutes one of these dimensions and the number of sexual intercourse partners in particular seems to be of interest. A sample of 106 couples who were either dating, cohabiting, or married were questioned about the number of sexual intercourse partners they had before their current relationship. With the exception of cohabiting couples, romantic partners matched in the numbers of prior intercourse partners. Among married couples, similar numbers of prior intercourse partners between men and women were linked to higher levels of love, satisfaction, and commitment in the marriage. In other words, the old formula of experienced male and virgin bride does not guarantee marital happiness anymore.[26]

As sexual attraction and sexual activities are significant aspects of married life, they have been given attention in previous research, and the findings that the frequency of marital sex generally declines with the duration of the marriage does not surprise many. And extramarital sex is a frequently cited reason for divorce.[27]

Considering the frequency of sexual activity in marriages within the context of diminishing marginal utility and human capital investment would suggest that initially the frequency of sexual activity between spouses would be high in satisfaction, and with that, sexual activity would increase in frequency. However, the increase of sex tends to reduce the level of satisfaction and the frequency of sexual activity decreases. On the other hand, people make rational choices and marriages are generally thought to be long-term relationships where both partners have incentives for investing specific human capital, such as companionship and sexual pleasures among many other benefits. Thus, the human capital investment functions in slowing down somewhat the rate of declining frequency of sexual activity within the marriage.

As the marital utility of sex with an old partner is lower than that of sex with a new partner, the marital utility keeps declining with marital duration. In addition, for those couples who work harder to keep their sex life stimulating, the investment of the additional effort becomes much greater than the effort involved in sexual activities with a new partner—at least, for a while. In other words, sex with a long-term partner requires an investment greater than the pleasure experienced, while the opposite would be true for investments in the sexual relationship with a new partner.[28]

Another factor figuring into this scenario is the generally accepted notion that physical pleasure in a sexual relationship is more important to men than to women, while for women the emotional attachment is expected to be more important than the physical pleasure in the sexual relationship. Then as a man's extramarital sexual involvement increases over the life of a marriage, the woman's satisfaction is expected to decrease because of the declining emotional attachment she shares with her spouse. Under these circumstances the woman's human capital investment can be expected to decline as she becomes aware of her spouse's interest and involvement with extramarital partners. Her physical and emotional interests will decline, regardless of the duration of the marriage. Most often it is the woman's wish for intimacy that prompts her to engage in sexual actions, but if the wish for intimacy remains unfulfilled in the sexual relationship, her sexual desire will plummet and her human capital investment in the marriage will decrease significantly.[29]

The picture for long-term romantic relationships appears bleak. Long-term romantic relationships require greater investments than the pleasure and satisfaction received for the investment. Is it surprising then that the number of repeatedly single individuals seems to continue to grow as a function of the overall population growth? But there are people who refuse to settle for the seeming inevitability of short-term relationships and reality proves them right, just as it seems to confirm the opposite. For some individuals long-term romantic relationships are achievable because they are willing to forgo the temptations of passionate whirlwind romances and hasty commitments in favor of undergoing a more mature selection process. Achieving what one wants in the end becomes a matter of making educated choices that are in one's best interest.

Sexual satisfaction with the same partner does not have to dwindle with the increasing duration of the relationship. A study conducted of 104 couples in heterosexual relationships lasting on average fourteen and a half years revealed that both male and female participants who openly disclosed more about their sexual likes and dislikes reported greater sexual satisfaction. There was, however, a difference in the effectiveness of verbal sexual self-disclosure for men and women. Although men and women did not differ in the extent to which they had shared their sexual likes and dislikes with their partners, men were more likely than women to adopt verbal sexual self-disclosure as intentional or instrumental actions in sexual situations for achieving greater intimacy or sexual satisfaction. For women, nonverbal communication seems important in achieving their partner's understanding and their own sexual satisfaction.

Certainly, there is room for experimentation about which type of sexual self-disclosure works best for sexual partners in a meaningful relationship. The willingness to communicate is the important factor; withholding feedback about one's sexual likes and dislikes is the surest way of not getting what one wants.

To hear divorcing or divorced individuals discuss their past relationships, one is often amazed by how surprised they seem by what they call changes in their partners from the time they first dated to the dissolution of the relationship. It appears that at the time of the breakup they found out what their partners were really like. Might there be a way to minimize this aspect of surprise? The answer might be part of the question some researchers focused on. They wanted to know if it was possible to predict from the psychological makeup of partners and the way their courtships unfolded whether the couples would be delighted, distressed, or divorced years later. Their answer was "yes, in terms of probabilities but not as a prediction with certitude."[30] The researchers regarded their project as a case study of people who either failed to see the warning signs or who saw them and experienced some misgivings but married in spite of their doubts.

Other researchers, making the case for promoting marriage, stated the basic assumption that marriages and long-term relationships are fashioned in the images of the relationships' partners and are shaped by the opportunities and constraints of the ecological settings in which they are situated. Therefore, the promotion of family health and stability will demand an approach that focuses on the couples' psychological, social, and economic needs.[31]

Based on the study of their participants' courtships, the researchers developed a protocol and compared it to how their marriages turned out nearly fourteen years after they were wed. The protocol defined three prototypical courtship experiences: (1) rocky and turbulent, (2) sweet and nondramatic, and (3) passionate.

Rocky courtships are the ones that give rise to conflict-prone, unhappy, and fragile marriages. Themes operating in rocky courtships include distress over potential rivals, and are characterized by periods of suspicion and anger about giving love to undeserving partners. With the use of standard personality tests, the researchers identified the personality traits individuals in rocky courtships seem to possess and ordered them into the following three categories: lack of conscientiousness, independent-mindedness, and anxiety. For instance, men with an independent temperament are often difficult to keep within the constraint of marriage, while anxiety-prone individuals may remain in their marriages but are unhappy because they are emotionally labile and their moodiness leads to emotional compromises, misunderstandings, and suspicions.

On the other hand, couples who experience *sweet, nondramatic courtships* enjoy each other's company, and they are individuals who are generally helpful and sensitively attuned to others. These individuals' nature is good-hearted, warm, gentle, and understanding. Their relationships run along smoothly and their marriages are likely to endure in a mutually satisfying atmosphere.

The third category of courtships is *passionate courtships*, which are characterized by a sudden plunge into love, almost instantaneous sexual activities, and early progression to marriage. The passion of the individuals involved is rooted more often in the personality of the lover than in the object of that person's love. In the early stages of marriage, individuals representing this courtship category are far more affectionate toward each other than most couples during the first two years of marriage, but with time their passion fizzles.

As stated earlier, marriages and relationships are assumed here to be created partly in the images of the partners and these images will be revealed during courtship, allowing glimpses of the other person that would be helpful in deciding whether a particular prospective lover presents good "marriage material." The levels of love/affection and antagonism in relationships create different emotional climates, such as warm/friendly, tempestuous/stormy, bland/"empty shell," and hostile/distressed.

The data collected by the researchers in the study discussed above made it possible to place each couple in the study within this framework at different intervals: as newlyweds, during the early years of their marriage, and almost fourteen years into their marriage. As a broad generalization, newlyweds are expected to fall into the warm/friendly category of emotional climate. One year into the marriage, average spouses express loving feelings verbally and physically, including sexual intercourse about half as often as when they were first married. Unpleasant interactions do occur with passing time, but in a generally warm climate their sting is less sharp than if they happen between spouses within a hostile/distressed emotional atmosphere.

As the goal of their study was to identify early signs of marital disintegration, the researchers who made the case for promoting marriage focused on the *loss of love and affection* early in the marriage as the primary symptom, signaling the breakup of the marriage soon after the wedding in weak marital bonds or years later if the spouses entered marriage on a romantic high. In general, what sends marriages into a downward spiral seems to be the loss of good feelings rather than emerging conflicts early in marriage.

Among those marriages that were still intact after more than a decade into the study, distinctive emotional climates had been generated at the onset of the marriages, in those marriages that were happy as well as those that were not. The happy couples had created a warm emotional climate early in the marriage and remained there through the ups and downs of their relationship. Emotionally warm and friendly climates are created by the individuals' psychological makeup of being even-tempered and warmhearted as well as low in anxiety.

The researchers called "mixed blessing" marriages those that survive because of a favorable balance between the positive and negative elements in the relationship. Some tempestuous marriages may survive the high drama because the spouses view each other as being difficult but having a heart of gold. Other stable mixed blessing marriages may have an emotionally neutral, almost bland atmosphere.

People's personalities are important; they affect both the dynamics of their courtships and the success of their marriages. Some qualities determine whether people are likely to create a stable, happy marriage while others are effective in keeping the spouses in the marriage. For a stable, happy marriage it is crucial that people know each other well and recognize the qualities in them that create an atmosphere of fondness and admiration. By adulthood people's personality characteristics and social attitudes have become relatively stable entities and careful observation over a significant period of time can provide predictive information about an individual's marriage potential, but people often marry in spite of the evidence that a prospective partner may be unsuitable.[32]

The discussion so far has focused on just some of the reasons for the deterioration and eventual death of intimate relationships. This list is far from complete; additional reasons will be attended to in the following chapters.

After the breakup of a meaningful relationship people's most likely immediate goal is to search for ways to cope with the devastating loss, finding out how to survive that hurt and go on with life. Those issues are important, and while survival is necessary, it is not sufficient for future happiness. It is only a first step on the healing path. Following, and simultaneously with, the healing, a kind of inoculation to safeguard against future recurrences of this emotional injury can take place within a process of exploration and discovery. Except for those individuals who have decided not to enter into an intimate relationship again, the many others, it is hoped, will be brave enough to embark upon a journey of discovery on how to avoid being repeatedly single while wanting desperately to be half of a long-term harmonious and emotionally rewarding partnership.

Following the end of relationships many individuals wake up every morning with the question: "why me?" Another period filled with excitement and hopes for having found the "significant other" with whom to travel on life's journey has come to a premature end. Facing the reality of being single again is too painful for many to endure; drugs and alcohol may work for some in numbing the pain of yet another disappointment. Others may jump into a new relationship at the first opportunity in order to delay the painful reaction. And a delay it usually is because this sort of "cure" is not a lasting one. The quick escape usually ends with greater disappointments and bigger bruises to one's ego. Relationships formed in haste have a low probability for permanence and two rejections in a row can make a dent in the sturdiest of egos.

As the focus of this book is not primarily on how to improve already existing relationships, it is also not on how to recover from the losses of relationship dissolution. There are many excellent books on the market about coping with loss and grief. The main purpose of this book is to explore how different combinations of personality traits and other factors interact to result in unique relationships between two people—good and bad, compatible and incompatible, happy and unhappy. An understanding of how these combinations function in making or breaking romantic unions can benefit those attempting to avoid the pain and disappointment of becoming single once again while desiring to be in a meaningful and long-lasting relationship.

· 2 ·

Journeys Following Old Road Maps

The breakup of a marriage or any other romantic relationship is painful. Understandably, people tend to distract themselves in order to gain relief from the painful feelings; only a masochist would want to wallow in pain. However, by distracting oneself, a person may miss out on gaining valuable information. Investigating the dynamics of a past relationship and focusing on the factors that contributed to the breakup can unearth knowledge about oneself.

Unfortunately—perhaps in an effort to justify their part in the breakup—people instead focus on the faults of the other person involved. Justification and confirmation contribute to one's feeling comfortable about oneself. And because that other person will not be around any longer, people decide to make a fresh start by doing the same things they had done before but now expect different results. Behavior like that is similar to traveling on an outdated road map and expecting to reach a destination that has not been recorded on the old map. This is one way to find oneself single again and again.

COMFORT VERSUS COMPATIBILITY

People frequently report that they felt comfortable with a person they just met and they interpret this as a sign that they must have found their "soul mate," somebody they will be compatible with. It is almost as if they found their "other half." However, comfort does not necessarily assure compatibility. A certain type of comfort can be based on familiarity rather than on compatibility and—with time—familiarity can breed contempt.

There are perfectly logical explanations for why individuals feel familiar or comfortable in interactions with a new person. Most likely, they have previously interacted in similar ways with other significant persons in their life who demonstrated similar behaviors. For many people, relationship styles are first learned from parents and may be modified later through interactions with friends. When becoming aware of feeling instantly comfortable with a new person it would be wise to search one's memory for comparable feelings or similarities that are reminiscent of interactions with another person in the past.

After locating this other person in their memory, individuals might examine their feelings about that past relationship. Did they feel good and did they receive the treatment they wanted in that relationship? Or did the relationship cause them pain and grief? What was gained as a result of their involvement in this relationship? What was lost? How did the relationship end? Why did it end? Was the termination brought on by outside forces or was it because of insurmountable differences in opinion? Was it due to personality clashes? A word of caution for that feeling of comfort or familiarity—one may have been there before and not liked it.

WALTZING DOWN THE FAMILIAR PATH

Rita, a young divorced mother of two daughters, sought counseling because she could not understand why her new romantic relationship did not develop as she had hoped. Through friends she had met Glen and was instantly attracted to him. Glen was not particularly handsome, so what had drawn her to him so magically? Rita explained that Glen was very intelligent and knowledgeable. Although somewhat intimidating, the attention he paid her was immensely flattering. He seemed different from most of the men she knew, except for her ex-husband. Something in the way Glen spoke reminded her of her ex-husband, who was also very intelligent and displayed a certain level of arrogance in his interactions with Rita. Thus, the feeling of intimidation in Glen's presence was familiar to Rita. Rita's formal education ended with her graduation from high school. She worked in an office to make ends meet. Fortunately, her ex-husband provided well for their two daughters.

Rita's new relationship developed in ways similar to her involvement with her former husband. What she thought she lacked in mental brilliance, she made up for in the way she cared for him. She cooked and did laundry for the men in her life and was grateful when they accepted her efforts and spent some time with her. Her previous husband, while satisfied with her housewifely duties, had taken her for granted. He regarded her more as a housekeeper than a wife. But he was young enough not to give up on exciting romance and became involved with an attractive career woman in the law firm where he worked. The divorce had been a tremendous emotional blow for Rita, but now she was ready to attend to the needs of another man.

Glen enjoyed Rita's pampering. Although he did not move in with her and her daughters, he regularly came for dinner once a week and most weekends. On those weekends when Rita's daughters visited with their father, Glen stayed overnight with Rita. It was a good opportunity to get his laundry taken care of. Rita never asked for financial contributions in exchange for the meals she provided. She was grateful for Glen's attention when they went for walks or watched TV in her home. They rarely went out for dinner or a show. Glen's finances were tight; he spent significant amounts of money in what he called "investments." Judging by his occasional urgent need for substantial sums of money, the investments seemed to be more characteristic of gambling activities. There were a few times when Rita bailed him out financially because he had no other source available. Of course, Rita never requested any documentation regarding the money she had lent Glen. He had made a few payments to Rita, but lately he seemed to be more financially strapped than ever.

Gradually, Glen's visits became less regular; he would just not show up some weekends. His explanations were vague and his visits occurred on an intermittent schedule, which behavioral psychologists consider the most likely schedule to resist extinction. Glen's unpredictable visiting schedule kept Rita dangling with hopes that had little basis in reality. Even though Rita had recognized the similarities in the two men's behaviors toward her, she did not want to abandon her efforts to capture Glen. Even more surprising, she did not consider changing the way she approached relationships and responded to men. On the contrary, she increased her efforts to win Glen's affection as she delivered cooked meals along with clean laundry to his house. Rita increased her efforts at doing the same thing, but expected different results.

Expressing her beliefs to her therapist, Rita asked, "Shouldn't kindness beget kindness and love get love in return?" Apparently she felt comfortable maintaining the beliefs of her childhood and most people would agree that responding with kindness and love might make our world a better one. But when expecting kindness and love in return, one needs to select the appropriate targets for one's kindness. After two failed attempts, how long will she continue with her endeavors? What advice would be helpful for Rita? Her therapist gave Rita a rating form titled "Giving and Getting in Love Relations" and encouraged her to independently assess her status in her current relationship. In cases of ambivalence about a romantic relationship, using a written record is helpful in remaining objective in the overall evaluation process.

As pointed out earlier, Rita could recognize some of the characteristics that the two men in her life had in common and she was aware of the attraction the men's intelligence held for her, but she did not apply the lesson from her emotional pain at the end of her marriage to this similar situation with Glen. She had been there before and had not liked it, but she did not recognize the signals when she traveled that road again. Or did she? And what about the signals she transmitted? Her behaviors were an expression of her intentions, not her wishes. Her poorly expressed wishes were to be in a loving relationship with a man who cared for her instead of taking advantage of her. She neglected to realize that if she did not want others to take advantage of her good nature, she better not issue an invitation for them to do so.[1]

Sometimes people are repeatedly drawn into similar circumstances with a person of similar characteristics believing that it will be different this time; that it will be better. Most people can think of friends or acquaintances who remain with the same partner for many years, eagerly swallowing a series of creative lies accompanied by promises of behavior changes only to face the same heartbreaking disappointments again. If it is possible to believe that a person can change, how much easier is it to expect different outcomes from an involvement with a different person? The difference—no matter how tiny—in the new person may just be the missing ingredient in the formula for a happy ending.

THE EASE OF FAMILIAR BEHAVIORS

There are, however, advantages to choosing the same type of partner. A person does not have to implement significant behavioral changes in response to a new lover. What worked (or did not work) with the previous one probably will (or won't) work with the next one and the next one. The knowledge of what to expect can be reassuring; indeed, it can present a tempting proposition. It saves time and energy; it eliminates questions or guesswork; one just responds as in past similar situations. Sure, there will be minor differences: the new lover might place his wine glass to the left of the dinner plate where the previous one liked the glass positioned on the right side. The new woman's preference might be the enjoyment of a leisurely bath and her towel might hang close to the bathtub instead of next to the shower. These are minor details that will not seriously derail anyone's habitual behavior repertoire.

Additional comfort can be derived from the hope that more of the good behavior will achieve better results if the initial attempts fail. Just as Rita stepped up her good deeds with the hope of winning Glen's love and commitment to her, there may be the unexpressed thought that if one goes to the very limits of one's abilities, the desired partner in the end will surrender in the conviction that he or she will never find a greater love.

Nancy, a forty-two-year-old divorced woman, was coming out of a relationship that had lasted almost five years and she was devastated. When she first started dating Richard, it felt so comfortable. It seemed that she had known him all her life. She recalled that after a while Richard told her what he thought was wrong with her and what he didn't like about her. He always prefaced it with: "I care about you; that's why I am telling you this." All his criticism seemed intended for her own good, but Nancy did not feel good about it.

There was a reason for Nancy's feelings of comfort with Richard. Indeed, she had known him all her life—his behavior resembled that of her father and her first husband. She responded to Richard as she had to her father and her ex-husband, by defending herself and by finally withdrawing and crying about her own worthlessness.

All her life Nancy wanted to feel loved and accepted. She worked hard to please her father but never made the grade. She had similar experiences with her first husband and now with Richard. As Nancy admitted, "I realized there were signs with my previous marriage and with this relationship, telling me that it would be best to call things off. Especially with my husband I had my doubts because he was stingy even while we were dating. But then that reminded me of my father too. He never agreed to spend any money on me. It seemed that this was the way my life was supposed to be and there was no reason that it would get any better. I felt so bad about myself that I thought I was fortunate to find anyone who seemed to be interested in me."

FOLLOWING PARENTS' EXAMPLES

In Nancy's case, some of the behavioral foundations were laid in her childhood, seeking the approval of her father but never reaching that goal. She wanted to please but repeatedly found herself in the position of having to defend herself and then she withdrew disappointedly. Those were the lessons of her childhood. Valuing the lessons from one's parents is a sensible thing to do, but to do so without considering one's own personality characteristics and those of one's partner can spell disaster.

The simple rule of following parents' examples as they interacted in their marriage if it had been a relatively harmonious union, or doing the opposite if family life had been characterized by major arguments and upheavals, may seem logical but does not guarantee that spouses live happily ever after.

Spouses employing the same interaction styles as their parents are not guaranteed a happy marriage, or an unhappy one.

Timothy, recently divorced after twenty-six years of marriage, is looking back on his life. His four children have left the house; the two youngest ones are still in college but return home for holidays. About six months after the youngest entered college Timothy's wife filed for divorce. Timothy was shocked. They did not have any serious arguments. He did not have any extramarital affairs. What was wrong? His wife had been easygoing; she was not demanding. All of a sudden she wanted to be rid of him. He became suspicious: was she involved with another man? No, there was no other man in her life. His wife explained: "We have grown apart—I never felt important to you and I have become lonely. Now with the children gone, I might as well live alone."

Timothy's attempts at persuading his wife to reconsider her plans failed. Hesitatingly he admitted that he probably had taken his wife for granted and never made her feel special. He thought marriages were supposed to be that way. After the early passion subsides and the spouses settle in to raise a family, life around the home becomes divided into different roles. Timothy fulfilled his role by providing financially for the family and handling heavy labor around the house while his wife cooked, cleaned, and took care of the children. That's the way his parents and relatives lived and their marriages seemed to be stable.

By following the example of his parents Timothy felt he had done his part. The thought of talking to his mother about her feelings regarding her life in the family never occurred to him. She did not complain and that was information enough. Therefore, he never considered asking his wife about her feelings either. In retrospect, Timothy vaguely remembered that years ago his wife had mentioned that she would like to have more of his attention, but he had not taken it seriously, especially since his wife had not repeated her request. He considered it as just a passing phase.

Timothy is not alone; many men wake up after twenty or more years of marriage when their wives contemplate divorce. Timothy and others like him are not bad or inconsiderate or unfeeling men; they just did not know any better. In following his parents' example, Timothy was convinced that he was on the right path. He was ill prepared for the shock his wife had in store for him. As pointed out in chapter 1, it is amazing how perfectly intelligent people who spend a lot of energy and effort preparing themselves for a profession are not encouraged by our society to spend the same effort on learning about and preparing themselves for a commitment that is expected to last for a lifetime—certainly longer than many careers.

Timothy does not like the idea of living by himself, yet he is afraid about going out and seeking the acquaintance of other women. He does not know how to behave. After the failure of his marriage he feels unsure of himself. He would like to blame his wife for the failure but deep down he knows better. As bewildered as Timothy is about his life situation, he does not trust himself to make the necessary changes. Where and how is he going to learn to be different? Timothy is looking for a woman who will accept him as he is. He may not have to look very long; there are many lonely people out there. But how long will a new relationship last? How long will it take for the new woman to become tired of being taken for granted, leaving Timothy single once again?

In his desperation Timothy asked his ex-wife to teach him how to make a woman feel important within a relationship. After all, she must know what she missed. Sadly, his companion of so many years misinterpreted his helplessness. She thought Timothy's plea was offensive; now he wanted her to teach him how to treat his next companion better than he had treated her. Timothy had entertained a slim hope that his wife might be moved by his request and would renew her interest in him. However, he did not express this hope openly and she did not read the signs of his intentions in his communication.

FAMILY BACKGROUND IMPACTING RELATIONSHIP STABILITY

The impact of economic factors, such as the couple's financial situation and wives' participation in the labor force, upon marital stability has been emphasized by economists and sociologists. In addition, sociodemographic factors and family background characteristics, such as intergenerational transmission of relationship stability, are considered to be indicators of successful marriage foundations. Demographers have noted that parental divorce increased the odds for marital instability. Furthermore, parental divorce seems to have an impact on individuals' relationship characteristics. If parents model poor interpersonal styles while divorcing, their offspring may develop personality characteristics that lead to interpersonal behavior conflicts.[2]

To investigate connections between parental divorce and young adults' certainty regarding their own romantic relationships researchers studied a sample of 404 individuals. Of this group, 87 women and 75 men came from divorced families while 120 women and 122 men were from intact families. The investigators found that parental divorce played a part in shaping the experiences of young adults; however, this was more evident for women than for men, in particular regarding feelings of love and trust in a partner. Women with divorced parents reported more conflict and negativity in their own relationships than women from intact families. Regardless of the marital status of their own parents, men tended to be hesitant to trust women who were ambivalent about trust. But when paired with women from divorced families men from divorced parents exhibited significant lack of trust in their female partners' honesty.[3]

On the other hand, analyses of the data from the "Early Years of Marriage" study demonstrated that among all spouses, but especially among wives with divorced parents, an increased closeness to their spouses' families was predictive of increased happiness in their marriages and reduced risk of divorce. In general, the family's cohesiveness brings about psychological and behavioral consequences in offspring, but the wife's preferences are influential in the degree of cohesion of the family network because women are considered to function as the connecting links or "gatekeepers" within the family constellation.[4]

National longitudinal data from two generations served as the basis for exploring the intergenerational transmission of marital instability/stability in a study designed to measure explanatory factors that preceded the divorce of adult offspring as well as the divorces of their parents. The findings indicated that the nature of relationship skills and marital commitment were factors related to the transmission of marital disruption from parents to offspring. Poor relationship skills that jeopardize relationship stability include unclear communication, inattentive listening, expression of negative emotions, avoidance of problem-solving discussions, and a tendency to criticize, which leads to defensive behaviors in the other partner.[5]

Observing their parents' distressing interactions prior to the parents' divorce puts the children at risk to learn interpersonal behaviors that undermine intimate relationships and increase their own marital instability in adulthood. In addition, through their parents' divorces, young adults learn that relationship commitments can be broken when the relationship is unsatisfying.

Another critical point of change in marital relationships occurs with the arrival of children, as roles change from lovers and spouses to include those of parents. Here again, parents serve as role models for their offspring's behaviors, often on a subconscious level. If the two spouses have not seriously discussed the sharing of responsibilities that will be necessary for the well-being of their family, they have not prepared themselves for the change in roles, and significant conflicts can be expected to disrupt their union.

THE IMPACT OF PERSONALITY TRAITS ON RELATIONSHIP QUALITY

Mark, a thirty-four-year-old attorney, is the picture of self-assurance. Mark knows the answers. He became widowed after four years of marriage to

Cindy. Cindy wanted a child but Mark was not ready for fatherhood yet. He was still busy developing his career. He assured Cindy that they would start a family in a few years. Cindy did not complain; but then she died of cancer. She died as quietly as she had lived. As an eligible bachelor, Mark had no trouble finding women to date but most of his dates fizzled out. Some dates were spoiled by arguments when a woman expressed a different opinion; others, with less outspoken women, just seemed to fade out.

One young woman raised the question of whether he felt guilty of having deprived Cindy of the motherhood experience after Mark had told her the sad story of his first marriage. Mark seemed shocked about the question and proceeded to lecture the young woman about the irresponsibility of planning for parenthood when one of the parents was to die. He had made the right decision in postponing parenthood even though he did not know of Cindy's shortened life.

Then he met Karen, who was raised in a large family with two sisters and three brothers. Karen seemed agreeable and easygoing, characteristics that made her a perfect wife. Two years into the marriage, Karen left. The note she left behind stated that she was tired of Mark lecturing and analyzing her statements. His responses to her during their conversations gave her the feeling of being interrogated and she learned to dread them. She added that she was thinking of having children but could not imagine having children with Mark. She did not want to subject any of her children to Mark's habit of lecturing and interrogating.

Mark complained bitterly about Karen. She had kept her true nature hidden, he whined. She had no consideration for what she put him through after the tragic loss of his first wife and the difficulty adjusting to life with a new person. Her abrupt departure made him wonder if he would ever find a woman considerate of his needs. Mark was correct when he stated that he did not know the "real" Karen. He never bothered to meet her. There was no genuine interest in learning about Karen's desires and goals for the future. It was sufficient that he told her what he wanted and that she agreed to that. Talking mostly about himself, Mark never got to know the women he married or the ones he had dated between his marriages. He also did not realize that he was less than perfect because he blamed Karen for the disruption of the marriage; after all, Cindy had never complained about his behavior.

Psychologists call it "repetition compulsion" when people seem to be compelled to engage in the same behaviors or rituals over and over whether or not these behaviors actually bring desired results. Replacing the word "compulsion" with the word "determination" may remove the sting, but in the end, acting with overdone or exaggerated determination likely results in very similar outcomes as would be generated by compulsive behavior. Determination and compulsion—among many other characteristics—are personality traits that people possess to varying degrees and that affect intimate relationships in different ways. Unless one makes a conscious effort to change, personality traits are durable characteristics that become more and more ingrained into an individual's overall personality pattern over time.

The very first college course on the topic of personality ever taught in the United States had the title "Personality: Its Psychological and Social Aspects" and was presented in 1924 at Harvard University by a psychologist from "middle America." According to this early psychologist, the social aspects of individuals' personalities are the important determinants of the nature and quality of their personal and intimate relationships because a person's personality is "the dynamic organization within the individual of those psychophysical systems that determine his characteristic behavior and thought."[6]

Individuals' personality traits generally influence their behaviors in interaction with others, and in turn, they impact the relationships they have with others, as was demonstrated earlier in Mark's case. People's behaviors are the main ingredients of their interactions with others and with that they become significant determinants within their relationships. Behaviors within interactions define the quality of the relationship and become the messengers of expectations and hopes for a particular relationship. Over time, through their recurring nature, behaviors in interactions combine to form individuals' relationship style or interaction style. A major relationship pattern that can be observed in couples is that of "demand-withdraw"—with one partner attempting to get closer and receiving attention while the other responds by withdrawing. In general, women fall more into the demand category as they tend to be more interconnected and affected by the quality of the relationship whereas men more typically withdraw, especially if the situation is perceived as conflict ridden.[7]

Congruent with earlier mentioned formulations, research in the area of marital and family studies has demonstrated that personality is related to marital adjustment. Perfectionism as a personality trait has been of special interest because this trait can be understood along three dimensions. In self-oriented perfectionism the individual demands the self to be perfect. Other-directed perfectionism requires others to be perfect. The third dimension involves a socially prescribed perfectionism, which is based on the belief that others hold unrealistic expectations for the self.[8]

In order to examine the associations among perfectionism, marital coping, and marital adjustment, investigators in psychology studied a community sample of 76 couples. The results of the study indicated that socially prescribed perfectionism functions as an important predictor of marital adjustment for both husbands and wives. The belief that one is expected by others to be perfect is strongly linked to relationship problems. The spouse who feels those expectations from the partner knows that he or she can never measure up and begins to feel resentful and angry, and perhaps depressed from a sense of futility or desperation.[9]

Conrad was a master in developing and maintaining a system of other-oriented perfectionism. He was convinced that he knew better and could perform better than most people he had met. However, he did not want to spend the rest of his life performing all sorts of tasks just because he could do them best. There were more interesting things to do in life. His wife, Alice, willingly volunteered to take on many of the work projects around the house and garden. Sadly, it was a rare occasion when Alice would earn Conrad's praise for a task well done. More often, her performance did not reach his level of acceptance, and what was worse, Conrad scolded her for even beginning the project. After all, she should know what she could not do well (which—according to him—included most things). It was better not to start something she knew she could not do, just to leave it for him to finish. His frequent response to Alice's less than successful attempts was "know—don't think!" In other words, don't think you can do it, know that you cannot do it. This piece of advice did not improve Alice's self-confidence, which had not been at a healthy level to begin with.

Conrad, perhaps thinking that Alice was trying to control him, considered leaving the projects half-done for extended periods of time a reasonable response to Alice's feeble attempts at either doing something herself or forcing him to do what she wanted done. Although Alice was a patient and willing-to-learn person, after almost seven years, her patience ran out. But despite Conrad's criticism of her limited capabilities, she embarked upon one more task—the search for a competent divorce lawyer.

Actually, it is not difficult to imagine that all three dimensions of the perfectionism trait can be detrimental to the quality of intimate relationships. A person consumed with self-oriented perfectionism will never be happy with him- or herself and tends to self-denigrate and complain, which eventually displeases the partner. Other-oriented perfectionism leads to blaming the partner and demanding improvement, just another way of eroding the quality of any relationship.

UNRESOLVED ISSUES FROM PREVIOUS RELATIONSHIPS

Many relationships do not end with a well-defined "good-bye" and no further contact between the ex-partners. This is particularly true—and expected to some degree—when the situation involves ex-spouses with children. Many contacts are still necessary, often to the annoyance of new partners, to make decisions about the children's well-being. Sometimes contact between ex-spouses lingers long after the children are grown. One female advice seeker to Annie's Mailbox, calling herself "Crowded by the Ex," wrote that she is disturbed that after twenty years of marriage her husband's ex-wife still comes to their house to greet his relatives when they visit. In addition, the ex-wife drives to the airport to see her ex-husband off when he leaves on business trips. Although the current wife has asked her husband to set stricter boundaries with his ex-wife, he does not consider the situation as unusual and is not willing to make any changes in his approach.

"Annie" did not see it as unusual that the ex-wife would appear at the husband's home on those occasions when his relatives were visiting; however, seeing the ex-husband off at the airport was regarded as inappropriate behavior for an ex-wife. One important question in this scenario would be: how long is the current wife going to tolerate the situation? After twenty years, she might have lost some of her energy to make life-changing decisions. The other question would be: how does this situation affect the quality of her marriage? One could speculate that the marital bliss has already lost some of its luster and perhaps the husband does not want to cut the ties to his ex-wife in case he wants to return to her.[10]

Similarly, another female reader writing to a different advice column admitted that she is encouraging daily online communications for hours with her ex-partner even though this is upsetting to his new girlfriend. "Lost Unfaithful Love" cannot cut the strings to her ex-husband whom she left because of his unfaithfulness. While separated from her ex-husband, she became involved with her current boyfriend with whom she has a beautiful son. However, she wonders if there is a chance that she and her ex-husband will find happiness again. Another question she asks herself is whether there is someone better out there for her.

"In Turmoil" seems to entertain similar questions. At the age of fifty-two she has been in a platonic marriage for thirty-two years. For the past eight years she has been involved with another man who apparently accepted her decision that she would not leave her marriage as long as her children were still at home. Now that her children are gone, her controlling boyfriend is giving her trouble, demanding that she start divorce proceedings. She describes him as jealous, suspicious, and quick tempered. Now her question is: should she leave the safety of her husband and home or should she break up the relationship with the boyfriend she loves—even though he is controlling?

A somewhat different slant to unresolved ties from the past can be found in the complaint of a woman dating a widower with a forty-one-year-old married stepdaughter. Although her mother, the man's previous wife, has been buried for some time, the stepdaughter objects strongly and successfully to the stepfather's dating another woman. Whatever the stepdaughter's power over the man is, it seems that he is unable to cut the "stepfatherly" strings.

Obviously, these advice seekers are involved in serious struggles regarding some significant life-altering decisions. All of the situations described above include the inability to break ties with the past. And no matter what decision they make regarding their current relationships, their difficulty in letting go will most likely adversely affect their next relationship. They appear to be doomed to be fellow travelers on the path of the repeatedly single.[11]

FEAR OF ABANDONMENT

Ron and Melissa married soon after Melissa's graduation from high school. She had plans for attending college but Ron, who had inherited his father's small business, persuaded her to forget her college ideas. In his opinion, her time would be better spent in helping him in the business. He wanted a trusted teammate, he declared, not a career woman who did not care about family loyalties. Melissa gave in and their married life was spent in almost constant presence of the other. Melissa's friends called less and less frequently after phone communications with Ron. They realized that their calls were not welcome.

Melissa's complaints about their boring life resulted in lectures from Ron about the importance of their roles as husband and wife as well as business partners. Melissa did not really feel like a partner in the business because Ron made the important decisions without regarding her input. Although he listened to her opinions, he rarely gave them serious consideration. One day Melissa disappeared with a male customer never to return. Ron was devastated by her betrayal. He swore he would never trust anyone again. If he were ever to marry again, he would increase his vigilance, making sure that the woman could not leave his side.

The few women he dated after the divorce from Melissa did not inspire trust in him. It looked like he was destined to remain single until he thought that a woman from a foreign country, who did not speak much English and who did not have any resources here, might make an ideal wife. Through an agency he established contact with a young woman from Sri Lanka, who displayed a quietly pleasing demeanor. Although the young woman could not be of much help in the business, he kept her with him in a back room, instructing her in some menial duties. After the birth of twin sons, Ron managed his wife's isolation in the nearby home.

Ron is still married to his second wife but he is not happy. Too many responsibilities rest on him. Ron's distrust of everyone requires his constant presence and attention at his business. And his refusal to let his wife obtain a driver's license places the responsibility for the family's doctors' appointments and shopping on him. He feels tired and anxious most of the time now. Where ostensibly in his first marriage he looked for a teammate, his increased fears of abandonment after Melissa's sudden departure have resulted in increased control tactics to the point where the master-and-slave type of relationship is the only affordable one for him.

But even this situation cannot put his mind at ease. A few times in the recent past he has overheard his wife talking on the telephone in a language Ron does not understand. What he thought would increase his security in the relationship (his wife's inability to speak and understand English) not only made communication between the spouses difficult, but in the end limited his knowledge about what might be going on around him. If it weren't for his sons, Ron thinks he would be better off without his wife. Does he see any connection between his distrust and fear of abandonment and the outcomes of his relationships with women? Not yet; in fact it seems to strengthen his belief that he has no reason for trusting anyone and has even more reason for increasing his vigilance.

Ron's insistence on complete control to avoid being abandoned may well stem from attachment problems in his early childhood. He was raised by a single mother, who did not tell him anything about his father, and he was left alone at home some evenings, not knowing where his mother was until she finally returned—apparently from visits at local bars.

Fear of abandonment is a powerful behavioral determinant in intimate relationships. According to well-known psychiatrist John Bowlby, the need for and ability to form strong emotional bonds to particular individuals are basic components of human nature. Attachment is the emotional tie experienced in infancy, usually to a parent, from which the child derives a sense of security. The development of secure attachment falls into a critical period of the infant's life. As believed by ethologists, the first two years of the infant's life constitute the sensitive period for attachment formation. Those individuals who are unsuccessful in establishing a close and trusting relationship with a primary caregiver are at risk for experiencing social and personality problems in the future. As it seemed important for survival in infancy, the affectional link with a special partner, a unique individual, is desired by most people in adulthood. The desire for maintaining closeness to the partner may express itself in extreme anxiety and clingy and dependent behaviors in individuals who have missed the healthy, secure bonding with a primary caregiver in early childhood. In men, dependent behaviors may take on the form of control-seeking actions, as was seen in Ron's case.[12]

ATTACHMENT PATTERNS AND PERSONALITY TRAITS

For decades researchers have attempted to determine the precursors of personality development. Even though there are some indications that normal personality traits can be inherited, sufficient evidence to support the notion that personality disorders are genetically transmitted has been lacking. In order to understand and treat personality disorders an approach based on a broad etiological framework appeared to be more promising. Research exploring various risk factors for dysfunctional personality traits has implicated several environmental factors, such as family dysfunction, early separation and loss, childhood abuse, parental neglect, and others. Those factors are linked to attachment theory, which proposes that the nature of caregiver and child relationships is instrumental in shaping a child's development and personality.[13]

As mentioned, specific attachment experiences in a child's life that occur consistently over time will become a part of the child's development into adulthood. At the time that the child adapted with certain responses to the attachment experiences, those responses may have been appropriate to the child's situation and cognitive functioning. However, those thoughts, feelings, and behaviors are no longer functional in the adult world and become characteristics of dysfunctional behavior.

In the study of close relationships, attachment theory has become an important area because it provides a wide-ranging perspective for understanding relationship processes. Attachment theory is based on the assumption that human beings form close emotional bonds in the interest of survival. These bonds promote the development of "internal working models," which are mental representations of the self and others and assist individuals in predicting and understanding their environment and in establishing a psychological sense of security.[14]

Extending Bowlby's concept of cognitive working models within the framework of attachment theory into the phase of adult attachment, it has been proposed that adult working models of self and others are characterized by positive or negative values. These working models represent individuals' views of self along a continuum of self-worth and the view they have of others as being trustworthy and available or rejecting and unreliable in regard to needs experienced in the relationship. Integrating these working models, Bartholomew and Horowitz developed a classification system with two orthogonal dimensions that in combination yield four main attachment styles, *secure, preoccupied, fearful,* and *dismissing.* One of the dimensions measures self-image along a positive or negative continuum, while the other measures one's positive or negative image of others.[15]

Individuals with a secure attachment style (positive self, positive other) have a flexible blend of positive and negative working models between a sense of self-worth and expectations of others as being accessible and trustworthy. Characterization of preoccupied attachment style (negative self, positive other) includes a sense of personal unworthiness combined with positive evaluations of others. Fearfully attached (negative self, negative other) individuals also exhibit a sense of personal unworthiness but linked with an expectation that others will reject them and therefore cannot be trusted. Similarly, mistrust of others is found in those who demonstrate a dismissing attachment style (positive self, negative other); however, here it is combined with a worthy sense of self.

Viewing personality disorders in terms of *developmental personality styles* (DPSs), where personality traits develop along a dimensional continuum over time starting as adaptive measures in response to critical situations early in life but may no longer be functional in adulthood, a group of researchers investigated DPSs within Bartholomew's attachment style theory. In other words, they hypothesized a relationship between adult attachment and DPSs. In particular, they proposed that preoccupied attachment would be related to obsessive-compulsive, histrionic, and dependent DPSs, while a blending of preoccupied and fearful attachments would be linked to avoidant DPSs among various other combinations. Overall, the investigators' findings indicated that adult attachment dimensions were able to predict seven of the ten personality styles defined in the *Diagnostic and Statistical Manual of Mental Disorders*.[16]

Discussing all the different personality traits and their association to attachment styles is beyond the scope of this book; however, it is not difficult to imagine how different personality traits and attachment styles may combine in couples, who are not aware of the possible negative effects that can lead them straight onto the path of the single again. Most romantic or sexual pair bonds are based on attachments, but they are not necessarily all secure attachments.[17]

As an example, in the case of Conrad and Alice mentioned above, Conrad would qualify as exhibiting a dismissive attachment style, which is not conducive to enhancing the quality of any relationship. Similarly, one might guess that the following male advice seeker shares Conrad's dismissive attachment style. "Alone" is in his midfifties and mourns the fact that after two divorces he cannot find a suitable companion. From his description of himself one can easily detect a strong sense of self-worth. Unfortunately, in his opinion all the women in his age group are "fuddy-duddies" who are only interested in their grandchildren, gardening, or quilting; whereas the younger women are looking for a man to start a family with. And this is not what he has in mind. He admits that he could lower his standards but after two divorces he seems to feel entitled to find a suitable life partner.[18]

THE LEGACY OF TOXIC RELATIONSHIPS

Toxic relationships are associations in which one or all of the participating members interact in ways that seem to establish a poisonous atmosphere within the system. Diminished trust, eroded self-confidence, tension, ambivalence, and negative emotions are just a few of the indicators of a toxic association. Sometimes the toxic atmosphere in a relationship can bring about a premature end to the union as in the case of a woman who, after being married for twenty-one years to a bullying husband who screamed and blamed her for everything that went wrong in the marriage, found that she and their two daughters, ages nine and seventeen, could live quite calmly without him. The husband had taken another job in a different state, which gave the family an opportunity to compare life with and without him. They opted to continue their lives without him.[19]

When a toxic relationship ends, will that be the end of the poisonous influence? Just as it is often difficult to sever the emotional strings to an ex-partner, many behaviors that were developed as adaptive or nonadaptive responses in past relationships have become habitual and will be carried into the next union, even though the person they were developed as a response to is no longer around. Life would be a lot easier if one could eliminate those influences by just divorcing one's spouse, parents, children, or siblings. But in many cases this easy answer does not provide a solution to the problem.

Depending on the duration of the relationship, the toxic influences continue and may well poison future relationships because human beings are creatures that adapt and bring learned adaptation skills to the next situation. The toxicity keeps reproducing itself from one relationship to the next as the poison invades the individuals' minds and directs them toward the next calamity—taking hold of their minds and emotions unless challenged and replaced by healthy cognitive habits.

Consider the union of Betty, a young woman who learned to silence herself and quietly withdraw from arguments with her mother, to Peter, a young man who grew up in an argumentative family. His learned adaptive response was to immediately and vehemently defend himself to any and all perceived attacks. The two spouses' learned adaptive responses surfaced automatically in any of their marital conflicts and did not provide any solutions or contribute to a harmonious marriage. In a few years' time their marriage turned into a toxic relationship heading for bitter disappointment and divorce.

During a last attempt at counseling, uncertain whether it would be marriage or divorce counseling, they were asked to identify their reasons for getting married. Both Betty and Peter agreed that they had entered their marriage because they were in love with each other, they were looking for companionship, and they wanted to be with one special person who thought that they were special, too. Betty added that she had believed that marriage promised happiness and Peter expressed his expectation of having an easily accessible sex partner. Were those reasons the wrong ones for getting married since they were now heading for divorce? Betty and Peter did not believe so; they confirmed that those would be the reasons for getting married again if this union dissolved.

However, both admitted that their behaviors had not been congruent with those reasons. Upon further exploration, Betty remembered that her way of responding in uncomfortable interactions had developed in her childhood during the many disagreements with her mother. Betty felt that she could not win in arguments with her mother because her mother was the parental power holder then, much more so than her father. She described her father as easygoing and silent when discussions seemed to turn into arguments. Betty also remembered that in the beginning stages of her marriage to Peter she had expressed her views and her opinions even in disagreements with Peter but as time went on her behavior reverted to what she had selected as a coping mechanism in interactions with her mother.

Furthermore, Betty pointed out that Peter's behavior during their arguments resembled his behavior in interactions with his mother. Peter admitted that his mother had been a blaming person and seemed to be in competition with him as he was growing up. With his mother he always felt the need to defend himself and he has allowed this defensive stand to direct most of his life.

Defense mechanisms learned in childhood are difficult to change, not only because of their duration but also because they usually were formed and adopted by the child in response to a powerful opponent, a parent. And because they served the child through the intense power struggle of their growing-up period, these defense mechanisms will likely remain stronger than other coping mechanisms unless a conscious attempt is made to explore their current utility.

What makes this occurrence so tragic is that the individuals are usually not aware of the origins of their troublesome behaviors. Again, Vickie and Larry's sad story (chapter 1) serves as an example here; explorations into their backgrounds revealed that both had problematic relationships with their mothers and both had developed a certain arguing style in response to their mothers' complaints and accusations. This bickering, as Vickie called it, was so entrenched in their behavior repertoire it seemed to have a life of its own, controlling both Vickie and Larry. As they are preparing to embark on separate journeys, it will only be a matter of time until their style of arguing poisons their next relationships, unless they make a determined effort to change.

COMMUNICATION PATTERNS

Communication is the vehicle for expressing what we want and making known what we don't want. While communication is the way to make ourselves understood as well as to learn about the wishes of those around us, communication, unfortunately, can also provide opportunities for misunderstandings.

Men and women employ different styles of communicating, according to a well-known sociolinguist's research. In their conversations women are often looking for responses that express understanding and support. But they are disappointed when men respond by addressing the problem described in the communication and offering solutions. Women tend to interpret this response as one of superiority, perceiving that men are telling them what to do. On the other hand, men become disappointed because their offered solution to the perceived problem does not receive the deserved appreciation. And this is just one aspect of many that impact relationships.[20]

Gender-linked styles of emotion exert their influences on the expression and perception of men and women's communication. In general, men's emotions are considered to be linked to rationality, which in our culture is regarded as higher in value than the feminine standards of expressiveness and as such exerts greater influence on male-female interactions and on the consequences of such interactions.[21]

The importance of the nature of male-female communication in predicting marital satisfaction and divorce has been emphasized in the literature on marital development. In particular, the manner in which spouses interact in marital conflict resolution has been observed to be a significant predictor of marital satisfaction and stability.[22]

It is important to remember that communication includes more than the spoken word; body language, facial expressions, and, equally important, what is not expressed verbally—what is left unsaid—are also parts of communication. For instance, when the live-in boyfriend promises to share all the chores equally but "forgets" to clean the dishes when it's his turn to prepare the meal and place the dishes in the dishwasher, his behavior may well communicate, "I don't clean dishes. That is your job."[23]

Communication styles and speech patterns like many other behaviors often occur automatically in response to the various stimuli in our environment. They develop early in life and unless there is a special need for changing them, they become part of our overall behavior repertoire. As such, communication styles can be conceived of as expressions of our individual personalities. Just like any other behavioral or personality trait, particular communication styles can lead to tension or irritability in interactions with others.

For many couples the seeds of marital distress and relationship termination are sown before the spouses' official commitments, a hypothesis tested by researchers. The Denver Family Development Project started in 1980 and followed a hundred couples for a period of thirteen years from the premarital phase through the primary risk period for divorce. An additional thirty-five couples were excluded from the study because their relationship had ended prior to marriage. The observation period included ten assessment points.[24]

The couples were categorized into groups according to marital status and satisfaction over time. Depending on their marital satisfaction eighty couples were differentiated into either the married but distressed group or the happily married group. In seventeen couples one or the other partner had been distressed at some time but had recovered to the point that the couple did not differ significantly from the forty-one continuously satisfied couples. Twenty-two couples were distressed but remained married while twenty couples divorced.

The spouses' scores were recorded for eight variables including premarital satisfaction, problem intensity, exchange orientation, problem-solving facilitation, emotional invalidation, and communication effects among others. Analysis of the data revealed that premarital interaction and conflict aspects played a key role in the marital outcomes. As observed in other studies, interaction patterns play a significant role in the development of marital dissatisfaction. Negative interactions before and early in the marriage lead to erosion of positive aspects over time. Negative interactions lead to defensive or accusing behaviors in one or the other partner and bring about a shift to pervasive negative attitudes, even in a previously positive or neutral emotional atmosphere.[25]

Usually, individuals have established these interaction patterns long before they meet their potential spouses and therefore, with careful observation during the dating period, they could be detected prior to committing one's future life to a partner with incompatible interaction patterns. But how many people pay attention to those aspects of their relationships? "In the glow of early infatuation, individuals see and hear what they wish to see and hear. Only with the dimming of the glow does reality slowly make its entry."[26]

THE EMOTIONAL INTERPRETATION
GRADIENT AND ITS GENDERED EFFECTS

Although we like to define and characterize relationships, their appearance as well as their function change over time. Relationships are not static entities and the forces operating within them change in strength and direction with the passage of time. An interesting concept to consider at this point is that of *global sentiment*, or *sentiment override*, originally proposed by a researcher in 1980 and later regarded by other theorists as a type of *marriage bond*. Sentiment override can be viewed as a global dimension of affection or disaffection that spouses feel for their partners and for their marriages and which, in turn, influence the individual's perception of the partner's behavior during interactions. Individuals with positive sentiment override tend to interpret their spouses' behavior and messages in positive terms regardless of the objective quality of the message. Negative sentiment override, on the other hand, would lead to negative interpretations of a partner's communication.[27]

A surprising fact emerged when global sentiment was explored in terms of its functioning as a marriage bond. It was found that global sentiment functions as a perceptual filter through which wives evaluate their husbands' behaviors but it does not seem to serve the same function in husbands. Thus, in wives, through the operation of positive sentiment override, the marital bond may protect couples at times of disagreement. Unfortunately, as the husbands seem to be unaware of this effect, they are unlikely to consider the importance of the marital bond when opportunities for its development arise.[28]

Timothy's situation can be understood in terms of sentiment override's impact on the marital bond. At the beginning of the relationship when partners have invested a lot of positive feelings in each other, the absence of clearly defined affective behavior and communication will most likely be interpreted in positive terms by wives and Timothy's wife was willing to follow this direction in her evaluations. However, with passing time and evolving disappointments, the sentiment and perceptual filter changed into a negative direction. And it was within that framework that she interpreted Timothy's request to help him learn how to make a woman feel important.

With each opportunity for disagreement and disappointment, the emotional atmosphere in a couple's interaction space loses some of the positive valence, at least in the wives' perception, and is replaced by increments of negative regard. This reduction in positive valence and increase in negative valence can be understood as an emotional gradient, along which communications or the absence of clearly defined communication will be interpreted by the wife. In the case of Betty and Peter, with the increasing frequency of their arguments, often ending with Betty's silent withdrawal, it is not difficult to understand how the emotional interpretation gradient affects the emotional atmosphere of a marriage over time.

COHABITATION: PRELUDE TO MARRIAGE OR DISSOLUTION?

Ever since the 1960s, the number of cohabiting couples and families has increased significantly. Once frowned upon, cohabitation has gained widespread acceptance. Cohabitation has become less of a moral issue, and currently many parents, relatives, and friends of those who decide to cohabit seem to be less concerned than they would have been fifty to sixty years ago. Although cohabitation is more frequent among divorced than never married individuals, living together as an alternative lifestyle—temporary or permanent—has been chosen by persons from all social, educational, and age groups. Living together without the formality of marriage has become a popular way of life for people across all ages.[29]

In general, in the United States it is expected that cohabiting units do not last very long, with roughly half of them ending within the first year and only one out of ten unions will last five or more years.[30] Although cohabitation seems to be here to stay, some people do not consider it an alternative to marriage in the sense of being equal to marriage in the kinship system, with its formal and informal support of marriage.[31] However, many marriages today begin with cohabitation and the question arises, what is the effect, if any, of cohabitation on the marital quality later on? In a study that obtained data from 3,598 married—previously cohabiting—women, it was found that premarital cohabitation had a negative effect on the marital quality in women with premarital birth; but premarital cohabiting women without nonmarital births reported the same marital quality as women who did not cohabit prior to marriage.[32]

Considering relationship histories pertaining to both premarital sex and premarital cohabitation, another study found that when premarital sex and premarital cohabitation were involving the women's future husbands only, there was no elevated risk of subsequent marital disruption. However, women with more than one premarital intimate relationship seemed to be at risk for marital dissolution. The investigator interpreted these findings to suggest that premarital sex and cohabitation limited to one's future spouse has become part of the normal courtship process for marriage. Unfortunately, data for men's risks of marriage dissolution linked to premarital sex or cohabitation is not available yet.[33]

Some researchers have been interested in the trajectory of cohabiting and married couples with their separations, periods of living apart, and reconciliations. A panel study of white young adults collected complete marital and cohabiting partnership histories from age fifteen through thirty-one, tracking and comparing the paths along which they arranged and timed the entries and exits from marital and cohabiting unions. The researchers' first goal for the study was to examine the nature of transitions that mark the dissolution of the union, either temporarily or permanently. A second goal was to compare union trajectories between marital and cohabiting unions.

A view of the path of separations, living apart, and reconciliations revealed that overall cohabiting couples have five times as many separations as married couples, and if cohabiting people decide to separate, their rate of reconciliation is only 33 percent as high as that of married people. Cohabiting couples living apart do so at a rate sixteen times as high as married couples. However, looking at new union formation at separation, cohabitors and marrieds seem to do so at about the same speed.

Transitions back into the union after separation seem to occur significantly slower for cohabiting partners than for married partners. Actually, the different rates for transitioning into and out of their respective relationships can be seen as reflecting the higher degree of commitment and durability in married couples compared with cohabiting relationships. Cohabiting unions end either in marriage or separation; within the first six months the number of exits is about equal—one-quarter of them. At one year the number rises to about one-half for each type of exit and at the end of two years it is about three-quarters, with marriage being slightly more likely at this point. Among marital unions, on the other hand, one out of ten couples separate within the first two years and about one in four by the end of six years.

Focusing on the effects of premarital cohabitation, it was noted that married couples who had cohabited prior to marriage and had lived apart during their cohabitation had rates of living apart during their marriage four times higher than couples who did not live apart while cohabiting. It seems that those who cohabit and then live apart continue the pattern in their marriage.

When examining the paths of cohabiting couples who separated due to discord, it was found that only one in ten couples reconciled within four years after separation (and most of these did so within the first three months). Furthermore, reconciliations were often short-lived, soon to be followed by a second separation. Higher and fairly steady monthly rates of initiating a cohabiting relationship with another partner were characteristic for this group. Within the first six months of separation about 10 percent were already cohabiting with another partner. This increased to about 16 percent by the end of the first year of separation and to 25 percent by two years. It is likely that one-tenth of separated cohabiting people will enter directly into a new marriage within four years.

What can be said of the role of premarital cohabitation in transition to marriage? Scholars in the field of marriage and family argue that the commitment in cohabitation is generally lower than in marriage and the lower commitment experienced during cohabitation continues into the marriage and presents a higher risk of dissolution of the marriage (about 65 percent) among those with premarital cohabitation experience compared with those who did not live together prior to marriage.

In the present study, out of the sample of 800 couples who had formed a cohabitation or marital unit by age thirty-one, 423 couples first cohabited (226 later married their cohabiting partners) and 377 married directly. The data collected from these couples indicated that the trajectories of their unions showed no significant difference. In other words, the transitions of living apart, resuming the relationship, reconciling after separations, and initiating new unions were not statistically different for those couples whether they had cohabited prior to marriage or not. In general, for the majority of young adults in cohabiting and married unions, it can be expected that the first separation taken due to discord signals the permanent dissolution of the union. However, despite some similarities, marriage is considered to be qualitatively different from cohabitation; marriage has a higher degree of commitment and stability than cohabitation.[34]

What are the ingredients that seemingly render the traditional path of marriage more stable or powerful than the decision made by two adult individuals to move in together without the blessing, pomp, illusion, or spectacle of a wedding ceremony?

There is a slight difference in the scenes of marriage proposal and cohabitation initiation. Imagine a young man in his best suit down on one knee, holding a ring in his outstretched hand, and asking the question, "Will you marry me?" Then shift to the guy in jeans, preoccupied with operating the apps of his cell phone, who mumbles, "Hey, why don't we move in together? We'll save on rent and utilities."

The differences continue. When the young woman tells her friends about the marriage proposal, they ooh and aah, inspect the ring, and—according to the size of the diamond—more or less elaborately congratulate her. It is a rare occasion that an announcement of cohabitation is greeted with congratulations. The joyous squealing "I am so happy for you" so often encountered at wedding announcements is painfully absent when the news of one's cohabitation is shared. Planning for the future conjoint living space of the cohabiting couple is mainly limited to how to arrange their different pieces of furniture and equipment. Well-meaning friends may contribute some secondhand items useful or needed in setting up house. But for an upcoming wedding no friend would dare offer unwanted items. Everything has to be shiny and new for this important event.

The comparisons could go on and on but for those who are insensitive to the differences, the point is made clear with the event of the wedding itself. The bride appears as an angel in white. "An enduring symbol of female redemption in wedlock and a means by which women announce their adherence to traditional marriage ideals, the white dress is the most salient visual object of the modern wedding."[35] In front of parents, siblings, relatives, friends, and acquaintances the vows are spoken for all to hear. The following honeymoon represents the stamp of approval for the couple's sexual activities as well as an opportunity to form an intimate union that is expected to withstand the winds of change after the couple returns to the everyday world they had escaped temporarily.

It is conceivable that the excitement of the marriage proposal, engagement period, wedding ceremony, and official honeymoon experience has a more lasting effect in the participants' minds than a brief verbal agreement to combine one's living spaces. The vows made in front of all those witnesses will be harder to forget and to break than the promises uttered by the two cohabiting partners. The veil, the white gown, and all the symbolism bestow a glow on the bride and groom's life that can be expected to shine and glimmer for a while; and to make sure that all that glory will not be soon forgotten, there are the photographs and videotapes that commemorate the significant event.

If we accept and believe the research and the experimental evidence regarding the duration of romantic relationships, it seems as though there is at least one situation where the older road maps outlast the more modern shortcuts to life's journey.

• 3 •

If Honesty Is an Issue

Just as some people are repeatedly drawn into relationships with individuals who seem to embody characteristics similar to partners they had been involved with before, there are also people who, while pronouncing the importance of honesty in intimate relationships, repeatedly swallow lies and empty promises from their current partners. Perhaps these individuals believe that stressing the importance of honesty is sufficient to extinguish their partners' behaviors of camouflaging the truth and concealing their reasons for doing so. A better approach might be to consider the fact that the liability for dishonest behavior belongs to the person who utters the lie, but the responsibility for repeatedly believing lies or half-truths from the same person ultimately rests with the believer.

A MENU OF LIES AND EMPTY PROMISES

It took Mary almost thirty years to realize that Jim's promises were nothing more than a smoke screen. Jim believed in marriage as long as it was a convenient arrangement. Jim also believed in satisfying his curiosity and yearning for sexual conquests. Each time Mary found out about his escapades, he had a menu of lies and tearful promises handy. Mary loved many aspects about Jim, she had invested a lot in their marriage, and she wanted to believe him, so she did believe him. Finally there was a slight change in the menu. The lies were just as creative as ever but there were no promises for changed future behaviors. Jim had found a younger version of Mary, one with whom he could start all over again.

In the meantime, what is Mary's outlook for the future? What she had considered to be an investment in her marriage, at the end, did not amount to much. Half of the furniture they had purchased together and some old dishes—along with a big bag full of painful memories—were the dividends of her investment. As it turned out, Jim had lied not only about his extramarital affairs, but also about money issues. The amounts he deposited from his paycheck to their joint checking/savings account had been significantly less than the checks he received from his employer. He explained that the difference went to an investment fund, shared with colleagues. At the time of the divorce the investment fund existed but Jim had not been an active member of it for a long time. Where did the money go? Jim was evasive in his explanations.

Randolph, a respected university professor, had been married to his wife, a registered nurse, for twenty years when he realized that his colleagues as well as many of his students had known more about his wife's affairs than he did. Beth and Randolph had married young, lived mostly in college or university towns, and raised two children. Periodically Beth became bored with the predictability of their life. At the hospital where she worked she found a supply of male physicians and nurses as well as other professionals who were eager to provide a little excitement in her life. None of these relationships had the promise of permanence though; the men were mostly married or in committed relationships. From time to time Randolph found out about Beth's affairs and confronted her with the threat of divorce. Tearfully, Beth begged for forgiveness and promised changed behavior and eternal devotion to Randolph. It worked three times before Randolph decided not to be blinded by empty promises anymore. He finally faced the reality he had wanted to deny for so long.

When did Mary and Randolph become aware of their extreme willingness to accept their partners' lies? Randolph decided to end his marriage to Beth after he realized that he had been lied to three times; but did his realization include the fact that he had been a likely target due to his strong wish to believe her or had he focused only on Beth's tendency to withhold the truth? In Mary's case, she would probably have continued to stay married to Jim if he had not left her for another woman.

As long as the Marys and Randolphs do not recognize their own weakness when wanting to trust the significant others in their lives, they remain vulnerable. Focusing primarily on the dishonesty of the other may distract them from realizing their own part in the relationship scenario. Or is it perhaps less an issue of being gullible than a matter of ill-founded determination and insisting that the other person change his or her ways? In continuing to believe that the other person will be honest in the future, even though they have evidence to the contrary, are they perhaps trying to enforce their demands on reality?

LIED TO TWICE: ASSUMING RESPONSIBILITY FOR THE OTHER'S LIES

Years ago the author of the book *101 Lies Men Tell Women and Why Women Believe Them* asked why women who have suffered through men's lies in their previous relationships convince themselves that these episodes of dishonesty were just characteristic of those particular men and were limited to their relationships with them. Sometimes the women might even blame themselves and their own behavior for being lied to. They might tell themselves, "If I had been more tolerant of his needs, he would not have had to lie." As they assumed responsibility for the men's lies, the women managed to assure themselves that it would not happen again in the next relationship.[1]

There is a strange logic to this argument: If indeed the women had caused—or at least tolerated—the men's dishonest behavior (as the women tried to convince themselves), then they could eliminate the men's lies through changed responses to the lies. In other words, if through one's own behavior one were in control of someone else's behavior (the men's lying), then one would also be in a position to prevent its occurrence by simply altering one's own actions. But the only way that this argument would hold water is if the women's behavior was to walk out of the relationship instead of remaining and tolerating it. That change in behavior would be the only guarantee that the men would not lie to them anymore because the women wouldn't be there to listen.

Answering her own question about why women continue to believe men's lies, Hollander explained that the women do not recognize the patterns that develop from the difference in men's and women's agendas and from the ways men and women have been socialized to perceive each other. In general, according to many sources, men's agendas are focused on pleasure while women's agendas are concerned with emotions and lasting relationships. As a result, men, having heard of women's goals, perceive women as a potential threat to their independence. But a word of caution is in order: not all men should be stereotyped on the basis of a few disappointing experiences; as in the case of Randolph and Beth, everybody has the ability to be dishonest, regardless of gender.

THE MEANING AND CONCEPT OF LIES

Howard was a master in the fine art of omitting the truth. As a twice-divorced man with romantic entanglements between and during marriages, he had plenty of practice with the skillful avoidance of the truth when he thought it was in his best interest. Howard did not consider himself a dishonest man; he regarded his behavior as a diplomatic strategy that combined an absence of direct lies with sensitivity for sparing other people's feelings. Megan, his most recent dating partner, did not share Howard's appraisal of his behaviors. In her opinion, omission of the truth equaled a lie. Megan had a difficult time understanding the underlying reasons for Howard's behavior, especially since she detected most of his sins of omission.

Megan did not hesitate to confront Howard with his omissions of the truth. But Howard was resourceful. He made use of the occasion by offering a vague explanation, followed by the accusation that Megan was spying on him. Megan displayed a lack of trust in him, he pointed out emphatically. This strategy placed Megan in a defensive position and by the time the argument ended, Howard was in control of the situation as he played the role of the innocent, persecuted victim.

Instead of accepting Howard's behavior for what it was—avoiding the truth when it caused him inconvenience—Megan continued her search for explanations of Howard's reasons. Her focus thus was on him and not on any goals for herself. If she desired a relationship characterized by honesty, Howard was not a good prospect. Her hunt for his motives in omitting the truth conveyed the message that perhaps under certain circumstances she was willing to accept a reduced level of honesty—if she could understand the reason for it. When asked about her goals, it became apparent that Megan expected absolute truth and she was not aware that she had been communicating messages, even to herself, that did not clearly express her objectives.

Perhaps there is another basic element that explains the tenacity with which some people insist on wanting to understand why their partners lie to them. Normally one would think that people who are so intent on finding reasons and explanations would contemplate changes in themselves that would provide allowances for dishonest behavior, depending on the validity of the reasons for the lies. But as the inquiry into Megan's goals demonstrated, that was not the case. She continued to insist on absolute honesty, but there was an underlying belief that if she knew Howard's reason for omitting the truth, she would be able to challenge his reason and persuade him to change. Further probing into Megan's thoughts confirmed that this was her line of thinking.

Megan is not the only one engaged in this thought process; the statement "If I only understood why he or she is doing or saying that . . ." can be found frequently among people struggling with relationships. What these individuals fail to realize is that in effect they are assuming the responsibility for their partners' behaviors because they believe they can effect a change in that behavior if they only knew the reason for its existence.

Just as people have different reasons to lie, they place different meanings on the concept of lies. And the concept of "truth" falls into a range of great latitude. Does the omission of truth count as a lie? Some people might say it is a function of how much information the other person really needs to know. Do husbands or wives need to know that their spouse married them without ever loving them? Nobody can answer that question for them because it may vary from person to person. A forty-seven-year-old woman who married her husband twenty-five years ago without loving him apparently did not think he needed to know that. At the time she thought nobody else would propose marriage to her. Now she wants to divorce him for a chance to meet a passionate man she can fall in love with.[2]

In trying to decide about the concept of lying or not telling the truth, one might ask: "Who reaps the benefits from omission of the truth?" Consider the proverb "What people don't know can't hurt them." This is an invitation to omit the truth under the guise of sparing another person pain, which is only a small first step on the path to dishonesty and should be considered as such, a first step that might well lead to further lies.

This might be the answer for an advice seeker in the syndicated column of a daily newspaper. A young woman reported having caught her boyfriend in a lie. He had attended a company party that according to him invited only employees. However, as the young woman later found out, spouses and significant others were also included in the invitation. Why had the boyfriend lied? He had wanted to attend the party by himself for, as he said, schmoozing purposes, but he did not know how to tell his girlfriend without hurting her feelings. The young woman requesting advice seemed ambivalent; one could sense her wanting to believe him with her tiny question about whether his explanation was OK.[3]

On the other hand, people worry about forgiving someone's omission of the truth without even bothering about the reasons for the omission. As a sixty-five-year-old man who had been involved in an exclusive relationship for four years with a fifty-six-year-old woman reported, he thought the relationship was good but then he noticed a few months ago that his lady friend was becoming distant emotionally and physically. By accident he found out that the woman had been active on a dating website and he somehow found four months' worth of e-mail exchanges, with some of them being of a sexual and intimate nature. When he confronted her the woman initially denied it but then—faced with the evidence—admitted to the communication and that she had seen the other man twice without anything sexual occurring between them.

Now this sixty-five-year-old man's concern is that he cannot get the woman's betrayal out of his mind and that he will never be able to trust her. "How does one forget?" he asked. The advice giver suggested—among other things—that he make a conscious effort to push this betrayal out of his mind. Wouldn't the man be better advised to find out why his lady friend became involved in the dating website? It would indicate that she did not find the relationship as satisfying as he did. Under those circumstances she might be tempted again to look elsewhere for a companion. Besides, if one is willing to forgive one betrayal, he might just be able to repeat the forgiveness. Before considering forgiveness, the man should look deeper into the relationship; something needs fixing there if the two of them want to consider a continuation. What lesson would the man learn from forgiving her?[4]

Sometimes it is difficult to determine when and where the first step on the path to dishonesty occurred. In the union of two spouses who each have been divorced twice, it might be expected—and perhaps unjustly so—that lies or omissions of truth had occurred in their lives. And a woman whose two previous husbands had left her for other women would understandably be anxious about the possibility of a third such occurrence. The two spouses have been in their current marriage for ten years and recently the husband reestablished contact with his former fiancée, who had broken off their engagement about twenty years ago but is now getting a divorce. The husband explained that his new contact with his old fiancée was out of concern about her well-being. When his upset wife told him that she would not tolerate it the husband said he would stop.

In the meantime, the wife found out that the husband had opened another e-mail account and continued to communicate with his former fiancée. Technically speaking, if the husband did not clearly state what he would stop, he possibly did not lie. He might have meant that he would stop the communication using his regular e-mail account. Thus, when not clarified in detail, the meaning of truth is somewhat stretchable, according to the needs of the communicators.[5]

GUILT: THE FLIP SIDE OF THE COIN

Dishonesty and betrayal often have a companion in guilt feelings. Except for sociopaths to whom we generally ascribe a lack of remorse and guilt feelings, most people's conscience makes them feel uncomfortable when they realize that with their lies they have harmed another person. There are different ways to cope with the discomfort of feeling guilty; one can find fault with the person lied to and in this way the dishonesty can almost be justified—they had it coming! Another strategy used by many to relieve the stress is to confess. With the burden dropping from the confessor's shoulders the expectation of forgiveness spreads into his or her mind. This expectation of forgiveness does not just revolve around the dishonesty; it tends to include the betrayal, the actual wrongdoing. Often to the confessor's surprise the person betrayed, the victim, is not ready or willing to issue this blanket forgiveness.

Andrew, a handsome physician in his late thirties, found himself in that position. He and Linda had been happily married and Andrew was a good father to their three children. But lately there had not been much excitement in their small rural town. Things changed when Andrew ran into Jessica, a physical therapist at the local hospital. Jessica was young, pretty, and vibrant and, like many of the young female hospital employees, admired some of the staff physicians. Andrew felt vitalized talking to the young woman. He increased the professional connection by referring patients to physical therapy more regularly than before and, naturally, he checked with the therapist about his patients' progress. As their relationship entered a more intimate phase Andrew invited Jessica for lunch at the local country club a couple of times. He believed people would think it was just a lunch meeting of two medical professionals, and because he was in the elevated position of physician it would only be customary that he sign their lunch tickets.

However, people in the small town started to talk and Linda heard some of the rumors, but she did not confront Andrew with any suspicions she might have had. At the same time Jessica's behavior became more clinging, which, in turn, made coworkers more aware of the situation. Andrew could smell trouble and he started to feel guilty. As the second son of a minister, he knew he had sinned in his little lies to Linda about some of the time spent with Jessica and with the adulterous affair itself. His father would never forgive him. Andrew's older brother, Henry, was the evidence for that. Henry, a hospital administrator in a different town, had been married to Jill, his high school sweetheart. Henry had been engaged in a brief affair with a nurse at the hospital and even though the affair ended without a lot of publicity when the nurse was terminated from her job, Henry's father never forgave him. To this day, at family gatherings Jill, who divorced Henry, and the couple's two children are welcome but Henry is not included in that welcome.

To relieve the onslaught of uncomfortable feelings that may have been a combination of guilt feelings about Linda and anxiety connected to the memory of his older brother's fate, Andrew decided to confess to Linda about his by-now-ended affair with Jessica. At least Linda would be prepared in case Jessica would be less than discreet about their relationship. Confessing to the affair and getting it off his chest felt good, especially since he expected Linda to be grateful that he had already terminated the relationship with Jessica. However, Linda did not respond with gratitude to his confession but neither did she divorce Andrew. She dealt with it in her own way and the marriage limped along for another year or so.

Andrew found a promising position at a hospital in a larger city and he moved ahead, leaving Linda and their three children behind to finish out the school year in the small town. Hospitals with their many female employees of all ages and varying degrees of attractiveness constitute a pool of temptations for the male physicians. It did not take long for Andrew to connect with a very attractive divorced female employee. The two embarked upon a passionate and volatile affair that did not remain a secret for long. The hospital administrator had a talk with Andrew, explaining the moral values of the hospital founders. In another meeting with the female employee, the administrator terminated her contract. But this young woman was not to be pushed aside easily; she made the reason for her termination public although she could not change it because the contract included a clause about romantic relationships between employees. Although physicians don't feel the brunt from moral indignation as much as other employees, Andrew's position at the hospital was not as respected and stable as it had been when he started to work there. Again, he confessed his guilt to Linda but this time she opted for a divorce. She thought one confession was enough and it entered her mind that Andrew might appreciate the feeling of relief when getting rid of his guilty feelings because it freed him to do it again.

A midlife crisis was the explanation for a man in his early fifties who, after an extramarital affair of six weeks' duration, confessed to his lovely and intelligent wife of thirty-one years. His guilt over the affair just became too much to handle. The relief he felt as a consequence of his confession was immediate and cathartic; it made him eager to start his new life with the woman he thought he could not live without. Eight years later he still has not married the woman even though she gave up her previous relationship for him. He feels paralyzed by guilt and a sense of responsibility for his former wife and their children to the point that a new life is impossible for him.[6]

Some people experience guilt feelings about their lies or betrayals; others may think they scored a victory. It is rare, however, for the person who utters a first lie to never distort the truth again. The act of lying, especially if the person gets away with it, has a built-in mechanism for repetition. Often the second lie follows soon, made necessary as some cover-up for the first lie. Furthermore, the ease with which a lie can be applied as a problem-solving tool is too seductive to resist. Once its usefulness has been experienced, the temptation of repeated application as needed is too powerful. Well practiced and skillfully applied, the act of lying can take on the semblance of a sport. Each successfully applied lie will reinforce the act of lying and its continuation.

THE EFFECTS OF LIES ON RECEIVER'S SELF-ESTEEM

While some people who resort to the use of lies may justify their actions by proclaiming that they wanted to spare another person pain, others may defend themselves with the statement that they lied out of distress and fear of being rejected or abandoned. However, neither explanation is likely to pacify the angry feelings of the recipient of the lies. In fact, many people tend to regard another person's dishonest behavior toward them as an insult and judgment of their level of intelligence or degree of significance. For instance, if this person thinks he or she can get away with lying to me, the person must think I am not intelligent enough to detect the lie or I am too insignificant a person to bother telling the truth to.

Thus, people's deceitful behaviors can have negative effects on the recipients' self-esteem. Following Megan's example above, the continuation of others' deceitful behaviors can imply that the individual—like Megan—does not have the power to persuade the partner to modify or eliminate dishonest behavior. In other words, the Megans are not important enough to the Howards in the scenario for the Howards to increase the degree of honesty in their behaviors.

There are several coping strategies available for the resolution of situations like that. One way is to deny the person's deceitful behavior, which leaves the self-esteem intact; another is to become angry over the perceived insult in the lie and perhaps to retaliate in some way; a third way is to accept reality and adjust one's behavior to reduce vulnerability to similar events in the future. One of the simplest—but not pain-free—behavioral adjustments would be inaccessibility to the other's dishonest behaviors.

Another word of caution is indicated here: ill-advised vanity about one's intelligence, significance, or judgment can result in personal vulnerability in situations that lend themselves to dishonesty from one or the other party involved. There are individuals who pride themselves on their ability to accurately detect dishonesty in others, much like a "lie detector" test might function, but in general, most people would admit limited ability when it comes to detecting the lies of others.

According to some psychologists, "feeling duped is an aversive emotional response to the perception of having been taken advantage of in an interpersonal transaction." Being duped or suckered is just another instance of having been exposed to dishonest behavior, which is not uncommon in human social interactions. But because of the frequent risk of being duped, people have developed various structures for the prevention of being repeatedly exploited. These structures include cognitive, emotional, motivational, and personality aspects. When a person feels duped, he or she also experiences the notion of having lost. The partner who has gained more in the interaction is viewed as a winner, whereas the self is the loser. Having lost or having been taken advantage of gives rise to suspicion and increased vigilance in the person, not only toward the particular partner who took advantage, but to others in general.[7]

The risk of self-blame is inherent in being duped. The self-blame usually centers on the implication that the self is stupid or gullible. Insofar as the victim has voluntarily interacted in some way with the other person, by making a decision or by believing what was promised, the victim has assumed a certain degree of responsibility for what happened. The emotional reactions to having been victimized in this manner are complex and may range from anger, regret, shame, and guilt, to embarrassment. In some cases, the embarrassment seems to be the strongest emotional reaction, as it motivates people to hide the fact that they have been duped. By hiding this in order to protect their self-esteem, people give the dishonest person the freedom to pursue his or her tactics with other victims.[8]

Aside from the emotional reactions, how do people evaluate deceitful behavior that they experienced? How important is what the person telling a lie meant by it and why they did it, compared with the significance the recipient attaches to the lie? Research indicates that people's attributions about honesty based on having been duped follow an asymmetrical pattern. For instance, one dishonest behavior is considered sufficient evidence for labeling a person a cheat, but one honest behavior is far from being enough evidence to consider that person honest. This would follow the notion proposed by some psychologists that bad is stronger than good.[9]

While this trend may be relevant to issues of being duped or taken advantage of in economic situations, it may not be as readily applicable to individuals' romantic involvements. Considering the significant impact on one's self-esteem, in romantic relationships the deceit may present an even stronger temptation to overlook or explain away the lie. With that another lie is added—the recipient's own lie. In romantic relationships, the impact goes beyond simple lies; individuals often have dreams and hopes invested in the other person. The recognition of deceit would seriously implicate the collapse of the dreams. A factor permitting significant influence on the likelihood of dishonesty in intimate relationships—more so than in any other relationship—is that of wishful thinking.

WHEN WISHFUL THINKING BECOMES STRONGER THAN OBJECTIVE EVIDENCE

Why do people repeatedly believe lies and empty promises in romantic relationships? One reason might be that they feel uncomfortable confronting anyone with their lies, let alone someone they promised to trust and support emotionally. Another reason for swallowing the lies may be that they have an investment—not only in the relationship, but also in their own judgment. At some time in the past they had made the judgment that this was the right person to share their lives with. Now the protection of the judgment's validity becomes more important than the protection of their own well-being.

The admission of an error in judgment is difficult for most people. If instead they could manage the acceptance of the lies and empty promises as true, they could deny the error. Denying the signs of deceit and refusing to admit mistakes in judgment for the protection of one's self-esteem only makes the error grow bigger and bigger—it does not go away and eventually the price in pain and disappointment skyrockets.

Of course, the realization that one's judgment is not impeccable can be scary. It may impact individuals' self-confidence in negative ways, such as refusing to trust anyone in the future or doubting their own decisions. But it is more discomforting to acknowledge that they blinded themselves to what they had first perceived objectively, perhaps only for a moment, until they decided to accept cognitively and emotionally, alone or in corroboration with the offender, the distortion of that perception.

The power of wishful thinking readily combines with attempts to camouflage errors in judgment for the continued acceptance of another's lies or meaningless promises. People want good things to come their way. Most people want to be involved in a happy, lasting relationship; they want *this* relationship to be the one that will provide them with eternal happiness. The wish to believe is often so strong that people hide it under an apparent investigative façade by saying, "If I only knew why he or she is lying, I could understand it better and could understand the person" (a line of reasoning very similar to that explained in Megan's case above). But even with improved understanding, a lie is still a lie and an empty promise remains a promise unfulfilled. Does it really matter whether the person is a habitual liar or only changes the truth occasionally for some immediate gain? As the target person, one pays each time unless one cuts the strings.

HALF-TRUTHS SUPPORTED BY WISHFUL THINKING

After discussing the occurrences and effects of lies and omissions of the truth, there is another element of partial dishonesty that is worth looking at in more detail. Statements of incomplete truth are as common as other breaches of the truth and they are also greatly aided by wishful thinking on the part of the target person. Consider for example this statement often made by a man to a female partner in a tentative relationship (let's call them Fred and Tina): "I enjoy so much being with you, but I am not ready to make a commitment. It's too early . . ." This is not a complete lie. Fred is not ready to commit—at least not to Tina. He may be totally committed to himself, however, and to what he wants.

What are Tina's most likely translations of his statement? "He is afraid of making a commitment; many men are because they don't quite know what it entails. He is not ready *yet* (but with more time he will be). He might have been hurt by another woman in the past. Poor Fred, he doesn't trust me yet, but if he gets to know me better . . ." And she expresses understanding. This male-female interchange clears the path to continued enjoyable dating, at least for a while. Tina is acting on hope and tries her best to put his mind at ease, which is not really necessary because he has nothing to worry about. Fred has not made a promise he doesn't intend to keep. He has not told her a lie either. For him, there is nothing to feel uncomfortable about.

There are, of course, occurrences where the male and female roles in this type of interchange are reversed, where the noncommitting partner is a female and the man is the understanding, translating, and waiting partner. However, the Fred-Tina scenario appears to be in the majority among contemporary dating couples.

There are various outcomes to Fred and Tina's continuing relationship. Perhaps Fred will be able to overcome his fear of commitment (if this was his problem) and the two will happily walk into the sunset—hand in hand. Another version might demonstrate a reduction in the frequency of their dates. Fred will call less often or at the last minute. Or there may even be weekends when Tina does not hear from him at all. Later when she asks him about it, he might say something like "Oh, it was my parents' anniversary. I thought I mentioned to you that I would have to attend." Tina does not remember having heard anything about it and she is upset but does not accuse Fred of anything dishonest, yet.

Similar events continue to occur from time to time. Now Tina expresses her displeasure. Fred accuses her of not listening when he tells her about some of his plans with others. She defends herself and accuses him of being inconsiderate, selfish, and superficial. But she continues meeting with him. Their quarrels become more frequent and their roles more established. It is usually Tina who is complaining; Fred is accusing Tina of behaviors that he doesn't like; and Tina is defending and complaining about him again.

In the meantime, what transpires in Fred's mind? From thinking "I can't wait to see her; she is cute, exciting, smart, and good in bed" to "She expects to see me, to be with her all the time. I have no breathing space." There has been a shift in his perception from a focus on what he wants to what he thinks she wants and he rebels against it. If he gives in to what she wants, he is hooked. He is not free and independent anymore. He may justify his withdrawal based on her attempts to control him.

Half-truths and wishful thinking make for a powerful combination. As discussed in the previous section, wishful thinking by itself can overshadow objective evidence; when the element of half-truths is added anything can be swallowed to contribute to one's happiness—even if it is temporary happiness. An example is the woman who is fortunate enough to have been living with the man of her dreams for the past three years. They have a son and she is the happiest she has ever been. There is a minor point of disturbance—the man's wife and children.

When the wife or one of the children call him, her husband jumps. Although the husband agrees that he should talk to his wife about a divorce, he never gets around to actually doing it because he does not want to do it in front of the children and the children are always around. Almost half of the man's paycheck goes toward supporting his wife and children, which sucks the cohabiting family dry, according to the new woman. She is especially upset that there is no court paper that limits how long the payments to the man's family will continue.[10]

The cohabiting woman seems to believe the man and blames his wife for the loss of part of his paycheck and that apparently there is no end in sight. The statement that the children are *always* around when the man talks to his wife raises the question, is that completely true or might it be a half-truth? It is difficult to imagine that the children never go to bed when the adults are still awake and able to discuss things. In other words, does the man really want a divorce from his wife? How does he explain to the children why he is not living with them? Being a mother herself, one would think that those thoughts would enter the woman's mind. Does the man really need a divorce? Perhaps he is not legally married and in due time there might be a third woman with whom he could live and have children. Those are all questions worth contemplating.

RECOGNIZING THE SIGNS OF LIES AND BROKEN PROMISES (HOW RELIABLE IS YOUR LIE DETECTOR?)

There are few guidelines on how to spot a lie. Common belief has it that some people are unable to look others in the eye when they are lying; others may be bothered by a nervous cough or nervous giggling when they are distorting the truth. There are also other behavioral nuances one can observe over time. But there are not always overt signs that tip one off. In fact, research has shown that individuals tend to overestimate their ability to detect the deception tactics of those around them. In one study when individuals involved in romantic relationships were asked about lies their partners may tell them, they believed that it was not difficult to detect their partners' lies; at the same time they believed that their own lies were much more successful than their partners' attempts at distortion of the truth.[11]

It is not clear from the results if the surveyed individuals believed that their partners were not as sophisticated in spotting lies or if they declined to make an issue of it. As a likely explanation it was considered that those interviewed saw themselves as more highly skilled in their deception than those around them. But there is no basis for this self-confidence. People's ability to detect the lies of their romantic partners is only about 59 percent—a little better than chance. Thus, the high levels of confidence in their own ability might make them more vulnerable to becoming victims of their partners' dishonesty.

Some researchers have tried to explain this phenomenon on the basis of a motivational impairment, meaning that most people would rather not know whether they are being lied to, particularly if the person lying to them is a partner in a close relationship. Acknowledging their partner's dishonesty would threaten to dissolve the relationship. "The bottom line is that much of the time, we really are not motivated to discover that our partner is lying to us, and will be happy to succumb to the 'Ostrich Syndrome': we will simply bury our heads in the sand and hope all the nastiness in the world around us will go away."[12]

Another factor operating in poor deception detection in close relationships can be seen in the truth bias. People who strongly believe in honesty in close relationships will naturally expect the same level of honesty from their partners as they believe they practice. Subscribing to the same type of values is just one of the reasons they have chosen each other. And if it turns out that their values are not in complete agreement, an open discussion of the importance of honesty in the relationship should convince the partner of the need to be absolutely truthful.

A close sibling to honesty is the issue of trust. Trust has been elevated to the level of sacredness in people's minds; we trust in god; we trust the president, king, queen, or whoever the current ruler of our society is; we trust our parents, our teachers, our priests and ministers; and we trust close friends. We also expect to be able to trust our spouses. But it is more complex than just trusting someone; trust carries with it certain demands and expectations. Because we consider trust to be so sacred, the person we trust has to be worthy of it; he or she better not disappoint us. Receiving someone's trust generally includes obligations; the trusting person expects to receive something of value in return. The something may be simple secrecy or it may be an act of assistance. Loyalty to the trust giver is an absolute demand; it cannot be permitted to fail.

PROTECTION: BECOMING ONE'S OWN BEST FRIEND

When the desire to search for the reason behind a person's dishonesty enters one's awareness, it is time to act as one's own best friend. To a friend one might even say something like "Once a liar always a liar." (Although some people—and rightly so—would object to defining a person on the basis of only one of his or her behaviors.) In a friend, errors in judgment can be accepted—why not in oneself? People might even assist their friends in sharpening their judgment skills as they point out what seems to be realistic and what could be the consequences of following some irrational path—so why not do as much for their own protection?

For those who have been told a story that leaves room for doubt or if they find out later the story was based on a lie, the first question should be, "Has this person ever lied to me before?"(And we are not talking here about little polite lies or "white lies" or some insignificant exaggerations.) In a new relationship, the answer may be "no" and will not provide additional information for the moment. However, it is beneficial to develop the habit of raising questions like that automatically. Furthermore, unless it is a life-or-death situation, an immediate answer to the question of whether or not a person has been dishonest is not absolutely necessary, but it helps set a basic level of awareness to the possibility of impaired honesty. There will be opportunities later in the relationship to find out more and the information will still be valuable and relevant for protection from future pain originating from this person's dishonesty.

This is not to suggest, however, that one should proceed blindly and wait for the rude awakening, hoping for increased strength in a confrontation with the person at a later time. As mentioned earlier, many people feel uncomfortable about confrontations of all kinds and especially about accusing another person of lying—how easy it would be to postpone the investigation.

The important issue here is that at the first shadow of doubt individuals should not attempt to explain away their doubts with something like, "He wasn't really aware that what he said was not the whole truth; anybody can make a mistake." That kind of reasoning could be a costly mistake. Instead, the indication here is to ask the question "If it is a lie, whose interest does it serve?" If the answer is "Mine, because she wants to protect me from the truth," this is a signal for the likelihood of self-deception. Another question would be, "What likely consequences will I encounter if I accept the lie as the truth or the empty promise as a sincere commitment?"

Returning for a moment to Randolph, the professor with the unfaithful wife, it happened that between the second and third periods of her affairs Randolph and his wife did not have sex very often because Randolph experienced erection difficulties. It may have protected him from contracting a sexually transmitted disease. People might say, "Randolph's wife was a nurse; she would know better than to catch a disease like that." Health professionals, such as nurses and physicians, are not immune to infections and some of them, just like other people, do suffer from sexually transmitted diseases such as genital herpes or chlamydia, or a number of other infections. Those can be expensive consequences for the Randolphs and Marys of our world.

Gina, a widowed registered nurse, was one who paid the consequences. Almost two years after her husband's death she went on a date with Tom, who had recently been divorced from his wife. Over a cup of coffee Tom confessed his loneliness and gave the impression that he had not dated anyone since the divorce. Gina understood; she still felt lonely after the loss of her husband. Gina and Tom helped each other over the rough spots of being on their own. Tom felt comfortable in Gina's home and appreciated her invitation to stay the weekends with her. She enjoyed caring for another person again and Tom was easy to pamper. He was so appreciative.

Several months later Gina found out that she had contracted genital herpes. Tom had been the only man she had sexual intercourse with after her husband's death. When she told him about it he became indignant and defensive; she could not have gotten it from him, he declared. Then, apparently for his own protection, he immediately left Gina's home and never returned or communicated with her again.

Gina met another young man she liked; however, she did not enter into a sexual relationship with him although he was persuasive in his attempts. About two months later he broke up with Gina not because she resisted his sexual advances but because he had been told by an acquaintance that Gina had herpes. How did he find out? He and Tom traveled in the same circles, and although they did not know each other personally, other people who knew both of them spread the news.

Making a case for the assumption that Tom had been the source of Gina's infection, then—unless he was unaware of being infected, which is unlikely—his path of dishonesty started with an omission of the truth followed by an outright lie as well as the spread of the rumor or "half-truth" about Gina's condition. If Gina had asked Tom about sexually transmitted diseases at the beginning of their sexual involvement, would Tom have told her the truth? Possibly not. When Tom, immersed in his loneliness, indicated that he had not dated anyone since his divorce, was that a true statement? Perhaps not.

What were the reasons for Tom's divorce from his wife? Might he have been involved in extramarital affairs? Could he have contracted genital herpes in one of those affairs and his wife divorced him when she found out? Or did his wife engage in affairs, where she contracted the disease and—in turn—infected Tom? Those are all questions Gina did not explore. Why not? Because she did not want to offend him, or hurt his feelings, or remind him of the pain involved in his unhappy marriage and the emotional turmoil of the divorce. As she protected him Gina made herself the victim.

All too often, people do not inquire about their partner's previous relationships because they think it might be interpreted as spying, as being nosy. Even if they do make an attempt to learn more about the prospective partner's history, a statement like "That's in the past, it's over with; I don't want to talk about it" prevents further inquiry. At times, the inquiring person may even feel guilty and apologize for his or her inquisitive behavior.

The disturbing effects of dishonesty can linger for years as experienced by one female advice seeker. While separated from her then husband, the woman met her current husband, a man who was in the service and told her that he was separated from his wife (even though his wife and children waited at home for his return). Technically, his statement had not been a lie because he was indeed separated from his family—at least geographically. Three years into the marriage the woman found out how devastated her husband's previous wife had been when he suddenly initiated the divorce. Now her husband is telling her that had it not been for her he would still be married to his first wife. The woman regrets having married this man and understandably is afraid that he will do the same to her. Telling a lie takes only a few moments, but the devastating effects of it can be felt for years.[13]

Before entering into a physically and emotionally close relationship, people would do well to seriously contemplate that their prospective partner's history might easily become their own history. Gina's situation is a lesson to heed. She was so considerate of Tom's feelings that she put her own safety at risk—and she paid dearly for it.

Thus, long before considering the other person in a relationship, it is advisable to scrutinize oneself, asking questions such as "Am I the kind of person who puts another's pain before my own?" or "To be a good person, do I always have to consider that I might be hurting the other before gathering information?" An affirmative answer to questions like these would strongly indicate the need to closely examine one's personality characteristics and possibly make modifications before jumping into another relationship.

SENDING OUT SIGNALS

Jenny has learned not to express her wishes because she thinks she will make herself vulnerable to disappointments if she openly communicates her wishes. Apparently, at some time in her childhood Jenny did utter a wish for a certain toy. When Christmastime came Jenny found among her gifts something quite different, a toy she did not care for at all. The doll she had wished for was among her older sister's presents. Jenny was crushed but then thought it must have been a mix-up. In a soft, hesitating voice she asked her mother about it. Her mother's answer, that the doll was designated to be her sister's, dealt Jenny a double blow of pain.

As a consequence, at that moment Jenny decided that she would never again tell anybody what she really wanted. It was her way of ensuring that she would not be disappointed again. If people did not know what she wanted, they could not hurt her by giving her something different. The underlying reasoning in Jenny's attempts to control the experience of pain was, as one could guess, the assumption that people would disappoint her on purpose. What a harsh picture of the world Jenny had constructed in her mind, a world where people would disillusion her on purpose. Her protection was that nobody would be allowed to obtain that much knowledge of her and her desires.

Jenny's dating history was, as she called it, "unremarkable." The few young men who asked her out did not remain in her company for long. She thinks they did not quite know what to do with her. They might have felt uncomfortable in her presence because they did not get to know her. Jenny has kept her promise to this day; her husband is at a loss regarding any gifts she might want for Christmas or her birthday or their anniversary. He does not know what would please her. Jenny knows what he wants and she provides it as much as she can. She loves and protects her husband but that does not include giving him the knowledge about her secret wishes.

Jenny's control mechanism keeps her protected from disappointments but also safe from those pleasant surprises that are the actions of a loving person. Jenny's signal to the world broadcasts that it is not necessary to spend thought on what would please her because it is not important enough to her or she would express her desires. With that signal, Jenny confirms what she thought was happening in her childhood and ensures that it will continue to happen for the rest of her life. She will not be given what she desires.

One of the reasons for meeting and connecting with the same type of person repeatedly is that people's behaviors contain many signals about themselves, so it is logical that they might attract the same or similar type of person over and over again. For instance, a person who repeatedly puts others first in attempts to help or please them, will most likely attract people who want the help of others—even to the point of taking advantage of them. It seems like a match made in heaven. Surely, they would be compatible—except for the fact that being taken advantage of for significant periods of time finally breeds resentment in the helper person.

The person who never voices a preference, such as where to meet for lunch, will eat most often in places determined by others because they attract those who care more about their own preferences than about those of their companions. Of course, there are situations when it is more important that we be with a certain person than where we will be together.

Most people probably know a person who when deciding to meet for lunch, dinner, or other occasion usually responds with "Wherever you want," "You decide, whatever is convenient for you," or "It doesn't matter to me." After a while, this type of interchange may cause some people to feel ambivalent about the person and the relationship. Do they feel relieved because the other person is so agreeable that they don't have to worry about his or her wishes? Many do. Do they feel frustrated because it seems that the whole responsibility for the decision about where to go rests on them? Some do. Or do they feel uncomfortable due to the realization that they don't really know that person—they don't know what that person wants and they don't know what the person is really like? A few do. Finally out of frustration those few give up on that person and fade out of the relationship. But that person will be spotted and recognized by someone else, someone who cares most about his or her own preferences. And the "agreeable" person will gravitate toward the one whose behavior is so familiar.

What does the "agreeable" person think of his or her behavior? What signals does she think she is transmitting? "I want you to be pleased" or "Our meeting is not that important to me; I didn't take the time to think about where to meet" or "Our meeting is more important to me than the place we meet at" or "I don't want you to know my preferences because then you cannot disappoint me on purpose" or "If I let you choose the place, I am not to blame if we don't like it"—there are many different interpretations of the agreeable person's signals and in all probability she is not aware of them except for the one she intends (but most likely fails) to send.

Returning for a moment to the story of Fred and Tina, what signals did Fred send out? I want to spend time with you as long as it is interesting and for my pleasure, but I am not promising you a permanent or exclusive relationship. And he may have hoped, banking on past experiences, that Tina would not read his signals correctly. Did Tina know what signals she transmitted? Was she aware that her message let Fred know that she was willing to continue their relationship even without his commitment? Apparently, she did not consider the actual content of her message because she focused on the content of her unexpressed goals. Was Tina aware of her self-defeating communication behaviors? Probably not.

Sending out signals that are different from what the person actually means or wishes can be understood as a form of dishonesty—or at least, lacking a significant degree of honesty because it leaves the other person in the dark about important aspects of a relationship.

ONLINE PORNOGRAPHY, INTERNET AFFAIRS, AND CYBERSEX

Emily was still in love with Anthony, her husband of almost ten years. They had two children and Anthony worked long hours in his profession as financial advisor. There were evening appointments with clients when Emily had to feed the children and get them to bed by herself. She would wait for Anthony to come home and have dinner with him before they could relax for the night. In recent years Anthony didn't feel like having dinner after a meeting with a client and preferred to spend time in his study to go over the paperwork concerning the case he had just worked on. Emily still had a healthy sex drive and many evenings waited for Anthony to come to bed. Sometimes she dozed off and awoke later to find the other side of the bed still empty. Concerned, one night she got up and searched for Anthony, thinking he might have gone to the kitchen to fix himself a snack. But she did not find him in the kitchen. He was still in his study in front of his computer, watching pornography and masturbating.

She did not understand what she saw. Here she had been all ready for him but he preferred the impersonal involvement with pornography over the pleasure of playing with her living body. When she asked Anthony about it he explained that it was less stressful for him to be watching pornography, getting aroused, and finding relief through masturbation than being involved with, thinking about, and satisfying another person. There was no requirement on his performance; he could just relax on his own terms. Obviously, he did not worry about Emily's sexual desires and satisfaction; that was going to be her problem.

Emily did not know whether Anthony was involved in cybersex or not; he refused to discuss it and she did not feel up to snooping around in his study. It was painful enough for her to acknowledge that his sexual desire for her was not strong enough to take the steps of seducing her or simply to be there ready for her to seduce him. It was a big blow to her self-esteem as a woman. She knew the marriage could not survive for long.

The Internet is easily accessible, it is affordable, and it preserves the anonymity of its users—if some precautions are taken. Those characteristics make it a popular vehicle for a new type of cheating and dishonesty among spouses and romantic partners. Many of those who engage in it insist that it cannot be counted as infidelity because there is no physical contact or actual sex involved. Others point to the fact that Internet affairs include emotional infidelity because those affairs frequently involve intimate chat sessions and sexually stimulating conversations. To the nonparticipating partners of those who engage in Internet affairs or cybersex the nonphysical infidelity can be just as devastating as a physical affair.

Because of the secretive nature of online affairs, it is difficult to obtain reliable statistics. However, some studies have been conducted. One study of 1,828 web users in Sweden revealed that almost a third of the participants had engaged in cybersex interactions. Furthermore, it was found that people in committed relationships were just as likely to be involved in cybersex as those who were single. There were, however, differences according to gender and age. While men's interest in cybersex declined with age, women's interest increased somewhat. For women age thirty-five to forty-nine, 37 percent admitted cybersexual experiences as compared with only a quarter of the men in the same age group.

An Australian study found that of 183 adult individuals in romantic relationships, more than 10 percent had become involved in intimate online relationships, 8 percent had engaged in cybersex, and 6 percent had actually met their Internet partners in person. Another gender difference was observed by a practitioner in the United States who counseled online affair participants and excessive users of online pornography. Overall, men are more drawn to pornography while women gravitate more toward erotic chats and webcam sessions (including filming mutual masturbation with a web camera). The results of another study revealed that almost two-thirds of the participants acknowledged that they had met and had sex with their Internet partners and only 44 percent of them used condoms.[14]

Online affairs live on fantasy. Considering the study results above, did those 56 percent of people who did not use condoms think they knew their Internet correspondents well enough not to be concerned about sexually transmitted diseases or pregnancies? Fantasy is the main ingredient when thinking about and communicating with the online affair partner. And if at some point they meet in real life, fantasy will bridge the actual encounter, at least for a while. Fantasy helps in remaking oneself into the most desirable individual imaginable. The computer keyboard is a willing design tool. The real-life situations of most people cannot compete with the seductive aspects of fantasy. Real-life relationships are at best mediocre compared with fantasy intimacy and they require more work—a definite loser.

Outside sexual involvement, whether it is of a physical nature or through some fantasy channels, hardly enhances a marital or otherwise committed relationship. Reduced sexual desire for the spouse is a common consequence as the fascination with the third person increases. Thus the extramarital involvement relegates the neglected spouse to the position of an outsider because the partner chooses to communicate his or her most intimate thoughts and desires to someone else, a person outside the intimate sphere of the original two partners' union. A cruel displacement indeed.

A partner in a committed relationship who decides to replace the interactive sexual relationship between the partners with a one-sided affair—physical or virtual—is secretly divorcing him- or herself from an important part of the relationship. As most extramarital affairs are kept a secret, at least for a while, the partner is placed at a disadvantage when trying to make sense out of the other's changed behaviors. Anxiety and self-blame might keep the unsuspecting partner occupied for a while until the truth comes out and he or she experiences the shock of the betrayal.

• *4* •

In the Name of Love

A review of marriage's political history in the United States might begin with a comparison of American marriages and marriages in other parts of the world. While in the early twentieth century marriages in countries such as China, Japan, Russia, and Poland were arranged, Americans were committed to the notion that marriage should be founded on love. People consented to marry each other based on the "true love" they felt for the other. For instance, sociologists observing a Midwestern town found that the inhabitants believed that the only valid basis for marriage was the partners' romantic love for each other. The arranged marriages customary in other parts of the world were seen as an expression of coercion, which seemed un-American in its philosophy. The "love match" came to be the American ideal of marriage.[1]

Elevating love to such importance in the minds of people opens the door to misuse of the wonderful concept of love. Love can serve as a justification for poor judgment. If one is in love, it is understandable to make mistakes, never mind that these mistakes can be costly for the individual who errs in the context of love. If love is so all-important, one may be tempted to *believe* to be in love in order not to lose out on this wonderful experience.

ACTING ON THE NOTION OF LOVE

Sue, the divorced mother of a three-year-old son, had just turned thirty. She described herself as being high-strung, impatient, goal-directed, but flexible. Right out of graduate school she married her boyfriend from high school. He had been her first love and while he attended college in a different town, they had kept in touch. Sue believed that she had done well in following her plans to get her career started first and then get married. She did not know much about men because she had not dated anybody but her boyfriend. Due to the geographical distance between them while both were in college, she was not aware of interests beyond what he wrote to her in letters and e-mails. Both returned to their hometown after graduation and—believing that they were still very much in love—made wedding plans.

Although they had practically grown up together, now they were strangers without realizing it. She remembered experiencing some doubts concerning the commitment that she and Jeff were about to make. But the wedding invitations had already been mailed, and Sue did not dare talk to anyone about her misgivings. Their honeymoon was disappointing; neither one had much sexual experience. Nevertheless, their son was conceived during their brief honeymoon. Married life proved hardly less disappointing than their honeymoon had been. And when they got to know each other again after their wedding, they did not seem to fit into each other's idea of a spouse. They could not reconcile their expectations of married life. They were not ready for the burden of a baby. The divorce did not take long. The only issue that Jeff contested was the child support, but he grudgingly accepted the amount ordered by the court. Sue found another job in a different town. Jeff did not object to her move; he had little interest in spending time with his young son.

Sue and Jeff are two of the many young people who were never really single before they married each other. Except for their college years, they had lived with their parents, and being in college, still at least partially supported by parents, does not constitute single life with all the responsibilities that it includes. Neither one had been responsible for meal preparation and household chores. If singleness is a time for being a totally responsible adult, Sue and Jeff did not fit that description.

In a different town with a new job, a baby, and no support system, Sue tried to put her life back together again. One of her friends at home had given Sue a book about singles published some years ago. Sue found the book helpful. She used the advice in the book to her advantage and diligently followed most of the exercises.[2]

Her life had become manageable again; she even made some new female friends. However, her attitude toward men remained bitter and resentful. She considered them to be superficial and selfish. Although she was satisfied with her adjustment, the question of how she could have gotten into such an unhealthy marriage kept nagging at her. An announcement for a personal growth group called "Single—Again" caught her eye.

LOVE EXPLAINS MANY THINGS

Love can be used as an explanation or excuse for many actions. Love can make a person forget his or her values and goals in life. Sally, a pretty brunette with lively blue eyes, had been infatuated before when dating a few men in her early twenties. She had been popular among her fellow college students. But now she was truly in love; she knew Kevin was the man for her. They shared many interests and she loved Kevin's sense of determination. Their sex life was exciting as well as filled with tender moments. More and more often Sally's thoughts strayed into wedding-related topics. But when Kevin's proposal came it did not include the word marriage; Kevin proposed living together for a while.

As would be expected, Sally was disappointed, even angry. She did not believe in living together without being married. But the more she thought about it, the more she believed that cohabiting would be safer than continuing to date. At least she and Kevin would spend much more time together, meaning that there would be fewer occasions for meeting other prospective partners. So she agreed to his proposal of cohabitation. Their life together was generally pleasant and satisfying, except Sally could not help thinking that Kevin did not love her as much as she loved him because he had not wanted to marry her.

During the third year of their cohabitation Sally got pregnant. Did she forget to take her birth control pills regularly? They did not talk about that; instead Kevin suggested that they get married soon, and so they did. Sally gave birth to a healthy baby boy and everybody should have been happy. But Sally could not forget that Kevin had made no move toward marriage until her pregnancy. Was she by herself not good enough to marry? This was a recurring thought that brought up feelings of anger every time it occurred to her. At first Sally did not communicate her anger and the reason for it, but as her bad feelings grew with the passage of time she started accusing Kevin of not loving her and claimed that he only married her because of their son. Kevin tried to convince Sally that he loved her and that in time they would have gotten married anyway.

For a while Sally calmed down but those recurrent thoughts had taken on a life of their own and Sally's anger erupted intermittently. Their arguments became more frequent, especially when Kevin developed stronger feelings for his son. He took Ken out on weekends to the zoo and other children's activities to shield the boy from his mother's anger. Of course, that fueled Sally's anger even more. At one of those outings Kevin and his son ran into Tana, a previous girlfriend whom Kevin had dated before he met Sally. They became engaged in a lively conversation. Suddenly, Tana seemed so much more fun to be with than Sally. Sadly, Kevin said good-bye to Tana, and took Ken by the hand and went home.

In all innocence little Ken told his mother about the smiling young woman they had met. Sally's ears perked up: "Who was that woman?" Kevin explained that they had met Tana, his old girlfriend, by accident and she had been interested in little Ken, so they talked for a while. Sally remained suspicious and arguments erupted more frequently, leading them finally into the divorce court—a confirmation to the sad statistics regarding cohabitation and marriage as discussed in chapter 2.

Sally's anger seemed justified when she found out that Kevin was dating Tana again. She told Kevin she would take him to court, demanding sole custody of Ken if Kevin was with Tana on his visitation days with Ken. Her threat did not have the desired effect; Kevin married Tana and there was nothing Sally could complain about to the courts. During the visits with his father little Ken was in the safety of a family, morally and legally united in marriage. Sally would like to be married again but has not found the right candidate yet.

Love may be stated as the reason, explanation, or excuse for many self-defeating behaviors that are difficult to comprehend, but what is often more difficult to understand is individuals' basis for loving a certain person. What are the criteria that the person to be loved should incorporate into his or her personality? Apparently, some people do not worry about their partner's personality traits—as long as they believe they love the other person. This seems to be the case for a young woman, let's call her Nancy, who has been in love with a man for several years. The problem is that the man has been going out with another woman who not only works at the same place Nancy does, but also lives in the same apartment complex. The man tells Nancy that he only goes out with the other woman for the sake of her grandchildren; he doesn't really like her. Although the man's stated reason for going out with this woman is an unusual one, other people who know him are not convinced of the veracity of his explanation. When he has the opportunity, the man sneaks over to Nancy and they sleep together, but he never takes her out in public even though she begs him to.

Now Nancy wonders if she should talk to the other woman about this triangle situation or if she should just be happy with what little attention she receives from the man. Judging by Nancy's description, the man apparently does not tell her the whole truth about his involvement with the other woman, but this does not seem to reduce her love for him in any way. The author of the newspaper advice column expressed the concern that any help offered to Nancy will be rationalized away by her as she will insist on loving him instead of seeing the man for what he is and herself for what she is. Yes, in the name of love, some individuals can manage to explain away reality and remain stuck in the cage of their own fantasies and denial.[3]

Falling in and out of love in short order is just one area where convenient explanations (or excuses) for behaviors can result in some undesired consequences. Historically, abuse—or even murder—of the love object has been claimed as a consequence of overwhelming feelings of love. In modern times, some places to look for examples of misuse of the love concept are shelters for battered women and children. A therapist who treated more than two hundred women over a period of two years found that most of them had been involved in abusive dating relationships that began while they were still in high school. Many of these young females had been choked, punched in the face, or kicked in the stomach by their boyfriends. They arrived in emergency rooms or the shelter with cracked ribs or broken jaws. Several of them had children with more than one abuser. Yet many of them returned to their abusers because they could not imagine a life without them. Statistically speaking, abused women will return to their abusers seven to nine times before finally leaving them.[4]

JEALOUSY AND POSSESSIVENESS AS JUSTIFICATION FOR ABUSE AND ISOLATION

There are also women who might not return to the same abuser but repeatedly end up in other abusive relationships. The boyfriends' abusive behaviors are often explained—by the boyfriends as well as by the girls—as a result of the men's jealousy and the general interpretation is that jealousy equals love. Parents may ask their teenage daughters why they remain in a dating relationship that is abusive: what do they see in a boy or young man who treats them poorly, verbally or physically? The answer most often heard is "But I love him."

What many young girls and women regard as love becomes an emotional dependency, which translates into a need for nurturance, support, and protection or belonging—even in persons who are capable of functioning independently. The degrees of emotional dependency are generally operationalized psychologically within symptoms and diagnoses of dependent personality disorder (DPD). Dependent individuals exhibit certain partner-specific influence strategies, designed to emphasize the dependent person's vulnerability and submissiveness as well as to minimize the possibility of abandonment.[5]

Julie divorced her husband after six years of marriage. She had a difficult time understanding the turn of events. Matt was so easygoing when they met. Not much seemed to disturb him. Although his parents did not approve of the marriage, Matt was committed to Julie and their future. In fact, he insisted that they not invite his parents to their small wedding ceremony. Julie was curious about his parents; she had never met them. Matt explained that his parents could not accept the divorce from his first wife. He did not say much about that marriage either. "We were too young for the responsibility of a marriage," Matt stated when Julie inquired about it.

During the early years of their marriage everything seemed perfect. They were very much in love with each other and aside from their work schedules spent all their time together. During this time neither Julie nor Matt kept up with friends they had known before the marriage. They lived for each other.

Julie's competence and hard work impressed her employer and she was promoted to a supervisory position. Julie could hardly wait to tell her husband about the promotion but she was not prepared for his response. Matt expressed concern that the new position would drain Julie's attention and energy away from their personal life. Matt's concerns had a basis in reality because Julie's new position required some overtime work on her part. Although it was not excessive, Matt was unhappy about it. For a while he gave Julie the silent treatment when she returned home later than usual. Soon he resorted to arguments and accused her of flirting with her boss. He called several times at her office, demanding that she come home.

His expressions of jealousy became nastier, especially when he spent his time drinking while waiting for her. Finally one evening he became physically violent. Later he tearfully apologized, explaining that it was only his great love for her and his concern about her working late that made him hit her. Julie forgave him and for a while things were quiet. Several months later at the mention of a business trip for her company Matt's violence erupted again.

Were there any signs about Matt's jealousy before she married him? Julie did not think so, but then she remembered that before their marriage every time she had gone out with friends, which was not very often, Matt had called, asking where she had been and with whom. No matter how late she returned home there were always calls from him. At the time she equated those calls and his questioning with his love and concern for her safety. She also remembered that when she told him that she had had a good time with her friends he criticized her for going out with friends in the evening and coming home by herself. It was not safe for a young woman to be alone on the streets.

Also, one time when she had been a few minutes late for their date Matt had questioned her in detail about where she had been and she remembered him making a gesture as if to hit her, but he caught himself and changed the movement to pointing his finger at her. Did he mean to hit her? Were those signs serious enough for Julie to become alarmed? Probably; but she explained them away, making herself believe that she misinterpreted his movements.

WHEN ABUSE BECOMES A WAY OF LIFE

In longer-lasting relationships, partners come to respond to each other in habitual ways. They develop a particular style or pattern of behaving with each other that becomes automatic. They don't have to think about it. Responding to an abusive partner can become a routine as much as any repeated behavior. As actress Ellen Burstyn explained, even when meeting another man with that abusive trait, one responds in the same way as one has done to a previous abusive partner. While operating in those behavior patterns, people do not see what they are involved in.[6]

What does one say to fourteen- and fifteen-year-old girls who "love" their boyfriends in spite of the boys' potentially abusive behaviors? Mothers are desperate for advice about their daughters being involved in abusive relationships. Whether it is a fourteen-year-old girl or a twenty-one-year-old daughter, mothers see the abusive behavior or potential for abuse in their daughters' boyfriends but are helpless against their daughters as they exclaim, "But I love him!"

As one woman reported in a syndicated advice column, she divorced her abusive husband after twenty-one years of marriage and is now dating a wonderful man who treats her well. Her current concern is that her twenty-year-old daughter is dating a young man who seems to resemble the woman's ex-husband in behavior, such as being critical and possessive and picking on her beyond what might be accepted as "good-natured teasing." The daughter denies the seriousness of her boyfriend's behaviors and one is left to wonder if she does not consider the boyfriend's behaviors as alarming because she had been exposed to similar behaviors from her father while growing up. It may seem like normal behavior to her.

In response to the request for advice from a woman whose boyfriend exhibits signs of being abusive, one reader offered advice and encouragement. This woman had in her teens dated a man who beat her, stalked her, and controlled her. She loved him and apparently stayed with him from the age of sixteen. It took fourteen years and the appearance of her current fiancé for her to leave. Simple calculations estimate the woman's age now to be thirty years old.[7]

If the fiancé had not appeared, one wonders, would she still be with her abusive lover? How far have we come since the days of our favorite childhood fairy tales if women still need a rescuer like the Cinderellas, Sleeping Beauties, and other helpless maidens of the past?

An encouraging sign comes from a fifteen-year-old girl who thinks she has been involved with the greatest boyfriend for the past six months. Dane, two years older than the young girl, is sweet and respects her. But she is concerned (and rightly so) that he has difficulty controlling his anger.

He punches walls and breaks things although he has never hurt her. But if she were ever to "cheat" on him, Dane threatens that he would kill that guy because he would die without her. Fortunately, the young girl recognizes this as controlling behavior and she is asking for advice. For her sake, let's hope she will heed the advice.

Abusive relationships are not the only scenario where the concept of love is used to explain self-defeating behaviors. Many repeatedly single individuals enter and exit relationships because they are in love repeatedly, or so they believe. Some of us might be tempted to call it infatuation but they insist that it was love that drew them to the next person—every single time. Without love they would not enter into a sexual relationship; they are practicing serial monogamy unless they are married during the periods of change in their love status. As described in chapter 1, this is different from the Don Juan syndrome. The pursuits of the Don Juan–type person are conquest-oriented rather than love-oriented and are characterized by variety- and adventure-seeking behaviors. The "repeatedly-in-love" individual sometimes believes in the permanence of love, even though when confronted with reality it seems elusive.

DESTINED OR DOOMED?

Under the umbrella of "love" we can accept practical strangers into our bed. Who has not heard of "love at first sight" and who has not believed its magic? As a forty-five-year-old woman, married for twenty-three years to a wonderful man, confessed, the second she shook hands with a man she met ten years ago "fireworks went off." She felt like she had known him all her life. The two had lunch together but nothing else developed except for some e-mail contacts over the past couple of years. However, recently they met again by accident and there was an immediate glow on both their faces. Now the woman is contemplating how to tell this man that she believes they are soul mates. And although she insists she loves her husband, her attraction to the other man is so powerful that she seems ready to dump the husband. How long does it take to know someone's soul—five minutes, five years?[8]

Many who knew her, considered Lenore to be a free spirit—both in thought and action. She experimented with her own sexuality while in college and she felt as independent and ambitious as the young men she dated. At a social gathering at the end of a professional conference Lenore thought she found her future husband. The strong feelings she experienced at the sight of this young man led her to approach him, stating that he should marry her.

Handling his surprise well, the young man responded in an agreeable way, suggesting that they have dinner first.

This was the beginning of a passionate relationship that led straight into marriage. Three years and two daughters later Lenore confessed to a friend that Hubert, her husband, was addicted to pornography, which over time had a devastating effect on her sex life. In an attempt to cope with her disappointment in their sexual interactions Lenore resorted to alcohol use. The fear of becoming addicted prompted her to seek professional help.

Looking back on the beginning of her relationship with Hubert, she recognized that she had blinded herself with her strong feelings and her deep belief in destiny and love at first sight. Her strong conviction kept her from obtaining information about the man she was to share her life with. Hubert did mention that he had been married before but Lenore did not ask for any details. It was enough that destiny had brought them together. Had she asked questions, she might have found out that Hubert's previous marriage dissolved due to his addiction to pornography—and not only the previous marriage, but several earlier relationships as well.[9]

Lenore's sad marital experience is not a rare occurrence; the increased availability and use of pornography is affecting many marriages. In the past, complaints of sexual deprivation were heard mostly from men; now more and more women feel neglected and deprived of sexual intimacy because their husbands find it easier to get aroused by watching pornography and masturbating to climax than taking the effort and time to engage in lovemaking activities with their wives. Reaching a similar level of arousal that is widely available through the use of pornography takes more effort and concentration within a permanent romantic relationship. To keep an ongoing relationship fresh and exciting requires some degree of creativity, playfulness, as well as a willingness to sincerely appreciate one's partner's need for pleasure. Changing sexual partners frequently relieves the individual of trying to be interesting and stimulating because with limited frequency, everything might seem new and exciting to the onetime partner. Similarly, relying on pornography for arousal and masturbation for relief does not require much ingenuity.

THE TINY REWARDS OF SMALL PROMISES

There are people who pride themselves on knowing what they want and often they believe that they will recognize it when they see it. Ted was married for three years before Arlene told him she wanted a divorce. At the time of their marriage Arlene was busy pursuing a master's degree. He knew her ambitions before they got married and he was proud of her. Ted believed his love was strong enough for both of them. He was supportive of Arlene's goal, expecting her to return his love once she recognized the full extent of his devotion to her.

However, married life was not at all what he had hoped for. He felt almost as single as he had living by himself, only with more household chores to do. In the evenings when Arlene was not in class she studied. Weekends were devoted to exercising and studying. Ted was lonely but he hoped that things would change after Arlene had obtained her degree. Change came but it was different from what Ted had expected. Arlene wanted to be free and independent to find out who she was. Ted felt used and taken advantage of.

While he was wallowing in self-pity, he forgot that it had been his insistence that persuaded Arlene to marry him. How much time had he invested in knowing Arlene as a person? As he prided himself, he knew what he wanted once he saw it. But did he see "it" accurately? Or was he blinded by his love for Arlene? She had been hesitant about getting married, but not taking no for an answer, Ted had tried hard to convince her that it would be good for her because he would be there to help and support her. And he had kept his promise. Arlene, on the other hand, had not promised him much and she may have given less than that, but he was in no position to argue with her decision.

LOVE GROWS BEST IN AN ATMOSPHERE OF IGNORANCE

In the initial stages romantic love is the most wonderful experience. It's so enchanting that many people search for it again and again. What makes it so wonderful is that the beloved is perfect in every way. Generally, the basis for this model of perfection is a lack of knowledge about the wonderful person's real traits and attitudes. When knowledge is replaced with blind belief, as in the case of Lenore above, the individual's mind is a fertile ground for infatuation to sprout and grow. As long as he or she looks somewhat similar to the type of individual we would like to fall in love with, we can fill in all the missing spaces with the delightful expectations we have of him or her and our strong beliefs about the blissful romance we are about to embark upon. Our expectations easily overshadow reality; it is only with repeated and continuous exposure to the dream person that reality makes a more pronounced impression on us. When that finally happens we can always explain our imaginary rose-colored glasses away by emphatically stating, "He (or she) has changed. This is not the person I met and fell in love with—that's a stranger!"

"He is a totally different person from the man I fell in love with. I am hurt, lonely, and scared." That cry of desperation came from a fifty-five-year-old woman who had been married for thirty-four years but got divorced two years ago. Within months she married a man whom she had met through an Internet dating site. The new man treated her like she was all he cared about. But he lied about his financial situation and soon after they got married she discovered that he drinks every evening, argues, and storms out. The woman had never lived independently and is on disability. She hopes she may be able to move out with the help of a friend.[10]

A forty-nine-year-old "heartbroken widow" recently lamented, "We were so in love. How can it be over so quickly after one little disagreement?" While dating the most wonderful gentleman the widow fell in love in just eight weeks. But then another widow entered the scene and the gentleman consoled her; when the heartbroken widow confronted him about not calling anymore he told her their relationship was over. But the heartbroken widow finds that difficult to accept; in fact, she believes the gentleman is not really interested in the other widow and she blames the other widow for crying on the gentleman's shoulder when she could have done so with a girlfriend instead of with a single man in a newly established relationship. Is this man just a helpless pawn in the hands of widows?[11]

Considering the widow's complaints, it is difficult to imagine that she really knew the man she was dating. That she considered him to be the most wonderful gentleman apparently was enough for her. She did not relate the basis for her beliefs but one would think it was shaky at best.

Another advice seeker is a fifty-five-year-old woman who is married to a verbally and emotionally abusive husband; she is ready to flee the home and seek happiness with a man she met online. Although she has never met him in person, she knows that they are in love with each other and want to be together. Her main concern is how to leave her husband because she is afraid of him. One could guess that the woman did not know much more about her husband when she married him than she currently knows about the man who is expected to rescue her.[12]

Considering the situations described above, expectations of a happy and lasting (until death do us part) marriage following certain romantic relationships can meet with disappointment. Researchers in the field of marriage and family report that about 30 percent of divorces occur within the first four years of marriage.[13] This is apparently the amount of time it takes for two partners to be confronted with and to accept reality.

After the veil of illusion is torn to shreds, the spouses may face each other as the total strangers they really are. To understand the process involving the variables of time and marital satisfaction, in 1978 two researchers gathered information from 162 couples at the beginning of their marriage and at different times in follow-up assessments with the use of personality questionnaires. Four years later the still married couples showed a more homogamous pattern of personality traits than those who divorced.[14]

Almost twenty years later, studies confirmed that unlike what fairy tales may lead us to believe, real-world differences between spouses in the areas of personality traits, attitudes, and socioeconomic status tend to be linked to high rates of marital tension and union dissolution. While waltzing in the dream world of romance, young lovers are blind to those differences in their personality characteristics and their attitudes, which a few years later may lead to disillusionment and separation.[15]

Studying various aspects of divorce, interviewers focused on individuals who had been the initiators in their divorce and found that a significant number of them reformulated their marriages in their own minds into "marriages that never existed." They justified the divorce initiation by symbolically voiding or annulling those marriages. Some of them regarded their marriage as having been bad from the beginning, rendering it a "fake" marriage. Others pointed to insurmountable personality differences in the spouses, claiming that they never really knew the "real" spouse when they made the commitment. Those differences seemed so overwhelming to the divorce initiators that they never seriously contemplated marriage counseling. There was nothing that one could do about this fundamentally flawed marriage other than get out. "It should never have happened to begin with."

Interestingly, very few of the initiators believed that they might have mistakenly elevated their partner and the wedding into an idealized version of marriage. The more frequent explanation for the failure of the marriage was found in the other spouse; they must have been less than truthful in presenting themselves and must have been less committed than the divorce initiators had been at the time. Of course, in many instances this argument was reversed as the noninitiators used it to explain their side of the story. Claiming that the other spouse initially misrepresented him- or herself or that the spouse changed significantly in personality is a convenient and logical-sounding explanation to cover up for a lack of patience or a realistic appraisal of the person one was committing one's future to.[16]

We might say that for those who insist on navigating the world of romance with blindfolds on their eyes, a rude awakening might be in store; but it does not have to be that way. Romantic relationships are powerful and meaningful undertakings that not only require but deserve our utmost focus and attention. For some the excitement in love relationships may come from not knowing the outcome of the relationship process; for others to be able to influence or determine at least in part that outcome is exhilarating enough. It is up to the individual to choose the path.

THE SINGLE AGAIN GROUP

"In the name of love" could well describe the basic reasoning that brought various individuals to a personal growth group experience titled "Single Again," as each participant had found him- or herself unpartnered once again. They all wanted to know how to avoid similar experiences in the future, all were ready and searching for the comfort of being in a lasting and meaningful intimate relationship with another human being they could trust in and depend on. The focus of the group experience was on relationship education. Rather than attempting to heal a currently ailing relationship, the goal for the participants was the avoidance of another painful breakup by probing into the reasons for past relationship failures.

When asked whether they had been involved in marital therapy prior to the final dissolution of the relationship, the current group of participants answered no. Interestingly, none of them had considered marital or any other type of counseling. Several gave the reason that it was too late for any kind of intervention. Others seemed to have a low level of trust in such intervention either because they thought the counselor would take sides or because they had heard from people who had resorted to marital counseling that "it didn't help." Sadly, that may be a general reflection of people's opinion regarding the efficacy of marital therapy.

Meet the Participants

Sue, the divorced mother of a three-year-old son, had just turned thirty. Right out of graduate school she married her boyfriend from high school. Her story is related earlier in this chapter.

Ted is a sincere, medium-built man in his early thirties. He was also introduced in this chapter.

Timothy, a man in his late forties and recently divorced after twenty-six years of marriage, has difficulty comprehending his situation (as described in chapter 2).

Julie, the woman described earlier in this chapter, divorced her husband several months ago after six years of marriage. She still has difficulty understanding the turn of events.

Michael, whose story is related in a later chapter, was very much in love with Diana when they married. But he overestimated his ability to accept some of her behaviors.

Sally, the divorced mother of a young son, was introduced earlier in this chapter.

Dorothy, always a follower, did not give herself a chance to develop her own person. Looking for a leader, she lost what little self-confidence she had in her marriage (she is introduced in chapter 5).

Marian has been waiting for years for her married lover to divorce his wife. How long is she going to believe his promises?

Gregory, a divorced man in his late twenties (briefly mentioned in chapter 1), is still looking for the right partner to provide the "chemistry" for a permanent relationship.

The Group Process

At the time of registration participants were given handouts as preparation for the group experience. Group members were encouraged to view the group experience as an autopsy-like examination of the dissolved relationship, identifying malfunctioning parts and—if possible—linking them to earlier observations of warning signs, including options that individuals could have used or can use in the future to determine the significance of such signals. Another aspect of the exploration would be directed to situations where individuals might feel comfortable with a new person, without quite knowing why. There may be memories involving similar feelings with another person in the past. If that's the case, what was the outcome of that relationship?

These issues are considered worth addressing. In addition, for those who have had repeated relationship experiences with similar dynamics, explorations into one's own behaviors for characteristics that may attract the same type of partner make up another part of the group experience—along with decisions about whether behavioral changes would be advantageous.

Homework assignments, such as writing narratives about their roles in various relationships as they perceived them, become part of the group experience. Less emphasis is placed on historical accuracy than on the individuals' perception of their part. These narratives often reveal important attitudes about the self. For instance, some individuals may see themselves as victims while others struggle to maintain control at all times and at any price. Such written accounts are valuable tools when attempting to define personality characteristics and behavioral traits that may be instrumental in repeatedly attracting certain types of prospective partners.

Invariably, participants have a list of questions they are eager to ask, such as "How can I ever trust another man (woman)?" "How do you start another committed relationship?" "How can I let somebody else know me after what I have gone through?" "If people knew how I really am, they would leave me. How can I afford to let my guard down?" "Do I have to give myself up in order to be with someone else? After all, the last one left me when I tried to be myself." Those questions are natural but cannot be answered individually. Most of them will be addressed in one way or another during the group process. More likely, the individual will find an answer without even asking the question again. Many of the answers will surface during the group experience.

Single Again Group Meeting

The participants had selected their seats for this first meeting and the group leader, following a brief greeting, presented a short outline of the proceedings of the course. "The basic assumption for your presence here is that you want to make inquiries into the death of your past relationship. What killed the relationship? Was it murder, suicide, or a slow grinding process of wear and tear?" After a brief pause the leader continued, "Some of you look surprised; perhaps my choice of words shocked you. Depending on how you now feel about your previous partner, you might think that he or she killed the relationship. On the other hand, you might be aware of some self-defeating aspects in your own behavior that were detrimental to the health of the relationship and you could conceive of that as some kind of suicide, as destroying your part of the relationship. On the other hand, the process of wear and tear may have come about through the combination of your and your partners' interactions and personality traits."

Pausing for a moment to observe the participants' facial expressions, the group leader looked encouragingly at Timothy, who was obviously ill at ease; joining the group was more an act of desperation than anything else. Having been married for twenty-six years made him feel like he was out of touch with today's dating situation. He did not know what to look for and what would be expected of him. Besides, he was not ready emotionally to let go of his ex-wife. Timothy looked around the room before he started to talk hesitatingly, "I can't remember any big arguments between my wife and me and, although she is the one who wanted the divorce, I would not see her as having killed our marriage. She said she never felt important to me, so now that the children will be gone, she might as well go, too, she said. Probably what you called the 'wear and tear process' is more likely to have happened to us; we just wore down the good feelings between us."

"That's an excellent observation on your part, Timothy," the leader responded. "Unfortunately, that 'wear and tear process' is what happens to many relationships and one of our goals is to focus on how to prevent that from happening in the future. Did you ever ask your wife what would make her feel special or important?"

Timothy blushed when he said, "She slammed the door in my face when I asked her some time after the divorce. I think she thought I was trying to learn how to make other women feel special and important."

Group members proceeded to tell Timothy that he needed to be more specific. His wife couldn't read his mind. He should try more openly to tell her how much he misses her and what he meant when he asked her about being special. If he still loved her and wanted her back, he could at least try harder than just to resign himself to thinking that she wanted no contact with him.

Timothy's facial expression reflected his internal struggle, but he nodded his head. "You are right; what do I have to lose? She's gone and another try won't make it any worse. I'll talk to her again—if she lets me." Everybody was cheering him on.

"If you were to compare just within this group the reasons why relationships failed to last, you would come up with quite a list of different factors. And that is what we are going to do because you joined this group in order to learn not only what caused the death of the relationship but also how to prevent the repetition of further pain and disappointments," said the group leader, directing the discussion to general topics. "This group experience will be divided into three parts: first we will look at ourselves—the possible 'suiciders,' if you will. What might there be in our behaviors and attitudes that could have contributed to the termination of one—or even several—relationships? Then we will attend to the others, your partners who might have caused the relationship's death."

"What you call the murderer would fit my ex-husband." Sally spoke up, somewhat impatiently. "I loved him and would have done anything for him—and I did. I was expecting him to propose marriage and when he suggested we live together I was devastated. I was not brought up to live with a man without being married. But for him I swallowed my pride and my beliefs and agreed to live with him. And what did I get for it? Nothing but disappointments and a son who prefers being with his father to living with me." As she ended her statement, the anger in Sally's voice left as she dissolved into tears.

"What did your ex-husband do to disappoint you?" The group leader tried to elicit information to understand Sally's position.

"He did not marry me until I was pregnant with our son. Without my being pregnant he would probably never have thought of marrying me," Sally responded.

"But he could also have *not* married you even though you were pregnant. He did the decent thing." Michael's statement had a challenging tone.

"I felt that Kevin did not marry me for me but for our son," Sally said looking down at her hand that had once worn her wedding ring.

"You didn't have to move in with him if you were so much against it," was Michael's quick reply.

"The breakup of relationships has many reasons, not least of all the mistakes we all make from time to time when dealing with those who are important to us," the group leader said, attempting to diffuse the emerging tension between Sally and Michael.

"It seems the arrival of children can turn a relationship in any direction," started Sue, who had been quiet so far. "I remember having some doubts before the wedding concerning the commitment that Jeff and I were about to make. And then I became pregnant right away. We were not ready for the commitment or for the burden of a baby. And as much as I love my son I was not willing to interrupt my career, which had just begun," Sue added in a slightly defensive tone.

Dorothy's voice sounded uncertain when she inquired, "Are you saying that you and your husband divorced because the two of you could not handle taking care of a child?"

"I expected more help from Jeff after we came home from work. But he was not willing to do so. Perhaps to make a point, he often stayed away from home after work, leaving me to cope with the baby and the household chores. Naturally, when he finally came home I was angry and complained. Our arguments increased until one day Jeff did not come home after work at all."

Sue took a breath; her voice quivered as she continued, "Much later in the evening Jeff called to tell me not to wait for him. He was not about to return. Before I could ask him where he was he hung up the phone." Sue paused for a moment before telling the group how she had sat on the bed with her young son in her arms, still holding the phone, tears streaming down her face. But the baby was hungry and his crying reminded her of the reality she had to face. She noticed that most of Jeff's clothes were missing. "I realized then that he must have secretly packed and prepared for his exit." She ended her story in a barely audible voice.

"I am so sorry, Sue. My difficulty was not because Kevin did not help me but I ended up feeling that Kevin loved our son more than he did me and it seemed like I had to compete with my son for Kevin's love," Sally said in a low voice, her anger leaving her momentarily.

"That is a most difficult position for a mother to be in; it will take a lot to resolve that feeling," the group leader responded. But before further elaboration of Sally's position some of the group members turned to Sue with the question, "Did Jeff ever return?" "No, he never came back and I knew it when I noticed his missing clothes," Sue replied.

"You mean he left you just like that?" Michael asked, his voice expressing disbelief. "How can he ever explain that to his son?" Michael wondered. "At least Diana and I did not have children yet before we split. I don't think I could have left—even if I had wanted to." Michael continued, "Of course I never thought that Diana and I would become so disagreeable and divorce. It is sad how things that start off so well can turn sour and disintegrate."

"It sounds like you experienced a few surprises in your short marriage." The group leader directed attention to Michael, who seemed tense as he spoke. "Are you ready to share with us how your difficulties started and had there been any warning signs you might have overlooked at the beginning? As Sue mentioned, she had misgivings before her wedding; you may remember some early signals."

"Well, I knew that Diana had difficulties being on time for some of our dates but I thought I could handle it. I was deeply in love with her and it seemed a minor thing at the time," Michael responded, "but what I did not expect to happen was that it would upset me so much when other people were involved, like when we had a date with another couple or an invitation for dinner—things like that I could not take in my stride."

"You found out something about yourself you had not been aware of. When other people got involved in the situation it caused you the most difficulties," the leader interpreted. "When it involved you as a possible cause for the delay or it somehow linked you with the reason for letting the other people wait, that's when you disliked your part in it but you did not clearly separate yourself from it and you resented Diana for it. But apparently you did not assert yourself by saying something like 'If we are not leaving here in time to get there on time, I will not accompany you.'"

"That's correct. I felt in a way that Diana determined the basis for every relationship I had with others at the time by putting me in a 'one down' position by having to apologize for being late at every meeting." Michael agreed and continued thoughtfully, "I resented to be put in that position but then I tried to make up for it by driving faster and more recklessly."

"You may have tried to make up for lost time or it may have been your anger about perceiving yourself as being helpless in the situation that made you drive recklessly, as you said," was the leader's answer.

"Yes, I was angry and I felt helpless, so I acted out in my driving, which is something I dislike in others as well as in myself. In fact, I probably disliked Diana more for the change in myself than for her tardiness. Somehow it seemed that she had more control over me than I did."

"Is there anything you could think of now that you might have done differently then?" asked the leader. "Some options you see now but were not aware of at the time?"

"I guess I could have explained my feelings to her. But I was angry and at the same time I thought I had no right to complain about her tardiness because I had been aware of it before we got married. Would she have listened if I had told her how uncomfortable I felt being late and having to apologize? I'll never know." Michael considered the options in retrospect.

"How would you describe your driving habits now?" Timothy asked.

"Funny you should ask," Michael answered sheepishly; Timothy's question took him by surprise. "I am driving as conservatively as I did before, but it took a ticket for speeding and reckless driving that really woke me up."

Wanting to give Michael time for reflection, the leader turned to Marian who had not said anything but looked tense. "Marian, would you like to tell us about what you are looking for that could be helpful to you?"

Marian's voice sounded shaky when she spoke, "When Sue told us about how her husband left I was wondering what might be worse, being left suddenly or being aware daily that the end is coming but hoping against hope that you are wrong?" Her fingers were tightly folded around the pen she was holding in her hand as if trying to draw strength from it.

Marian related her story, one that bears resemblance to Norma's situation, as mentioned in a later chapter: "There are no more arguments in my relationship with Bertram, a married man. It is too late for that. In the past we had argued about whether or not he would leave his wife and when that might occur. I had believed his lies and promises. According to Bertram, the marriage was one of convenience for the children's sake. He and his wife slept in separate bedrooms; they had not had sex in years. Bertram was waiting for the children's graduation from high school. Once they were in college that would be the time for working on the divorce, he had said."

Marian continued her story, describing how she had counted the years and in her mind quietly celebrated the passing of each one as a step toward her future with Bertram. Then Bertram's wife became pregnant. How did that happen if they did not have sex? Although he did not deny his part in it, Bertram came up with a complicated story about his wife's pregnancy. Marian again believed his lies. Would they have to wait another eighteen years, she asked? Bertram offered some vague promises. Why did Marian believe the lies? Because she wanted to. She could not face the reality of years of holding on to empty promises followed by shattered dreams.

Their relationship had experienced several transformations over the years. The passion of the early years turned into the emotional turmoil of waiting, along with the comfort of familiarity with each other's behaviors, and finally the anger, resignation, and acceptance of the inevitable.

Julie looked at Marian as she started to speak, "Those shattered dreams are the hardest to live with, even harder than the shattered body." The group members looked stunned at Julie's statement. In her introduction, Julie had mentioned that she had left an abusive relationship but had not related any details. That situation involved her ex-husband. Julie explained that her reason for joining the group was to learn to recognize danger signals in the other person, but the group's discussion directed her focus to arguments she and Matt had been involved in.

Their arguments began with Matt's complaining about her job; it coincided with Julie's promotion to a supervisory position. Julie was proud that her employers had recognized her competence and hard work. To her surprise, Matt did not share her happiness; he cautioned that her new position would drain her energy away from their personal life.

Julie admitted that on occasion working overtime was required. On those evenings Matt was at home by himself, but he had no additional responsibilities—at least he did not assume any. Instead he started drinking and was ready for arguments when she came home. He expressed jealousy and suspicion about her relationship with her boss and her coworkers. One evening apparently Matt had been drinking more than usual and was in an aggressive mood when she entered the house. He started to bombard her with his suspicions and as she defended herself he slapped her face really hard. Julie was stunned; she slept on the living room couch that night. The next morning Matt tearfully apologized with the explanation that it was only his deep love and concern for her that made him hit her.

"That's when you left him?" Sue's voice sounded like she expected a confirmation. Julie agreed that she should have left Matt then and there. But she did not. Why not? She loved him and believed his apology and his promise because she wanted to hang on to the dream of the happy marriage. It took another, more violent, beating to disrupt her dreams. Turning to the group leader, Julie stated that the argument assignment prompted her to think back to earlier times to find signs of possible abuse and there were signs. Julie would keep that part for later in the group discussions.

"I came here because I felt that my ex-husband had betrayed me; by listening to Sue, Julie, and Marian it seems that most men are mistreating us even though Michael seems to feel that it was Diana's fault that he became a reckless driver," Sally threw in.

"Your thoughts are quite normal, Sally; we automatically look at the other person for the blame when our loving feelings have been disappointed." Then turning to Julie, the group leader continued, "Julie, focusing on arguments would be a natural link when exploring danger signals in the other person. But your discovery of earlier trouble signs in the relationship with your husband indicates that our tendency to overlook early signs can be costly," the group leader explained. "It is important to realize how much our wishful thinking can prevent us from getting out of harm's way. The wish to believe the best about the person we chose to share our life with is natural. After all, if we believed our partners to be bad or even dangerous, we would run before we started any serious involvement."

Ted wanted to make a point in response to Julie's and Sally's comments or implications that men are not supportive of their wives' career goals. In his previous marriage to Arlene his support for her career had not worked for him. Arlene had left him soon after she had accomplished her career goal with his help and support. As Ted told the group, Arlene hesitated about getting married. To her, marriage was not as important as finishing her master's degree. But Ted had promised that he would support her and she finally agreed to marry him. Ted kept his promise and did all the chores around the house so that she would have time for her studies. Their arguments started when Ted complained that his wife never had time or energy for sex. His complaints did not improve her feelings for him. After she obtained her degree she left. She wanted to be free to pursue a promising career.

Now Ted asked, "Was my behavior—except for the complaining about the lack of sex—something that made her take me for granted and therefore not value me as a person? Of course, I expected sex to be part of the marriage. I put so much into the relationship and came out with nothing. Where did I go wrong?"

Michael offered his opinion that Ted's wife could have interpreted Ted's push for marriage as his being dependent on her in some way and she thought he would not complain no matter what she did. But when he became dissatisfied about her lack of interest in sex, his complaints became a nuisance to her and she wanted to get rid of him, especially since she had achieved her goal.

The group leader summarized the situation, "By making a blanket offer of support and not mentioning any wishes on your part, Ted, you might—as Michael suggested—have given her the message that you were willing to do whatever Arlene wanted just for her presence in your life. You did not communicate any conditions or any of your own wishes and hopes. You probably quietly hoped that Arlene would learn to love you as she realized the strength of your love for her. And the one thing that you wanted in return, sexual intimacy, you did not mention because you expected it as a given, as a part of marriage, independent of what type of marriage it would be. It seems that as you did not communicate much of what you wanted, you got even less than you expected."

Leaving Ted time to contemplate the discussion, the leader turned to another male group member who had not said anything so far. "Gregory, we haven't had a chance to hear from you and your personal reasons for joining this group."

Gregory, a handsome young man in his late twenties, obviously felt awkward as the group's attention shifted to him, but he started to speak, hesitantly at first. "I have been married before but it didn't last long, just like my other relationships—it starts out great but the sparks burn out."

"When you say 'the sparks burn out' I guess you mean the excitement in the relationship is gone. How do you see that as happening, Gregory?" The leader encouraged Gregory to be more specific.

"Well, when I meet a new girl or woman I feel energized and I want to be with her all the time. Usually we have fantastic sex for a while but then the excitement fades. Like with my wife, Lynn, at first we really got along well but then we had some arguments about how to run the house and which friends to be with. She had a lot of friends that were interested in sports. I don't mind watching a few games, but overall, I'd like to be outside and work in the garden after sitting all day at the computer."

"It sounds as if you and Lynn did not have much in common. What made you decide to marry her?" asked Julie.

"Initially, we had this great attraction for each other; it was just like magic." Gregory's response raised the leader's curiosity. "Did you experience a similar kind of magic with your other relationships?" the group leader asked.

"Yes, they were similar. There was this instant chemistry with them. I believe in that. If you don't have that, the excitement won't last long. I won't even get involved in a relationship unless I feel that chemistry."

"When you talk about chemistry, don't you mean sexual arousal?" Julie asked again. Gregory squirmed a little in his seat. It was obvious that Julie's question made him feel uneasy. Perhaps he did not expect a young woman to talk about sexual arousal in a conversational tone.

The group leader turned to Gregory, asking him how his belief in the significance of what he called chemistry had developed. Although Gregory felt relieved that he did not have to answer Julie directly, he realized that the group leader's question meant that additional disclosure on his part was requested. "I think it started when I was a lifeguard at a community pool during the summers in my early college years and before." Gregory related his memories about the beautiful tall blond girl with bright blue eyes, who was perhaps a year or so older. She seemed so self-assured and all the guys were trying to impress her. She did not even notice Gregory; he was just part of the pool.

One evening after closing he observed the girl with one of her admirers in a tight embrace. Their bodies seemed to melt into one and Gregory could hear the girl's moaning as the man's hands moved over her body, cupping and squeezing her breasts with one hand while the other hand moved down her body and legs and between her thighs. Gregory became aroused as he was watching them. Later that night he experienced the most powerful climax as he was masturbating, fantasizing about the girl. In his fantasy, Gregory was the man with the girl, kissing her and moving his hands over her body and legs. The strength of that night's climax made him believe in the special chemistry between a man and a woman.

When Gregory stopped his story the group leader's voice indicated knowing the answer to the next question, "Was Lynn blond and blue-eyed like the girl from the pool?" "Yes, she and the others I became involved with" was Gregory's response. A murmur of surprise could be heard from some of the group members.

"Could it be that the real chemistry is between you and the fantasies you have about the girl from the pool years ago?" the group leader finally asked. "In other words, the chemistry is in your mind, what your mind expects a woman of a certain look to be like in a romantic relationship. In fact, it is very likely that the woman does not exist in reality at all; it is your imagination. And even if she looks like the girl from the pool, she cannot match what is in your mind. That's why with the real women, the look-alikes, the chemistry cannot last."

For a moment there was absolute silence; group members seemed to hold their breath. Gregory appeared stunned. But it was time for the meeting to end. The group leader gave a summary of this first meeting: "When we look at the reasons why your past relationships dissolved, several factors emerge. As Timothy said, in his case it was the 'wear and tear' process that brought his marriage to an end. Several of you (Ted, Sue, Julie) had expectations of your partners but did not really know your partners and even though some of you (Julie and Sue) had signals or misgivings, you went ahead with your commitments. Marian believed her lover's promises, not really knowing him well or not wanting to know him. Some of you looked for something in your partners, characteristics, such as the chemistry Gregory was looking for that seemed to communicate to him he had found the right partner. Sally's and Michael's choices could have been good ones, except they did not know themselves well enough to make the best of it."

After a pause the leader continued: "While the endings sound sad, to say the least, they indicate, however, that people are not doomed to stumble into relationships that do not last. With more time, careful examination, and awareness of discrepancies in our partners' verbal and actual behaviors as well as being cognizant of our own tendencies to get carried away by our expectations, we could improve our decision-making abilities and give ourselves better chances at a satisfying permanent relationship." Looking around the room, the leader closed the session, encouraging everybody to think about how they might want to approach those decisions in the future.

• 5 •

Know Thyself

What is the purpose of exploring how a once promising relationship deteriorated to the point of no return if not to learn from looking back? The purpose is not to assign blame to one person or another. Both men and women stumble into relationships with insufficient knowledge about themselves, the other partner, or the requirements for successful adjustments to the coupled life. Very few individuals would knowingly and willingly want to commit themselves to an unhappy marriage. Looking back on the dissolved relationship is painful, but it provides one an opportunity to recognize the signs that went unnoticed prior to and during the ill-fated venture.

For many partners the termination of a relationship is a rude awakening in several ways. Not only do dreams come to a premature end, partners also learn through the termination proceedings how good or how bad their union had really been, what type of person they had been committed to, and how their own actions and responses may have escalated some of the stressful situations into unhappy or crisis encounters. Realizing one's own part in the scenario—although painful—can serve to remove some of the hopelessness of feeling doomed to have unhappy relationships for the rest of one's life. Instead it can bestow some power to the individual because it promises that one—with additional knowledge—can effect changes in the development of a new partnership.

ACHIEVING SELF-KNOWLEDGE

The most important ingredient in the process of achieving self-knowledge is memory of one's past. How has the person responded emotionally, verbally, and physically to certain situations in the past? Have the responses been successful in reaching goals or have they amounted to failures or even embarrassing events? It is certainly understandable that one would not want to dwell on the embarrassing moments in life while memories of successful actions are much more rewarding. However, banishing unsuccessful events from one's memory makes them unavailable as a basis for learning and controlling one's future. In fact, wiping those events from one's memory becomes an invitation to reexperience similar painful situations.

Furthermore, by avoiding awareness of one's own reactions to certain positive and negative occurrences, it is impossible to assess or estimate the impact of those occurrences on one's happiness. And with that lack of knowledge one does not know what to look for in a prospective romantic partner. Instead of tossing aside the power of one's past, engaging in a "willful act of imaginative remembering to overcome any form of amnesia" has been suggested as a better alternative.[1]

The process of self-knowledge is not a brief journey. It can take many years, as in the case of a sixty-one-year-old twice divorced female who is still trying to decide what qualities and characteristics she can tolerate in a partner. Her first husband was too sweet and passive and the second husband was abusive. It seems she tried both ends of the spectrum but now she is dating a really nice divorced guy who is smart and interesting and has good values, but unfortunately, he is also extremely passive. She finds his conflict-aversive behavior to be a total turnoff. While she is trying to decide if he is the one for her, she is also worried that this good guy could be snapped up by plenty of other women. Sadly, if she lets the concern about other women taking him away determine her decision, she still will not have discovered what she wants for herself.[2]

On the other hand, "Gold Digger," a twenty-seven-year-old divorced woman, seems to have already learned a few things about herself. Having married for love the first time around, and apparently the marriage had not been successful, she now believes that marrying for money would be a wiser choice for her. With money, she could engage in some of her expensive hobbies and would also be able to volunteer her time for a good cause. Overall, that would make her happier than making a living on her own without an academic degree. Although currently in a relationship with a really great guy, which had been convenient when she divorced her previous husband two years ago, she now realizes that he will not be able to take care of her financially because of his responsibilities to his former wife and children.[3]

Apparently, Gold Digger has learned that she cannot be truly happy without significant financial resources and is looking for an appropriate source. To her credit, she is willing to be open and truthful about her reasons for marrying the rich man. A lesser degree of self-knowledge appears to have operated in the life of a divorced female also turning to a syndicated advice column, as she finds herself pregnant with her ex-husband's child. The divorce was the husband's idea after the couple had been separated for almost two years. Although the former husband always treated the female advice seeker with disrespect and hostility, upon his initiation she went back to him, believing that she loved him. Now she is expecting her second child by him and wonders what to do because his behavior has not changed for the better.[4]

Before the separation, the woman admittedly put up with her husband's behavior because of her low self-esteem and out of fear of being alone. Apparently, after he had left her, she somehow translated those sentiments into feelings of love for him. One wonders how much this advice seeker knows about herself, and without knowing herself how can she find and recognize a male partner who would be compatible with her?

Connecting to our earlier discussion about achieving self-knowledge, becoming aware of behaviors or ways of thinking that are not helping us in our interactions with others and may eventually lead to painful or strained relationships, why wouldn't we want to learn to trade these self-defeating ways for more self-enhancing traits? Just because we have acted and thought this way for a number of years (or even decades) does not mean this constitutes a birth defect that cannot be modified or erased. Working on changing well-established ways of thinking, feeling, and behaving takes effort, time, and—above all—determination to construct a happier and more successful life.

Part of constructing a successful life is the elimination or reduction of self-deception. The concept of the persona or false self and its counterpoint, the authentic self, has been discussed in the literature across subdisciplines of psychology.[5] From Carl Jung's description of the persona as a social mask that individuals wear to present an acceptable public image and to adapt to the expectations of others and one's culture, it can be understood that the persona develops along the requirements of social norms. There is a risk that with excessive and prolonged focus on cultural and social norms, an individual's authentic and inwardly felt sense of identity fades from consciousness.[6] When that happens, the persona functions not only in the deception of others, which is its original purpose, but also in the individual's self-deception.[7]

Probably the most often applied act of self-deception is the use of self-justification. As our brains manipulate the information packaged in our thoughts and actions in order to protect us from unacceptable truths about ourselves, we are busy explaining, defending, and glorifying ourselves and our actions. Irrationally insisting on being innocent of any wrongdoing clouds our judgment and leaves us vulnerable to errors and delusions. It could indeed be troubling "to learn of the farce that passes for self-knowledge. Our conception of ourselves, we have discovered, is ever-changing, fluidly adapting itself to our circumstances and moods and the petulant demands of self-esteem."[8]

What propels us to repeatedly and continuously engage in self-justifying behaviors is the experience of an unpleasant feeling that in social psychology has been called "cognitive dissonance," a state of tension that occurs when individuals hold two cognitions (beliefs, thoughts, attitudes, opinions, etc.) that are psychologically contradictory. "Dissonance produces mental discomfort, ranging from minor pangs to deep anguish; people don't rest easy until they find a way to reduce it."[9] And marriage provides an arena for a seemingly unlimited need for self-justification.

In the beginning of a romantic relationship a good portion of self-justification works to explain why person A decided to make the relationship to person B a permanent one. Person A had the unfailing perception and good judgment to recognize person B's great attributes and characteristics. This state of affairs can generally be expected to last well past the honeymoon stage of the marriage. Newlyweds may avoid recognizing warning signs about their spouse and instead seek confirmation that they found the ideal partner in order to minimize cognitive dissonance. With passing time both A and B may realize that they did not marry the perfect person; they may justify that recognition by blaming the other for either having changed during the years of their marriage or for not having been honest to begin with. (More opportunities for exploring those situations will be available in the next chapter.) Unhappy spouses who decide to remain in the marriage despite conflicting temperaments and disappointments may avoid "facing the devastating possibility that they invested so many years, so much energy, so many arguments, in a failed effort to achieve even peaceful coexistence" by reassuring themselves that most marriages are like their own.[10]

But it is not only our judgment about the other person that might be compromised; what we believe we know about ourselves is often less than objective. As mentioned earlier, if we cannot accept imperfections in ourselves, we can resort to explaining them away or justifying them. There are many fascinating ways that we can blind ourselves to our true motivations, and with that, unwittingly sabotage our own efforts for achieving satisfaction and happiness in our relationships.[11]

David is a hardworking man; he views himself as a helpful, loving, and caring husband and father. He has many good qualities and his friends will readily testify to that. His parents are proud that although being ambitious in his career, he has been able to keep his sensitive and considerate nature alive where family and friends are involved. Then one night David woke up in the middle of the night, hearing what he thought might be a noise made by their cat, Prissy. But this noise seemed to come from outside the house and Prissy was a house cat; she did not stay outside at night. David looked over to his wife's side of the bed where Lori was sleeping soundly. He thought about getting up and checking on Prissy but he was tired and remaining in bed was so seductive.

Debating whether it had really been Prissy making that noise, David thought that she would meow again and the repeated noise would wake Lori who knew the cat's behaviors better than David did. With that thought he went back to sleep. Early the next morning, David awoke to his little daughter crying, "Prissy is gone; she is not in her bed." Lori woke up at about the same time and a frantic search for Prissy ensued. At first David felt a mixture of shock and embarrassment. He had let Lori and his little daughter down when he did not get up during the night to check on Prissy. But nobody knew that he had been awake, so nobody could really blame him. It was unlike David not to care about his family's happiness and the well-being of their pets.

His role in this situation—even if nobody knew about it—did not seem congruent with his view of himself. He was uncomfortable for a moment until he thought that it really was Lori's cat and therefore it was her responsibility to make sure Prissy was safe and to spare their daughter the disappointment of a lost pet. David had worked late last night like he had on many nights in order to provide well for his family. He was very tired and needed his sleep because he had to get back to work again. Lori can take a nap now and then during the daytime, he rationalized. Her life is not as regimented as his. Lori has more freedom, thanks to his hard work and dedication to the family.

Those thoughts improved David's mood and, fortunately, Prissy had not strayed too far from home. There was after all a happy reunion and everybody promised to be more careful in the future to make sure that Prissy was safely in the house before everybody went to sleep. A happy ending? Seemingly so, but without being aware of it, David's perception of Lori changed ever so slightly. She didn't seem as perfect anymore; her devotion to him and the family appeared slightly less sincere. She wasn't always there ready to comfort him when he felt sad or tired.

With the passage of time the glow of their relationship faded; what had been an exciting union became more of a partnership determined by needs rather than wishes and dreams. David's need to reconcile his behavior on the night of Prissy's disappearance with his self-view provided the stimulus to justify his behavior, and while doing so he placed some of the blame for the event on Lori. In other words, in order to protect his self-image Lori had to become less wonderful in his mind. As his admiration for her lessened slightly over time, so did the excitement in his marriage—all without his awareness of the role he played in the mental and emotional changes that occurred in the atmosphere of their relationship. The dynamics of a chain of events like this take on a life of their own that cannot be reversed without the deeper knowledge of their origin and development. The price for the restoration of David's self-image—or rather for the lack of his self-knowledge—was indeed high as he traded it for the emotional glow that had made his marriage to Lori so special.

When we see the world in a self-justifying way, our view of the world and the people in it becomes distorted—our reality becomes distorted. And above all, as our awareness of ourselves becomes distorted due to the mechanism of self-justification, we become strangers to ourselves. The one person we have to depend on, to have on our side, does not even recognize us, a tragic outcome indeed.

WAKING UP TO REALITY

Norma, a fifty-two-year-old woman, had been single on and off for the past thirty years. After a brief early marriage that did not last even two years, she had dated several young men without finding the partner she was looking for. She could live independently on her income as office manager for a medical practice but it was a modest living.

In her daydreams she saw herself as the hostess of a cultivated home filled with elegant furniture, beautiful table linens, china, and flatware as well as some original oil paintings covering the walls and an occasional tasteful sculpture occupying a corner in one or the other of the home's spacious rooms. All in all, it was a picture of a grand setting for entertaining, more gracious than she could ever afford on her salary. Norma knew she had excellent taste; all she needed was to find the kind of husband who could pay for it. Although quite intelligent, she did not particularly enjoy working in a mundane job day in and day out, especially since it would never pay enough for the lifestyle she felt entitled to.

Norma was attractive and caught the eye of Robert, the vice president of a large company in a neighboring town. His business brought him into Norma's town frequently. Robert was almost seventeen years older than Norma, but at that time it made him more distinguished looking than a man her own age would have been. In addition, he had a family, a wife and two children. But since they lived with him in the town where the business was located, Robert was on his own during business trips to Norma's location. For their first few dates they met in nice restaurants, but then Robert suggested they look for a little house for Norma to live in where Robert could stay overnight with her.

Norma was also able to accompany Robert on some of his business trips to interesting places with glamorous hotels and places of entertainment. Sometimes her sudden requests for vacation time according to Robert's business schedule raised questions and created resentment in Norma's coworkers because they were required to cover her workload on short notice. But Norma did not let that disturb her too much; she felt entitled to the benefits that came with Robert's position and her relationship with him. Her small house was nicely furnished and tastefully decorated. She loved to entertain her friends and family members there. Of course, Robert would not be around at those times.

Norma expected Robert to get a divorce when the children were a bit older; at least, one time he had contemplated the issue, saying that the two boys were still too young to be exposed to all the pain of a divorce. Norma waited. From time to time she dated some available men but they could not compete with the resources of Robert's position. When Robert found out about those other men he was displeased and stayed away for a while, which meant that those credit card charges that Norma made for entertaining Robert at her house went unpaid until Norma begged him to come back.

As the years passed, the supply of eligible young men dwindled away while at the same time Robert preferred that during his visits they stay in Norma's house rather than go out to dine in a restaurant or see a show. He had supplied Norma with a new TV/video home entertainment system and it was more comfortable just to stay in Norma's house after his business in town was taken care of. The frequency of his business trips also decreased as younger men were groomed to take on executive positions in the company. Norma's life more and more resembled that of a middle-aged matron, who did the shopping and cooking for her part-time partner while he relaxed with a cocktail before dinner and in Norma's bed after dinner. Life became boring. There were no more discussions about Robert's divorce; instead he started talking about his retirement. His life would change drastically as a consequence. There would be no reason for him to visit Norma's town and, unfortunately, there would also be no expense account anymore, which he had handled through the company without his wife's knowledge. In fact, Robert's wife had decided that the occasion of his retirement would be the perfect time for a move to Florida to be closer to her parents.

Norma's situation did not look promising. For the past almost twenty years she had been intermittently involved in an affair with a married man—a dead-end street. She had become accustomed to a lifestyle that she could not afford on her salary. Did she really believe that Robert would divorce his wife and marry her? While she was enjoying her surroundings and living in her pretty home, she wanted to believe it. When she encountered doubts, she tried to distract herself from the disturbing reality, as she admitted to her therapist. Now there was no escape into a dream world anymore. She would be fortunate if her employer kept her despite her coworkers' ill feelings toward her. Although she was only fifty-two years old, the look of resignation and depression made her appear older. Her voice had an edge of bitterness to it that in conversation tended to push people away. There was no promising admirer on the horizon and the future looked dim.

Norma's story is not a rare one, as can be seen in the case of Marian, one of the participants in the Single Again group. People do become involved in affairs with married partners, hoping for or believing promises of divorce but many of those promises are empty ones. In these dead-end affairs individuals waste time and energy that could be applied to exploring the possibilities for meaningful and mutually rewarding romantic relationships. As in Norma's case, closing one's eyes to reality can come at a high price. Although Norma can still find someone to love on a more permanent basis, it will take time and effort for her to overcome her current defeatist attitude and the bitterness that has evolved over the years of hiding from the truth. In those years she seemed to have been more involved with the house she wanted to live in than with the person who would share her life in that house.

CRITICISM AS A FOUNDATION FOR BUILDING A FALSE SENSE OF SECURITY

The repeated search for affirmation and validation is only one of many ways that individuals express personal insecurities. For some, a more efficient method is found in criticizing others before they themselves can be criticized. This approach uses the "offense is the best defense" tactic. This is how it works:

Adam and Eve fall in love. Each thinks that the other is just the greatest, most wonderful person they could ever have met. It is as if they were in paradise. Eve, however, is not convinced that she herself is that perfectly wonderful and starts worrying that if Adam finds out that she is less than perfect, he will leave her. What could prevent this from happening? If he was not really as great as he seemed to be, he might be concerned that she would leave him. Eve realizes that Adam's awareness of his shortcomings would be required for the successful functioning of this scheme. She can handle that by observing Adam's behaviors and pointing out any negative aspects of his actions. Surprisingly, Adam is not grateful for her efforts. He thinks Eve is nagging and he—in turn—notices some of Eve's imperfections, which he informs her about. Now there are two lovers focusing on the other's negative aspects.

How long will this romance last? Intense focus on the other's shortcomings logically results in a reduction of loving feelings for him or her. Eve's attempts at camouflaging her insecurities with a false sense of security built on her criticisms of Adam only accelerated the end of their once promising relationship. Their cohabitation in the Garden of Eden lasted little more than a year.

Will Eve learn from this experience? Most likely not; by now the intense focus on Adam's shortcomings has produced a different picture in her mind of the Adam she once knew. She has convinced herself of the significance of his imperfections and that—as she claims—his personality has changed. Where he once seemed to be sweet and loving, he now has nothing but complaints about her. She can actually congratulate herself on being rid of him, instead of having to spend a lifetime with such an ungrateful person, full of character flaws. This line of reasoning perfectly describes the self-justification scheme described above. Adam only seemed to be the ideal lover in the beginning because that was not the real Adam in Eve's mind, but did she ever recognize the real Eve? Adam either changed or played a role to get her to like him. Now that she recognized his true colors, it was better to end the relationship. For a moment she might even entertain a feeling of relief and with that she will not recognize her true colors. Eve is not the only one engaging in this maneuver; Adam is perfectly able to play this game, too. There are many Adams and Eves out there.

SWALLOWING AND REGURGITATING HURT FEELINGS

Marge, the divorced young mother of two daughters, learned at an early age that people would befriend her more readily if she agreed to activities they had chosen than if she were to insist on her own choices. Actually, the lesson was provided by her mother, a registered nurse who considered placing the well-being of others above her own as her destiny. For most of her life Marge had an extensive circle of friends but there were frequent replacements.

Replacements entered the circle after Marge had distanced herself from some of her previous friends. Marge's agreeableness wore thin after a while. Her turn never seemed to come and she developed feelings of anger and resentment. However, she did not permit herself the overt expression of these feelings. She quietly withdrew and collected a new friend to replace the old.

After a few early years of compliance with her husband's wishes, Marge's feelings for Fred cooled somewhat but not enough to leave him. She distanced herself from him emotionally and after a while physically in that she created elaborate excuses for not engaging in sex with him. However, she missed some of the closeness of being with a male partner and she became involved in an extramarital affair. When Fred discovered her infidelity, she explained that it was because he had neglected her wishes and preferences, which she had never openly communicated. He failed to accept the blame inherent in her explanations and filed for divorce.

Since then Marge had met several men for whom she felt an attraction but her behavior did not change. In due time her distancing techniques ushered in the termination of the relationship either by the man because he felt rejected or by Marge who blamed him for taking advantage of her good nature. Marge had no awareness of the consequences of her behavior; she assumed that if she put her friends' or lovers' wishes first, after a while they would have to inquire about her preferences and grant her wishes without her needing to request them. By refusing to communicate her wishes and assuming that others could read her mind and provide what she desired, Marge gained the unfair advantage of putting others on probation without their knowledge. As she silently waited for them to redeem themselves by fulfilling her unexpressed desires, the unfair advantage backfired and left her disappointed once again.

People express their hurt feelings in different ways. Those who can be described as self-defeating, depressed, fearful, and anxiously internalizing personalities respond to hurt feelings with distancing or distracting themselves. They may ruminate and establish links with emotions that are unrelated, such as grief, guilt, and sadness, which also lead to withdrawal. Some people avoid facing their own hurt feelings by placing the feelings of others higher in importance than their own.[12]

With this cautious dance in the dark the two people eliminate precious opportunities for learning about each other and for finding out if they are compatible. Beyond the fear of being rejected after disclosure of one's true self to the significant other in this scenario, what might be the reason for maintaining the façade? Might it be the hope that by the time the person can no longer hide the true self, the other has fallen so deeply in love with the outward reflection that he or she will not notice the difference to challenge or leave the "impersonator"? The outcome here is that rejection is postponed only for a time, not avoided indefinitely.

Will a final confession of having played a role out of deep affection and devotion convince the other person that this relationship will provide eternal happiness because the other person's happiness was considered more important than expressing one's real self? While its intent looks like deception, one could argue that this behavior also signals dependency and a readiness to be taken advantage of.

Whatever the line of reasoning behind hiding the real self within a relationship may be, one outcome is certain: intimacy between the players will not be achieved.[13] The degree of vigilance required for the maintenance of the façade will prevent the development of intimacy. Emotional closeness can only grow in an atmosphere of trust and comfort in the presence of the other. It is not difficult to imagine how stressed and tired one would be after hours of being on one's "best behavior" with a person one very much wants to impress and wants to develop a romantic relationship with. The constant self-observation and self-evaluation of one's behaviors according to self-imposed requirements of perfection or adherence to the simulated personality produce more stress than anyone can handle for a prolonged period of time without succumbing to mental and emotional fatigue. Feelings of resentment, depression, or anger toward oneself and/or the partner will most likely result.

THE COST OF SILENT COMPLIANCE

A level of awareness different from Marge's was reached by Dorothy, an attractive young woman who ended her first marriage to a man so judgmental and domineering that it severely damaged her self-confidence. Over the three years of their marriage Dorothy found complying with his demands easier than asserting herself. As she stopped voicing her opinions, she simultaneously extinguished her feelings for her husband until the prospect of divorce became more appealing than staying in the marriage. Her friends congratulated her on her decision but her problem was not resolved.

Following the divorce Dorothy dated several men. Some of the quiet ones she found boring and those who were interesting because of their own enthusiasm about some aspects of their life or a hobby they were actively involved in, she feared—or rather—she feared herself. The experience of her first marriage had shown her that she was a follower. Following the interests of another was easier than steadfastly pursuing her goals and desires. Considering the likelihood of submission to another man aroused in her the fear of losing herself. Somehow—without verbalizing it—Dorothy knew within herself that the possibility of self-abandonment existed for her and she knew that the harm of self-abandonment would be more fundamental and disastrous than abandonment by another person, such as a husband.

"What is the difference between Marge and Dorothy?" one might ask. "Both seem to follow others' preferences rather than persist in pursuing their own goals. Both are easy targets for others to persuade them to follow instead of determining their own path." Yes, they have those characteristics in common, but the difference between them is that Marge still lives and operates out of a perception that focuses on others while Dorothy has taken the first step in functioning within a self-focus frame of mind. With the focus on her, Dorothy can start learning about herself, and even though she does not yet know the self in all its aspects, she intuitively knows that it would be dangerous for her to abandon it—no matter how tempting it might be at the moment. Paying attention to her own attitudes and thought patterns, Dorothy "nurtures greater awareness, clarity and acceptance of present-moment reality" resulting in a state of mindfulness, as explained by Jon Kabat-Zinn, a leader in the field of mindfulness and founder of mindfulness-based stress reduction approaches.[14]

IGNORANCE ABOUT ONE'S LEVEL OF TOLERANCE

Thinking one can cope with a partner's irritating behaviors may end in desperation when there is no escape from those irritating interactions on a daily basis. As one married woman complained in a syndicated advice column, her husband, a functioning alcoholic, criticized many of her actions. Both spouses worked full-time and the wife thought she could manage to let his criticism of her pass for the few hours a day they were together. When the husband retired from work at the earliest opportunity she still could manage to be married to him because her work kept her away from home all day. The husband had decided that she needed to continue working for the next ten years so that they would not have to dip into their retirement fund too early. However, the situation changed drastically when she lost her job and could not find another one. Now the constant exposure to her alcoholic and critical husband is so distressing that she has difficulty getting out of bed in the morning.[15]

Financially the spouses are not in a position to live separately. Due to his early retirement, his income is less than it would have been had he retired at the regular age, and she has not reached retirement age yet. Having been unemployed for more than a year, her financial situation is precarious, at best. Had she paid more attention to her level of endurance while both of them were working and earning an income, she might have been able to prepare herself for an independent living arrangement.

"Barb in Boston" addressed the question of tolerance a little earlier in her life. She loves her boyfriend, who is a superb partner, but they are sharing their finances and most of it goes from her pocket to his. They are living together and his earnings are not enough to cover his half of their bills. As the young woman admitted, she has difficulty tolerating being the primary breadwinner.[16]

Michael did not believe that there would ever be a time in his life that he did not want to be with Diana. Petite, blue-eyed Diana was attractive, intelligent, witty, and lively. She had a way of making everybody feel that she was their friend. Diana's outgoing nature appeared to be the perfect match to Michael's caring but more reserved character. They fell in love and seemed destined to live happily ever after. During their dating period there were occasions when Michael had to wait ten or more minutes for Diana to appear at their meeting place. This did not occur on every date, usually more on weekends when Diana came from home or Michael picked her up at her home. Diana always apologized and with her warm smile and sparkling blue eyes Michael forgot his slight irritation when she looked at him.

Their marriage started out happily and for the first year of their marriage life was sheer bliss. They were passionately in love and spent most of their free time by themselves, setting up their new home together. But then they emerged from their seclusion and started to meet again with friends for dinner or a show. As had happened when they were dating, Diana had difficulty being ready on time for the outing. Michael was ready and dressed, walking nervously up and down their hallway to check on Diana's progress. It wasn't that she needed so much time to get dressed, but she always seemed to find a small task here or there that she completed as she went about getting ready.

When they finally left it was obvious they could not possibly make it on time to meet their friends. Michael's mood grew dim as he contemplated the apology he owed his friends for being late—"What a start for a fun evening," he thought. The friends did not seem to mind very much that they had to wait a little. Michael made his apologies and Diana chimed in admitting that their tardiness had really been her fault. "Michael knows from dating me that I have trouble with being on time. There seems to always be something else I need to do before I can leave." And then she added with a big smile, "But Michael married me anyway." Trying to diffuse any tension, Michael's friend laughingly remarked, "So you knew what you were getting into—too late to complain now." Michael agreed. They all had a great evening and forgot about Michael and Diana's tardiness.

But as it usually happens without change, things continue as before. If Michael and Diana went out for social events right after work, they arrived on time; leaving from home seemed to be the problem. As Diana hurried around finishing some last-minute tasks, Michael could feel tension mounting in him. Finally in the car, Michael started to drive faster than usual in an attempt to make up for the lost time. His driving became more risky and he adopted a style of weaving in and out of lanes, barely cutting in front of the driver he had just passed—all with the purpose of saving a few minutes and reducing the embarrassment of having to apologize once again for being late.

Diana did not like Michael's new manner of driving; it frightened her and she complained, sometimes in a shrieking voice. Soon they both came to dread going out because what were to be pleasurable events turned into anxiety-producing ordeals. It didn't help their situation when Michael's best friend and his wife stopped inviting them to join them for dinner or a show. In due time, the tension associated with outside events spread and invaded their life at home. Where in the beginning of their relationship smiles spread over their faces as they looked at each other, now frowns developed even while discussing topics other than outside events. The irresistible glow that had once characterized their union had faded into a dull resignation that turned into impatience and irritability after Michael took a closer look at Tiffany, his young new assistant at the office.

Most people would argue that Diana and Michael could have discussed resolving their different attitudes about punctuality to prevent the termination of their once happy marriage. But they did not address the issue that drove them apart. As Diana explained long ago to their friends, Michael knew prior to their commitment about her tendency to be tardy and he did not complain about it, which she interpreted to mean that it was not a significant issue. When she became annoyed about Michael's driving behavior, she expressed her displeasure. Michael, on the other hand, remembered Diana's tardiness when they were dating and did not take his friend's remarks about it being too late to complain seriously. Though he had known about it, he did not know he would not be able to tolerate this for the rest of their lives together. He had assumed that compared to Diana's other wonderful characteristics he could overlook her lack of punctuality. Unfortunately, Michael did not know himself well enough. He did not realize how much impact Diana's habit would have on his own emotional status.

Certainly, an open discussion and even a decision to seek marital therapy could have prevented this sad ending—if from the beginning the two spouses had been fully aware of the source of tension between them. But lacking sufficient awareness of their attitudes, Diana did not examine the reasons for her obsession with uncompleted tasks at home and Michael did not realize that his level of actual frustration tolerance did not match his imagined ability to tolerate Diana's irritating behavior. Once they had moved to the reality of married life the significance of their different attitudes became painfully clear.

FEELINGS OF INSECURITY AND THEIR EFFECTS ON RELATIONSHIPS

As in the story of Adam and Eve above, personal insecurities, whether they stem from attachment issues early in life or from a variety of other adjustment difficulties, will have a negative effect on most intimate relationships. In a social circle of friends one might encounter individuals who apparently need constant validation. Their complaints about their beauty, their charm, their skills, or their knowledge prompt assurances from those around them that they possess these qualities in sufficient quantities. The validation-seeking person may counter with responses like, "You are so kind, you want to make me feel good, but . . ." With that they turn around and inform the friendly bystanders how wrong they are. Another way of responding may be by gratefully accepting the assurances but pointing out another minor flaw that might not have been noticed yet. After a few of those interchanges most people would want to give up and avoid future interaction with the person.

If faced with this type of interchange with a significant other on a regular basis, how long would most people stay in such a relationship: a month, a year, a lifetime? Christine, a beautiful brunette, found out. She was constantly surrounded by a string of male admirers. When she was in her midtwenties she thought she had found the man of her dreams, a young financial advisor with a promising future. Stephen, like her other male admirers, paid her compliments on her beauty and the way she dressed, but after some time he got tired of the same question and answer game and he asked Christine why she sought his opinion on practically every piece of clothing she wore, every new hairstyle she tried out, and every line of cosmetics she experimented with. Christine was offended and an argument ensued, which ended with her leaving the room claiming to have a headache.

Stephen apologized the next morning, which may have been a tactical error because Christine's behavior continued. Instead of challenging her approach, Stephen resorted to giving brief affirmative answers. After the birth of their first child, a baby girl, Christine's inquiries centered mainly on her weight and figure. Had she lost all the weight necessary to fit into the same size clothes as before? About two years after the birth of their daughter, Christine considered having another child. Stephen, however, was not in favor of it and instead—in his quiet way—suggested a divorce.

Christine had no problem dating eligible men after the divorce. Stephen provided well for his little daughter and Christine managed nicely with a part-time job. Richard was the next likely candidate for a husband. Christine felt a strong attraction for him and he seemed passionately in love with her. They dated for about a year and considered a wedding around the Thanksgiving holiday. Richard did not utter compliments spontaneously, so Christine asked him what he liked about her. Poor Richard made the mistake of answering, "Everything." Everything was not enough for Christine; she questioned him about what in particular he liked about her. After a few attempts at listing some of her attributes, Richard gave up. Of course, he could not list "everything" individually. What if he left out an important asset? Christine would be sure to notice its absence from Richard's list. The scenario was repeated several times until Richard—frustrated—faded out of the relationship.

Was Christine aware that her seemingly bottomless need for validation had been a major factor causing the breakup of her relationships? Her friends listened as she complained and wondered how the men who had adored her at the beginning of the relationship could have been so cruel as to leave her without so much as an explanation. Apparently, neither Stephen nor Richard felt inclined to discuss in detail the reasons for their shrinking affection for Christine. One of her friends suggested therapy, but Christine did not see how that could explain the behaviors of the men in her life; if anything, they seemed to need help with their rude behavior.

With that attitude it is difficult to imagine that Christine will be embarking upon a self-searching journey in the near future. Her concerns about her attractiveness seem to take up all her time and energy. Not much is left for any efforts at understanding how her behaviors affect the mood and patience of her admirers. In their responses she does not perceive a reflection of her signals, only the expression of what she interprets as their rude behavior.

Can tardiness be classified as rude behavior? Many would agree; Rebecca doesn't think so. No matter where she is going, she is usually late. "My friends know that I will be ten to fifteen minutes late; they don't seem to mind. It's only with new people that I have to remember that they don't know about it. If we are supposed to meet in a restaurant, I better have the telephone number handy," explains Rebecca. In her mind it is not a big deal; her friends seem willing to tolerate her behavior. So why should she change? She is so busy, always trying to accomplish one more task before leaving for a date or an appointment, very much like Diana above. A system like that gives her the idea that she can stretch time; yet in reality, she has only twenty-four hours in each day—just like everybody else.

What does her behavior tell us about Rebecca? That she can do more than anybody else in the same amount of time? That she is hardworking and makes every minute count? What about the minutes her friends are waiting for her to arrive? Of course, they have the freedom to get to their agreed-upon destination with a time delay because it is understood that Rebecca will be late. It may even work out that sometimes they will arrive later than Rebecca. In that case, will Rebecca be annoyed? "No, I won't be annoyed," Rebecca answered. "That just gives me a few more minutes next time we meet." One can imagine that with this system the minutes can eventually stretch into hours and a lunch meeting may turn into a dinner date.

And another question comes to mind: Does Rebecca believe that her friends or other people she keeps waiting consider her a well-organized person, who handles her tasks efficiently and effectively? Or might they even think that Rebecca does not respect the value of their time? How much does she value their friendship? Is she even aware of how these people might interpret her behavior?

LEARNING TO READ ONE'S OWN SIGNALS

How do people know who would be the most likely person to fulfill their wishes? By careful observation of the behavioral signals people emit. If it can be assumed that people can "read" other people, would it also be possible for individuals to "read" their own behavioral signals as well as gain the knowledge of how others interpret these signals? The answer is yes, if it is important enough to spend the attention and effort on learning this. Obviously, this knowledge about others is important to some people—for whatever reason and not always for the others' benefit. Usually the most compelling reason for exerting the effort of observation and interpretation of those behaviors is for the benefit of the observer.

When bank robber Willie Sutton was asked why he robbed banks he answered, "Because that's where the money is." Similarly, people who want others to do their work for them and put their interests first will hardly approach persons who display selfish or egocentric behaviors; they will look for those agreeable, selfless individuals who are only too happy to help. In other words, it is in the selfless, empathic person where the good will to help others can be expected. Just as Willie Sutton observed over time that people deposit money in banks and interpreted and concluded from his observation that the money is kept in the bank, there are people who observe others' behaviors with the goal of learning what those others might have that is of value to them.

Perhaps some people might reject this approach to relationships as being too calculating. However, considering their wishes, most people would regard them as sufficiently important for learning where and how they could best be fulfilled. Rarely are people's desires so insignificant that it does not matter to them. Or, as in Jenny's case from chapter 3, are they so important that they must be hidden for fear of rendering oneself vulnerable to disillusionment? Those who consider their wishes as reasonably important will search for ways of getting what they want. And they probably also know what they don't want and how to avoid receiving what they don't want.

Behaviors are the vehicles people use for accomplishing what they want and behaviors are also the paths to communicate that to others. In Christine's case, she knew what she wanted: continuous affirmation of her physical attractiveness. She also thought she knew how to get it by requesting it constantly. What she did not know was what her signals communicated to those around her. The men in her life received the message that nothing was as important in their relationship with Christine as clear and frequently expressed admiration for her physical beauty. Nothing else came close in comparison. Christine's signals also made the men believe that their feelings and well-being were of little importance to her. If she had been aware of her own signals, would she really have wanted to transmit that message?

In the case of Mary and Jim, encountered in an earlier chapter, during their thirty years of marriage Mary's message to Jim was, "I want to believe you"; it was not "I insist on your honesty" and Jim complied—as long as it matched his wishes. If he had not wanted to replace Mary with a successor, Mary would probably have stayed in the marriage "until death do us part." It is doubtful that Mary ever realized the real content of her message.

On the other hand, Randolph, the university professor from chapter 3, communicated to his wife that he was willing to forgive a lot but three was the magic number, beyond which he did not want to continue with the marriage. Megan in her relationship with Howard expected the absolute truth from him, but that is not what she communicated to him. The message Howard received was that Megan wanted to know the reasons for Howard's less than honest behaviors. Megan also silently assumed that she would be able to change Howard's behavior. Would Howard have agreed with Megan's assumption if she had communicated that to him? Probably not.

Also from chapter 3, Tina's behavior in continuing the relationship with Fred signaled that she was not determined to establish limits on what was acceptable to her; instead, she was willing to bank on her hopes. When Fred informed her about his unwillingness to make commitments, she could have told him to give her a call when he was ready to commit to a relationship. Then they could get to know each other better to see if they were compatible. As for Gina, the widowed registered nurse, by her pampering of Tom and lack of inquiry into his past, she transmitted the statement that Tom was the significant one in the relationship, significant enough that she considered his feelings above her own safety.

As Lois, another registered nurse near retirement age, said, "I may not have known what I wanted but I certainly knew what I did not want and would not tolerate." Lois is in her second marriage. Between the divorce from her first husband and finally marrying her current husband, she had many years of dating several men. Having first married while still in her teens, Lois had not been aware of what she was looking for. But not accepting what she did not want gave her the strength to wait until she found what she could accept and fortunately it also turned out to be what she wanted. The quality of her second marriage would indicate that she not only knew what she wanted, she was also able to communicate that to herself as well as to her current husband.

When Tina defended herself in response to Fred's accusations and when she complained about his behaviors but continued to be available to him, did she think she let him know that his behavior was unacceptable to her? No, her message was that she did not like it but was willing to stay with him in spite of it. If she had determined that his behavior was not acceptable to her, she could have calmly told him once. There would not have been a need to keep on complaining about his shortcomings and defending herself. She could have saved her breath and time with the simple statement, "I don't think we are a good match, goodbye." Her continued complaining, in fact, provided Fred with enough ammunition and justification for deciding that committing himself to an intimate relationship with an angry, nagging female partner would not be in his best interest.

In all these relationships the partners communicated simultaneously on at least two levels, the spoken word and displayed behaviors. When the two levels contain different or even contradictory messages, the receiver usually focuses on the one that best suits his or her intentions and expectations and that may not be congruent with the sender's interest. For those who are not aware that the two levels of their communication contain incongruous messages, painful disappointments will be in store.

Throughout this chapter the importance of knowing oneself, one's wishes, dislikes, level of tolerance, and other characteristics that impact relationships has been stressed. And it is equally important to be aware of the messages one emits to those one interacts with. The story of a man who called himself "Alone" is a fitting illustration.

As mentioned in chapter 2, Alone describes himself as a twice divorced man in his midfifties with many talents, but he is having difficulty finding someone to connect with. In addition to knowing himself, he is also keenly aware of what he cannot tolerate in a companion. Alone lives in a conservative community and he is not about to relocate. This would mean that his search for an acceptable companion is restricted to that community unless he finds someone with the desired characteristics who is willing to move to his conservative community.[17]

Having this degree of knowledge about his own talents and attributes in addition to being aware of what he can and cannot tolerate is definitely an advantage when looking for a long-time partner. However, it is doubtful that his awareness includes a sense of what signals he gives out. Overall, his description of the women he encountered is not very flattering—and hopefully not very accurate. His words express criticism of what he has seen so far. For a moment he does contemplate the possibility of lowering his standards, but after two divorces, he would like to find a life partner.

Again, his verbal message is not designed to draw people to him; after all, who would want to be grateful for being accepted by the superior one on the basis of lowered standards? His words also seem to indicate that the two previous wives may have been chosen by him on the basis of lowered standards. While his message can be helpful to those who do not match his level of intelligence, talents, and success by discouraging them to consider sharing a life with him, it also might well be a negative signal to those who do match or even surpass his qualifications. This is unfortunate because with his many assets he could be a good candidate for a stimulating and mutually satisfying relationship.

The knowledge one can acquire about the language of one's behavior and its effects will be beneficial in placing oneself in a position of control over part of what happens. Of course, this is important knowledge not only for single people; it is vital for everybody. But our emphasis here is to provide an explanation of the underlying mechanism for those who may repeatedly end up in relationships where they feel used or even victimized.

WHEN SHOULD THE LEOPARD CHANGE HIS SPOTS?

When we want to attract a different type of lover, one who treats us better, interacts with us in more satisfying and self-enhancing ways, respects our opinions, and cares for us in an honest and open way—more so and better than the previous lover did—it is time to make some changes.

The purpose of self-exploration is to recognize behavioral patterns that might jeopardize the development and maintenance of satisfying personal relationships and to modify them if it seems worthwhile. It is important here to distinguish between emotions and behaviors a person expresses in order to camouflage or hide actual feelings and those that the person is developing or modifying in himself or herself because they are self-defeating and do not result in harmonious and appreciative relationships with others. Those deeper changes will involve more than altered superficial outward behaviors and will include modified ways of thinking and feeling.

Can't I just be "me" (whatever that is) or do I have to change everything? Is it even possible to change? What if I don't like the new me—will people think I don't know what I want and put me down for it? These are questions that discourage people from contemplating significant changes in themselves, even if they realize that it would be better for them. Instead of charting new waters they resign themselves to floating along the same river and to returning to the muddy swamp of their departure, to their previous way of acting and feeling. Sometimes they try to do more of what they have done before, banking on a "power law"—if I put more power behind it, I will succeed.

On the other hand, observing the behavior of others (using them as model) and noting desirable or successful consequences coming to the observed person can provide valuable road maps for those who want to improve their own effectiveness. Reportedly, as a young man, John F. Kennedy was fascinated by the attraction and magnetism that certain movie stars seemed to possess. While visiting Hollywood he was determined to meet and observe such stars as Clark Gable, Gary Cooper, and others. Many remember John F. Kennedy as a charismatic leader; if he took the time to learn from those who seemed to have what he desired, why wouldn't everyone else be tempted to do the same?[18]

THE SINGLE AGAIN GROUP

During the first group meeting participants were reflecting on the reasons for the dissolution of previous relationships as they remembered and understood them. The purpose for reviewing those reasons was an educational one, to learn from the possible mistakes and misinterpretations that had contributed to the breakup with the goal of preventing similar disappointments in the future. As soon as the participants had taken their seats the group leader asked for any responses to the previous meeting.

Timothy looked like he had waited for this moment; with a smile on his face he was the first to speak. "Our previous discussion made me understand that I had nothing to lose by approaching my wife again and trying to explain how I felt about her and myself and that I would truly want her guidance in expressing my appreciation of her. In fact, I wrote down my thoughts before talking to her, so I wouldn't lose my direction," he admitted somewhat sheepishly. It turned out that this time his ex-wife listened to him more closely and they had started to meet and talk about each other and the dreams they'd had when they first started out. Timothy emphasized that he did not just listen to his wife when they discussed some of their past experiences. He consciously tried to question and to make note of how they may have drifted apart by not fully discussing their feelings about some of the situations they had faced in the past. Probably there was something to learn from those experiences when he might have taken something for granted without really knowing how his wife had felt about them.

Group members were impressed by Timothy's swift action since he had appeared so hesitant about how to resolve his situation. But as he explained, once group members had expressed their opinion that he would be better off trying another approach than just resigning himself to his wife's decision, he was determined to act on what he had learned.

"Your openness to different approaches combined with your willingness to act on new realizations will be of great help on the way to reaching your goals. And I particularly like your taking notes in preparing yourself for what you want to say. That means you are seriously taking control of your situation," the group leader responded to Timothy's report. While the rest of the group members cheered for Timothy, the group leader turned toward Dorothy. "You haven't said much so far, Dorothy. How does our discussion relate to your goals for participating in this group experience?"

Dorothy blushed as the group's attention shifted to her. "I am trying to learn by listening to all the different opinions. For myself, I have to say I don't know where I am headed but I know I don't want to go back to where I was."

"It sounds like due to some circumstances you have learned some things about yourself but you are unsure of how to apply this learning to the steps you have to take in the future"; the group leader tried to interpret Dorothy's statement. "Perhaps with some details of what you did not like we could work on where you would want to go," said the leader, encouraging her to speak out.

"When I left my marriage my self-esteem was so low I thought about killing myself, but I was too worried that I would not even do that right. I had always been a follower; my older brother, Donald, knew what to do and I just did what he said. Donald was two years older and I worshipped him. He taught me things like roller skating and how to fish and build houses out of cardboard and glue. He was going to be an architect and he would let me be his assistant. But he was also protective of me. In high school he kept reminding me to keep my math grades up because architects and even their assistants needed to be good in mathematics."

Dorothy continued to tell the group how proud her parents had been of Donald. As young as he was, he knew what he wanted and he worked hard to get it. During Dorothy's last two years in high school Donald was away at college and naturally Dorothy would apply to the same college. Then one day all their plans came to an end. Donald had been killed in an accident. A group of his fraternity brothers had gone to a ball game at another college. On the way back they had a head-on collision with a truck. It was dark and a bit foggy. Donald had been sitting in the passenger seat next to the driver.

Apparently, the driver had had a couple of beers before they headed back. Although he wore his seatbelt, Donald was killed instantly. The driver sustained a serious head injury that left him with significant brain damage. One of the passengers in the back sustained a back injury that left him paralyzed from the waist down; the other rear passenger was the "lucky" one who got away with a broken arm and shoulder bone.

"That was a terrible tragedy," the group leader said to Dorothy, "for you to lose this important person in your young life. How did your parents get through this tremendous loss?"

"Interesting you would ask that question; perhaps you already know the answer." Before continuing, Dorothy looked straight at the group leader as the group leader's head moved in a slight nod. "The answer to that question changed my life more than even losing my brother. My parents had a difficult time dealing with my brother's death. They kind of forgot about me; it was almost as if I had died too, or rather that I should have died instead of my brother." Dorothy paused for a moment before continuing. During the rest of her high school years she felt isolated and lonely. Her parents did not take much notice of her, and when she was accepted at the college she had applied to before her brother died she just went there because she did not know what else to do or where to go. Her parents did not object nor did they suggest any alternative.

At the time she did not know how she would feel being at the same place her brother had attended. One time, the professor in her calculus class recognized her last name and asked if she was related to Donald. He remembered Donald as a very bright student in his class. The professor's memory of Donald did not hurt as much as she thought it would, and, compared with the pain over her parents' lack of interest in her, it was easier to take. Without Donald, architecture lost some of its attraction but she found graphic design more to her liking. She had a few brief romantic relationships while in college but nothing that developed into a serious relationship.

"I was always looking for someone like Donald," Dorothy tearfully explained. Another blow to her self-esteem came on graduation day. Her mother came by herself, embarrassed and explaining to Dorothy that her father could not bear to visit the college—in his mind it should have been Donald's graduation. Her graduation turned out to be one more occasion that taught her that she did not count. She found employment in a town where nobody knew about her or Donald and started the next phase of her life.

Dorothy made a few friends in her new environment but they were not close friends. She was agreeable to their wishes, where they would go and what they would do. She didn't want anybody to know more about her family background, especially that she was not important enough for her family to care about her. So she followed along on the sidelines of the groups she associated with.

When she met Robert, Dorothy thought she had finally found someone like her brother. Robert was intelligent and seemed interested in her abilities. He knew a lot about computers and seemed willing to help her improve her skills. Following his directions felt comfortable to Dorothy. She was grateful for the special attention Robert paid her. Finally there was someone who cared enough about her to be a mentor. They got married in a quiet civil ceremony.

"Did your parents attend your wedding?" was Marian's question.

"No, I didn't tell them until after the wedding. Actually, it's only my mother and I who communicate from time to time and only on a superficial level," Dorothy answered before continuing with her story. Sometime after the wedding the mentorship quality faded and Robert's expressions of guidance transformed into giving her directions on what to do. If her actions did not meet his expectations, he did not hesitate to inform Dorothy of his disappointment in her. The message was clear, once again she was not important enough to be accepted the way she was. But she did not really know how or what she was; all her life she had tried to follow others.

"I knew then that I had to leave Robert or I would never be a person in my own right. While the divorce proceedings went on I met a young man who seemed so gentle and sweet; it was easy to lean on him. But when I started to hope that we might have a future together, he pulled away. His behavior was confusing to me until I learned that he had been involved with a married woman before. Had he been hurt by her, hoping that she would leave her husband for him? That's what I thought to explain his withdrawal to myself. But then he mentioned that he had had an intimate relationship with another married woman before that."

Taking a deep breath, Dorothy continued, "It finally dawned on me that he was interested in married women because there was no risk of commitment for him. When my divorce became a reality, he lost interest in me. I felt like a freak; I didn't even understand this man's intentions. I ran again. I quit my job when I found my present position in this town. I saw it as another chance to start all over again and find out what makes me so unimportant in this world."

"You mentioned earlier that you communicate with your mother occasionally and on a superficial basis only," the group leader turned to Dorothy. "It seems that with the death of your brother your parents lost two children—of course, part of that is their decision. What is your opinion about your parents' behavior? Do you agree with them that your graduation and your future are not important enough to take notice?"

Group members' faces reflected an expression of shock at the leader's words and turned their eyes on Dorothy to watch her response. "No, I don't; it hurts my feelings to be treated as if I don't count," Dorothy stammered.

"If you don't agree with your parents' treatment of you, then it is time that you treat yourself as important rather than wasting time exploring what makes you unimportant. In those years that you followed your brother's lead, you may have missed the opportunity to find out what you are really like and what you want. It was a wonderful brother-sister relationship you had for a while, but now you need to become a person in your own right. You could not have lived through Donald for the rest of your life anyway, even if he had remained alive." Taking a breath, the leader continued, speaking slowly and emphasizing each word, "Every time you think of yourself as unimportant, you actually confirm your parents' treatment of you!"

There was a moment of silence; group members did not quite know how to respond until Ted turned to Dorothy and thanked her for the courage to disclose her doubts to the group. "In a way, what you said applies to me, too. When I used all my energy and focus in support of Arlene's plans I neglected myself, perhaps because I was afraid there was not enough in me to be important."

"Dorothy and Ted, it seems you made commitments to others in your life when you did not know much about yourself yet." The group leader addressed their situations. "It is difficult to know what to look for in a relationship when you are unsure of yourself and don't yet know what your needs are and what you can offer another person. Now is your opportunity to get to know yourself, which can be an exciting journey if you don't rush yourself with it."

The group leader closed the meeting, encouraging participants to devote some time to themselves, exploring what they wanted their future life to be like and what they thought they wanted to find in their next companion.

· 6 ·

Know the Other

*O*nce it is over, what is the purpose of looking back on how a relationship deteriorated? It is not to assign blame to one person or another. Both men and women stumble into relationships with insufficient knowledge about themselves, their partners, or the requirements for successful adjustment to the coupled life. Nobody would knowingly and willingly want to commit to an unhappy marriage. Reflecting on it after the relationship has ended provides an opportunity to learn the lessons that went unnoticed prior to the ill-fated venture.

As their dreams of an enduring happy relationship dissolve into disappointment individuals experience a rude awakening. It might appear to them that the divorce proceedings reflect the past union of a different couple, a couple whose only resemblance to the current case lies in their names, not their personalities. What became of the gentle and caring person who promised to make me happy? Surely it could not be the same as this cold, sarcastic man facing me or the whining, nagging woman talking to me in this high-pitched voice. Body snatchers must have been at work. But once individuals realize that their own expectations and wishful thinking blinded their vision, they might be ready to learn how to realistically get to know another person.

The relationship described at the beginning of the first chapter started like many others. Two people met and liked each other's company well enough to decide to date each other. The young man's commitment to her at the time might have been: "to be with you, enjoy your company, your thoughts, your wit, your smile, and to feel your kiss, your embrace for as long as I can." How long? Forever? "As long as I can" could mean as long as she holds still. Or as long as he can find her? Or, since he said "enjoy," that could mean that after some time he may not enjoy the relationship anymore;

he may become bored by it. So if he is bored, he cannot enjoy it anymore and it's over? His commitment is fulfilled and over, while she believes it will last forever. Some individuals keep committing and committing and it may never end, as one commitment flows right into the next one without one ever broken or fulfilled. The eternal committer—to whom does he or she commit? To what? To commitments!

DIFFERENT GOALS WITHIN THE SAME RELATIONSHIP?

"I wonder if this is a red flag or a period of adjustment," a young female reader asked in a newspaper advice column. As she explained the situation, she and the man she is engaged to recently combined their finances with savings and debts at different levels. According to her, the young man is finding fault with her financial attitudes even though her credit rating is better than his and she is willing to pay half of his graduate school loans. Are their goals the same in their commitment to marriage or is he attempting to establish a pecking order within their relationship where his status is somewhat more elevated than hers? It would seem that her perception of this situation as a red flag is appropriate and warrants further exploration.[1]

Lisa and Derek started on a promising relationship. But Derek did not know that Lisa was a staunch believer in the book *The Rules* because she never talked about it. Lisa had good reason for her support of the book as well as for keeping it quiet. Once one discovers effective advice, one follows it, but does not advertise its use.[2]

One of the premises of the book is that man pursues woman and woman seems to wait passively. Derek, being kind of an old-fashioned young man, would not have disagreed with that premise. Lisa's beauty would have turned any man into the pursuer. With her soft golden-blond hair, her dreamy brown eyes, and her dimpled smile, she captured his attention from the moment he laid eyes on her. When she agreed to meet him for a first date Derek could hardly believe his good luck. He tried to find out what restaurants and what shows she would prefer but Lisa wanted him to be in charge of that selection.

They had a wonderful first date. Derek was somewhat surprised at how reserved Lisa was. She did not talk much and seemed just to want to listen to him. Since Derek did not know that this was part of *The Rules*, he felt flattered by the attention Lisa seemed to focus on him in her quiet way. The next several dates did not change Lisa's behavior much; she appeared to possess a very agreeable nature. It was a refreshing change from some of his previous dates with other young women who were more talkative about topics he was not particularly interested in. Although at times he did wonder what Lisa was thinking about.

Questions about dating other men were handled by Lisa in such a way that he did not get a definitive answer. She seemed to be available for dates with him on most weekends, although every once in a while she had other plans, which sounded ambiguous. This seemed to happen especially on those occasions where he had not called her early in the week to arrange for the weekend date. A strange coincidence seemed to be at work on those few times that he did not call Lisa before Thursday afternoon; those were the times when she had already made other plans. Of course, Derek did not know that this was another very important behavioral prescription from *The Rules*.

There were little behavioral manifestations that Derek had difficulty reconciling in his mind. Lisa's restraint in talking about herself gave her existence an elusive quality, yet when the gaze of her beautiful brown eyes fell upon him, he felt secure in the attention she focused on him. The progress into the intimate phase of their relationship was slow. It was not until their third or fourth date that Lisa allowed him to kiss her lightly on the lips. Derek tried to push for more physical intimacy, but Lisa—while not strongly rejecting his advances—managed to delay them. Finally she allowed herself to be swept into passionate lovemaking. Derek was ecstatic and from the depth of his infatuation he proposed marriage. Lisa hesitantly accepted.

During the brief period of their engagement some changes could be observed in Lisa's behavior. Her previously displayed acquiescence became tempered with more assertiveness. Derek explained this change to himself as the fact that weddings were more important to women than to men and all those preparations were usually the responsibility of the bride. It was only natural that Lisa would show a more decisive side of herself. But this was only the beginning. Following their honeymoon Lisa's assertiveness increased. Her former agreeableness gradually got lost along the transition into married life and Derek was confronted with a wife he hardly knew.

In retrospect, one could describe this story in terms of different commitments. Derek committed to marrying the woman he loved and thought he knew. Lisa, on the other hand, seemed to have been committed to a marriage and the lessons she learned from *The Rules*.

Women are not the only readers who take such literary advice so literally. For men—if marriage is not necessarily the goal—detailed instructions are available on how to seduce women into participating in less permanent enjoyment. For instance, in one advice book for men they can learn how to penetrate the secret society of pickup artists. Following instructions on how to approach the desired woman by seemingly attending to other men and women in a group, which will arouse the woman's interest in the seducer, comes the promise: "Women breed with seducers, who understand how to trigger, through words and touch, the fantasy parts of the female brain."[3]

Efforts like those described above have the potential of turning the dating scene into one giant masked ball, where everybody tries to outguess or outsmart everybody else and whoever believes what he or she sees pays the piper. The cost in pain and disappointment can be significant for those who become involved in this subterfuge. All the more reason not to blindly rush into a new relationship without taking sufficient time to observe the new wonderful person's behavior, his or her verbal and physical expressions. And if something seems too good to be true, it probably is.

That appears to have been the experience of a fifty-five-year-old divorced woman who had been married for thirty-four years. Not long after the divorce from her husband she had met "Sam" on the Internet; they married soon thereafter. Sam made her laugh all the time and she had never felt so happy. He promised to provide for their old age with a pension and life insurance, but he forgot to mention that he had neither one in place even though now at sixty-one years of age, he is retired. The couple is embroiled in frequent arguments and the woman feels like she is walking on eggshells. Apparently she did not find out that he had been married five times before this marriage. She wants to get out of the situation; "I must have been blind. This man was married five times before me." It would be difficult to disagree with her last statement; five previous marriages would raise a red flag for most people.[4]

It is difficult to imagine how this middle-aged woman decided to make a commitment to marry a man she hardly knew and who apparently withheld major parts of his history from her. Was it fear of being alone after her marriage of thirty-four years had ended in divorce? Was it wishful thinking that made her believe his promises without inquiring into his past? She herself explains it as having been stupid. One might wonder if that brief explanation will be enough for her to learn the lesson about commitments. Without it she is likely to continue on the path of the repeatedly single.

How to convince her nineteen-year-old live-in boyfriend and father of her second child to look for a minimum-wage job to pay for his own living expenses, those of his child, and his frequent speeding tickets is the question raised by a twenty-two-year-old mother of two young children. Not surprisingly, the young man likes to sleep and party instead of getting a job and helping around the house—after all, he is only nineteen years old. Although not holding a job herself, the young woman reportedly is the sole financial support for this cohabiting family of four. At the age of twenty-two, this woman does not seem to have achieved a greater level of maturity than her boyfriend. If she expected him to assume the responsibilities of a man six or more years older, she could not have taken much time and effort to know him before she committed herself to another episode of motherhood.⁵

ACKNOWLEDGING EARLY SIGNALS

In most cases of ill-fated romantic relationships there are signals that the partners emit, exposing or disclosing some of their beliefs, attitudes, intentions, and personality traits. These signals may not be strong, and unfortunately, their existence will be overlooked because of the lovers' excited expectations or for other reasons already discussed in earlier parts of this book. However, because of the importance of those early signals, a section here will be devoted to this topic.

Cindy Chupack, writer and producer of *Sex and the City*, described the lowest moment of her life when she found out that her husband was gay; she also admitted that she "had a teeny gut feeling" when she first met him, but she did not know enough to listen to herself.⁶

Should she find a place of her own, a fifty-year-old divorced woman is asking after having moved in with a man she met about one year ago. According to the woman, her cohabiting partner travels a lot for his job and he receives many calls from women on his cell phone. When she is around he will not answer the calls. However, she also found lewd text messages from women and pictures of naked women on his phone. Confronted with those facts, the man accused her of snooping and claimed that although he loves her, he can't trust her anymore. It would seem that the signals in this scenario are loud and clear and she better heed the message that she might not be the only woman in this man's life and that he was not about to tell her of his other involvements.⁷

What might be the message in a husband's telling his wife of one year that he had been sexually involved with more than one hundred partners, along with the statement that he wished he could go back to one of them because she was so much better in bed than his wife? He says that mostly when they are arguing, although he also brags about his past sexual activities to his buddies. Naturally, the wife who had been a virgin until she met her husband feels criticized. After the arguments are over the husband claims he loves her and only says those things because he knows they upset her.⁸

The wife reportedly is depressed and has difficulty sleeping. She is trying to please her husband but it is never good enough. She better realize that he is upsetting her on purpose, which gives his proclaimed love for her a strange expression indeed. The messages in this signal could be foreshadowing an abusive relationship. If she did not detect any warning signals earlier in their relationship, now would be the time to pay attention. For instance, if he even admits that he is upsetting his wife on purpose, how great can his love for her be? It would seem a strange way to express one's love for another person by purposefully treating that person badly; most people would reserve the bad treatment for their enemies.

The wife may also consider that frequent bragging about one's conquests or achievements in order to belittle another person can be understood as a personality characteristic and personality traits are lasting entities. Unless there is a sincere wish to change, those personality traits will remain a part of the person and with that a part of the relationship. In other words, the wife may as well resign herself to being confronted with those behaviors as long as she remains with him.

When Cindy dated her future husband she realized that he had difficulty handling anger appropriately, but she thought with time he would change or she would be able to handle it without too much pain. At the time she was twenty-nine years old and wanted to start a family; the young man was entering a promising career and he was handsome enough to be likable. So she married him. Now, almost twenty years later, the anger is still there and she still does not like it when he screams and yells. She was wrong on two counts: he did not outgrow his temper tantrums and she did not learn how to accept them any better than before. Twenty years ago she did not know enough about her future husband nor did she know enough about herself.

RUDE AWAKENINGS

A well-educated, well-respected man in his late forties with a good career, friends and acquaintances, loving mother, siblings, and a son finds himself in the situation of being constantly criticized by his forty-one-year-old wife of two years. Whatever he does his wife berates him for it. Her criticism also extends to his eleven-year-old son from his first marriage who visits him every other weekend. His wife gossips and, except for her sister, nobody wants to be with her. The man insists that his current wife was fun to be with while dating and wonders how their relationship evolved into this mess. The only reason he stays in this marriage is because he does not want to be labeled a two-time loser.[9]

In his report the man did not state whether he divorced his first wife for the second one although that is likely to have happened. And now he is willing to sacrifice the rest of his life for an unhappy relationship because he does not want to admit he chose someone he hardly knew. As it is, he is not likely to learn from his unfortunate experience because he is not ready to admit that he made a mistake. And what is he teaching his eleven-year-old son on his visitation weekends? Whatever blinders he wore when he met his second wife, he is still willing to keep them on in confrontations with the world around him. It seems safe to say that while his awakening may be rude, it is not complete yet.

Thomas, thirty-four years old and divorced after six years of marriage, also wondered about the changes he thought he had observed in his wife during their marriage. "I thought she had a genuine interest in me. I felt she was concerned about me and would not do anything to hurt me. That's why it came as such a shock when she divorced me because I did not fulfill her needs. In the beginning I had been concerned about her self-criticism and low self-esteem. It put a lot of pressure on me, trying to make her feel good about herself. At the same time she was criticizing me in public about extremely minor things."

Although Thomas thought that his ex-wife had been responsive to his needs for the first three to four years of marriage, he continued his recollection with: "But as I look back now, I see that there were several times when I needed a special lift from her and didn't get it." He also remembered that on the occasion of their engagement she did not respond very well to his wishes. He had wanted to be alone with her when he proposed and gave her the engagement ring. But she interrupted the process and insisted that he wait with the proposal until her mother was with them. He had felt awkward about it because he had wanted it to be a memorable, intimate moment just between the two of them. His ex-wife, apparently, had not shared his desire for this intimate occasion and had in some way placed her mother between them. Although disappointed, he went along with her wishes.

As Thomas became increasingly more aware of her tendency to criticize others and especially him, he wondered whether his wife's self-criticism was her way of justifying her criticism of others. With the passing of time, Thomas had sufficient indications to doubt his earlier belief that his wife's concerns really centered on his needs. However, he wanted to be important in her life and therefore refused to accept any other possibility. Finally, when she decided the two of them should move into one of the smaller bedrooms to vacate the master bedroom for her widowed mother's use, Thomas blew up. She had not even discussed the situation with him before she had invited her mother to live with them.

Finally Thomas mustered all his courage and requested that his wife inform her mother that this living arrangement would not work. The wife complained bitterly about Thomas's cruelty; she said their life was boring

132   *Chapter 6*

and she felt lonely without her mother. She refused to revoke the commitment she had made to her mother and started divorce proceedings. Only later did he discover that an old boyfriend had reappeared in his wife's life. Thomas remembered that his mother-in-law occasionally talked about this young man in very favorable terms. Was he the reason for the divorce rather than Thomas's so-called cruelty? Thomas did not know and he realized that he had not really known his wife. His yearning for her love had blinded his perception and judgment. By refusing to acknowledge reality, his wishful thinking brought him six painful years and the experience of doubting his own perceptions.

MY MONEY IS MINE AND OUR HOME IS YOURS TO CLEAN

One might wonder how well a young woman seeking advice from Annie's Mailbox knew her future husband. Apparently, she did not expect her husband to go away on vacations without her. Their financial situation is such that her husband makes much more money than she does in her part-time job without the benefit of paid vacation time. After making payments for taxes and a student loan she is left with $10,000. From this amount she provides household necessities and pays for the food and care of their pets. Her husband, apparently the main breadwinner, takes care of the mortgage payments and utilities. With that he has enough money left over for vacations, but refuses to take his wife along and pay for her part. In addition, the wife does all the household chores; her husband believes this is a woman's job.[10]

Reading this sad story, one might ask what the two young people discussed before they made their commitments. What did they commit to? Obviously, they have different ideas of how their marriage should function and what their roles within this relationship are. If the young woman expected an equal standing in her marriage, she must not have checked this out with her groom-to-be before they tied the knot. From her description it appears that she did not know much about the man she was willing to tie her life to. Unless there will be an opportunity for negotiations and a change of commitment terms, this union will not last long.

But it is not only in new unions that we find individuals with a lack of knowledge about their partner. A man who describes himself as "Heartbroken" admitted that after many years of living with his partner he was totally unaware that she was unhappy. They never argued; he worked hard to provide for the family although he did not take the time to marry his partner. Now she left him for another man who has less to offer her in material things but perhaps is more willing to give of himself. After all, Heartbroken did not even give her his name.[11]

While she was still living with him he did not seem to worry about whether she was happy with him. Did he ever inquire about her happiness? Apparently not. They never argued, perhaps because she was afraid to complain about anything because he could have told her to leave and she did not enjoy all the rights of a legally married spouse.

BEHAVIOR IS PURPOSEFUL—
BOTH IN SPEECH AND IN ACTION

So often people express confusion about their partner's behaviors; they just cannot understand it. And it is difficult to comprehend because the partner usually refuses to explain the reasons for the behavior, which leaves the questioner with more questions. How should he or she interpret what is going on? The answer to that question is to take it seriously; never gloss it over, regarding it as just a passing fancy or an expression of the partner's mood of the moment. All behavior is purposeful. What is the purpose behind any given behavior becomes a more difficult question to answer, however, because more often than not the behaving person is not giving us all the answers.

Take for instance the case of a twenty-nine-year-old man who has been married to his high school sweetheart for seven years. They have a five-year-old daughter. The wife has lost all interest in sexual activities and is suggesting a separation and for her husband to find sex somewhere else. She denies having an affair and he believes and trusts her. From that description it appears obvious that the wife has no sexual desire for her husband and her behavior is telling him so; why she dislikes sex with her husband is something she does not communicate. This could be because she does not know why she now dislikes sex or that she does not want her husband to know the truth. As long as she keeps him at arm's length without letting him know why, she knows more than she wants him to know.[12]

Much has been said and written about men who shy away from making commitments to spend the rest of their lives with a particular female partner. Yet many women don't want to accept that and continue to pursue commitment-shy men. It is almost as if they were magically drawn to these men with the purpose of demonstrating how wrong the assessments of those men are. Unfortunately, many pay dearly for disregarding the warning.

A fifty-two-year-old divorced woman, involved in a relationship with a wonderful man, complains that he is not ready to make a commitment to her. The man lives with his parents at a distance of eighty miles from the woman's location. At fifty-three years of age he has never been married. The woman believes that they are madly in love and that he adores her children and grandchildren. They have looked at engagement rings but nothing else has developed; in fact, whenever the woman raises the question of commitment her lover avoids talking about it.[13]

What can we assume about the purpose of his avoidance behavior? He does not want to make a commitment. Is it because he might not be ready for it yet or he never wants to commit? It is not known, but since he avoids talking about it, we can assume that he does not want to give an answer to the question. Thus, both his verbal and his action behaviors demonstrate that he does not want to make a commitment. This is the message his female lover needs to attend to in order to prevent additional disappointment.

Yet another woman reports to be in love with a man she has dated for about a year, but he has been single for twenty years and is withdrawing from the relationship. She wonders whether she should continue this one-sided relationship or move on. From her description of the relationship her question is a moot one; most likely, he will continue his withdrawal until he is gone. His behavior tells her so. Even if she manages to keep him involved with her for a little longer, he has twenty years of experience and training in how to remain single and that most likely will eventually outweigh one year of dating.[14]

And then there are people who are willing to make a commitment, but perhaps only that one, as can be seen in those cases where individuals become involved in a romantic relationship with a partner who is already committed to his or her spouse. This is the case with "P. H.," who has been dating an older married man for the past two years after she and her husband split up. Since the older man is married, the time he can spend with P. H. is limited to once or twice during the week and every other weekend when her children are with their father. Although he has told P. H. that he will leave his wife, he has not done so. In fact, sometimes he does not appear at her place on a night she is expecting him. His response to her anger is an apology and she forgives him. The system works well; he does what he wants and then verbalizes an apology, at which point she forgives—and everything is back to normal.[15]

What does his behavior tell P. H.? His verbal statements convey to her that he will leave his wife and that he is sorry to disappoint his lover, but his actual behavior seems to indicate the opposite. He does not leave his wife and he does not always bother to visit his lover when she expects him. For "some reason" she believes his words more than his actions; when will she explore the reason for her selective beliefs? The act of lumping excuses together into a category of "some reason" makes them difficult to distinguish within a process of challenging those reasons. They remain mysterious and assume greater power than when explored in a logical and rational manner.

In a similar fashion, "Bob" made a commitment to his wife when he married her. But sometime later the handsome and charming young man met a single young woman whom he liked and he dated her for two years. To explain his restricted availability he told the young woman that he lived out of state and could see her only when he was in town for business. Then Bob ended the relationship without offering her a reason. The young woman was distraught. Relatives of the young woman did a little detective work and found out that Bob had been married for ten years, was the father of two children, and lived just about thirty minutes away from the young woman's home.[16]

The young woman dating Bob is fortunate to have relatives who cared enough to find out more about the young man. Without the information they obtained, she might have asked herself what she did to make Bob lose interest in her. While the information was undoubtedly painful to accept, it was an opportunity to free herself from self-recriminations regarding any of her behaviors that might have disenchanted him with the relationship. The information also helped her avoid any humiliation that might have resulted if the young woman had tried to find Bob in an attempt to make him explain his decision or to try to reconcile with him.

A young woman, experiencing difficulties with her boyfriend over the issue of moving in together, expressed her confusion to a syndicated advice columnist. Her boyfriend says that he wants to live with her, but he resists by stating that he thinks their relationship is too unstable to live together. Their arguments revolve around his belief that it is inappropriate for her to have a platonic relationship with ex-boyfriends. On the other hand, he communicates with his ex-wife on a regular basis. Their twenty-year-old daughter lives with the father but the communication between the ex-spouses does not really involve issues about the daughter. The ex-wife has permission to drop in on the ex-husband and daughter anytime she wants to and even has a key to the home.[17]

Although the advice-seeking woman thinks her boyfriend's behavior is hypocritical, she also believes that if she and her boyfriend were to cohabit, these visits from his ex-wife would stop. Indeed, he acts in ways that he is criticizing her for and that could certainly be called hypocritical behavior. However, the other important issue is that he engages in conflicting behaviors that each have meaning and purpose. His verbal behavior says he wants to live with his girlfriend and that keeps her in the relationship. His actual behavior is refusing to live with her and at the same time giving his ex-wife unlimited access to his home, which would make cohabiting with his girlfriend impossible. His actual behavior tells the girlfriend, "I don't want to live with you." Both of his behaviors are sincere and both have a purpose.

PROTECTIVENESS VERSUS POSSESSIVENESS

When does protectiveness turn into possessiveness? A fine line separates the two characteristics and the boundaries are often hazy. Much of the distinction may get lost in one's interpretation.

Talking about leaving her second husband, Irene strongly argued that he had changed his personality during their three-year marriage. "All of a sudden he became controlling. One day he cleaned out my closet because he considered it to be messy. He threw some of my things away without asking me!" Trying to show how her husband had been different at the time they met, Irene gave the following explanations: "He was easy to talk to. He was friendly to everyone in the neighborhood and played with the kids in the pool. He took responsibility to help the apartment manager with little jobs around the complex, such as checking out the fire alarm." When asked for more details Irene reported that he had taken on the responsibility for scheduling and executing fire drills in the apartment complex. He checked out the equipment and saw to it that the residents followed the prescribed procedures. From Irene's description it would appear that there was a controlling aspect to the execution of the fire drills, an aspect that was hidden from her view beneath the friendly and helpful demeanor.

Contemplating her earlier statement about the ease of communication she had experienced when they first dated, Irene said, "We never seemed to have any disagreements or arguments. I don't remember expressing many *wishes* to him. He usually decided what we would do or buy or how he structured our time together. I took it as a sign that he strongly cared about our relationship and it was worth it to him to take the time and plan for the two of us." While talking, Irene realized that from the beginning there had been signs about her husband's controlling attitudes, but she had been busy explaining them away by covering them with a benevolent interpretation. Even when he had planned an event that she would rather not have participated in, she did not voice any hesitation or dislike because she still explained her husband's decision in terms of caring and devoting his time to planning their time together.

While acting on her benevolent interpretation, Irene gave her husband the signal that it was acceptable to her when he made decisions for the two of them without consulting her first. Had she expressed her own opinions more strongly, he might have curbed his leadership tendencies in order not to risk her good feelings for him. There are opportunities for expressing one's wishes that can effect changes in the development of a new partnership. But Irene will never know if that would have been possible in her second marriage.

FORGOTTEN SECRETS FROM THE PAST

Isabel, a thirty-nine-year-old college English professor, was shocked when a young man, looking like a freshman in his first semester, approached her as she walked toward the faculty parking lot to get into her car. "Professor Linder, I believe I am your son, Francis," the young man said. After a moment Isabel collected herself, saying, "You are mistaken; my son is away at college" and proceeded to walk toward her car. But the young man was not easily discouraged; he followed her, explaining that he had been adopted twenty years ago in Cleveland by Don and Marie Henning. His birth mother's name had been Isabel Long, he added.

Isabel stopped in her tracks. "Where did you get that information?" she asked. "From my adoptive parents; my name is Francis Henning," the young man answered. Isabel thought for a moment before she asked him why he was approaching her this way. He explained that he did not want to cause any problems but he had wanted to know why his birth mother had given him away. He did not want to write or call her because at this point he did not want to involve anybody else and did not want to leave a paper trail. Isabel wondered if his words were meant to put her mind at ease or if he did not want to disclose more of himself. Perhaps he was not the real Francis but had found out about the adoption long ago and was impersonating the young man who would have been her son.

She was already late for an appointment but Isabel agreed to meet the young man the next day. She suggested he bring some evidence about his birth and his parents. She really did not want to believe that this young man had been the baby she had given up for adoption when she was nineteen years old, not knowing what to do. Except for her parents and her older brother nobody knew about this episode in her past. She had not even told her husband, firmly believing that this part of her past would remain buried forever. Her parents had died several years ago and her brother would not tell anyone. The only source of information could have been the adoptive parents. The name Henning sounded vaguely familiar; she had tried so hard not to remember the name of the young couple who had left the hospital with her baby.

As a college student Isabel had fallen in love with a brilliant young philosophy student from the Netherlands who was a year ahead of her. Jon had similar feelings for her and the two became lovers. They had big dreams for the future but could not quite decide whether they would live in Europe or in the United States. At the end of her sophomore year Isabel found herself pregnant. She asked Jon if they could get married and continue with their studies during her pregnancy and the birth of the baby. Jon's face reflected panic; no, they could not get married. His father would not allow it. In fact,

Jon's plans were for both of them to graduate and then to bring Isabel to the Netherlands for a visit with his parents. They could not possibly get married and have a child now. Jon was in favor of abortion, but Isabel could not imagine herself having an abortion. She could not murder her own child.

The other option was to give the child up for adoption. After many tearful nights Isabel agreed to the adoption solution; it should be done as soon after birth as possible. Isabel confided in her parents and her mother volunteered for the job of finding suitable parents for the baby. Isabel wanted to make sure that the baby had the best parents possible under the circumstances. Her mother interviewed several applicant couples and hired a psychologist for more formal evaluations of the prospective parents' character. Jon had no objections to the way Isabel's mother was handling the situation.

Isabel did not personally meet with the couples except for two that were rated highest by her mother according to her own impressions and the psychological evaluations. Those two couples met with Isabel and Jon to give them an opportunity to ask questions and get to know a bit more about the birth parents of the baby they wanted to adopt. The agreement at the time had been that the birth parents would never try to contact the child and that the adoptive parents would not reveal to the child or anybody else who the birth parents had been.

With all the work her mother did for her, Isabel could remain in school for the current semester and start the next semester with a smaller load because most likely she would have to take a few weeks off prior to the birth and hoped with fewer courses she would be able to make up what she missed. The rest of the credits she planned to pick up during the summer term. The agony of making the decision had been significantly lessened by her mother's support and search for suitable parents for Isabel's baby.

Jon and Isabel's relationship did not withstand the stress of undesired pregnancy and the subsequent decisions. They drifted apart and soon after Jon's graduation he left for Europe. He had planned to return to the United States for his graduate studies but Isabel did not hear from him again. Isabel continued with her education, achieving a Ph.D. in English literature. During her graduate studies she met Lawrence, her present husband. They seemed very compatible, both focusing on an academic career. When it seemed reasonable within the framework of their schedules they got married, found teaching positions at the same university, and in due course had two children, a boy and a girl. Life was agreeable.

That evening after meeting Francis, Isabel decided to tell Lawrence about the surprising appearance of what might be her first child. It was a difficult task but she knew she could not keep the information from him. She was not prepared for Lawrence's response; he appeared outraged about her confession. "How could she have given away her own flesh and blood to strangers? Didn't she ever wonder what had become of her child?" Those questions made up his first reaction. After a pause he inquired if this young man was a student at their local university. Isabel admitted that she had not asked Francis about that. "If he is a student here, just think of the scandal it could cause for both of us. And how are our children going to feel about this?" were Lawrence's additional questions.

Isabel felt like she was on trial and thought perhaps she deserved that for the sins she had committed so long ago. But she was surprised about her husband's stance in this situation. Without any consideration for her past pain and her current emotional upheaval, he was ready to judge and condemn her. Perhaps there would be professional repercussions if the facts about her relationship to Francis were known and Lawrence might be involved in something that he had no choice in. That would be unfair to him, she thought. How would this information affect the lives of her son and daughter? Would they judge her like their father seemed to, or would they try to understand the mistakes young people sometimes make?

In the end, Isabel decided to seek a position at another university. Francis had become a student at the university where Isabel and Lawrence were teaching. Francis had wanted to know more about his birth mother and finally his adoptive mother gave him Isabel's name. From there he tracked her down, just trying to understand more about himself. Marie Henning remained the person he associated with the mother figure and he owed it to her not to make any difficulties for Isabel and Lawrence Linder because that would be betraying Marie who had promised never to tell but did break down and told him who his birth mother was. Everything could have remained the same, except Isabel could not forget her husband's reaction to the secret of her past and she decided to set him free of her past by moving to a different place without him. The appearance of her son from long ago had made her painfully aware of her husband's judgmental nature and she was afraid that he would continue to worry as long as Francis remained on their campus.

Isabel wondered how she had been intimately involved with two men, not fully knowing either one. Long ago she had hoped that Jon would see a possibility to join their lives even with the burden of a baby. With Lawrence she had kept her past out of his life. Couldn't he have accepted it that way? Couldn't he have respected her past decisions without being frightened by them? He didn't have any responsibility for those decisions; he married the woman she was in the process of becoming and had finally turned out to be. But for him that was not enough reassurance; he demanded an unblemished past from the person who was his wife. And in a way, he had a right to know Isabel's past because it could have an influence on his life. If Isabel had told him the truth about Francis at the beginning of their relationship, would he have accepted it or would he have left her? One can only guess at the answer.

PUTTING ONE'S PAST TO REST

Burying or forgetting the past or putting it to rest is advice often heard from well-meaning friends and relatives and sometimes from the advice columns in daily newspapers. When people follow that advice how much do they learn from the past? What are the lessons gained that can be applied to the present and the future?

A forty-four-year-old man, being divorced for three years, expressed his concern about his current girlfriend maintaining a friendship with the man she had been engaged to in the past. The man's past is also providing reason for concern and suspicion. Although his former wife had numerous affairs during their marriage, he remained with her because of their three children. While he may think that he sacrificed for the children, what did the people in this family learn?[18]

This man would do well to explore his past before putting it to rest or he might be doomed to repeat earlier mistakes. One way to start his explorations would be to examine his own behaviors—might there be a connection to his wife's infidelity? In other words, could his behavior have contributed to her dissatisfaction with the marriage to the point where she looked outside for happiness? If that was not the case because the ex-wife had difficulty remaining faithful to anyone, what made him choose her in the first place? Perhaps his selection criteria need some modification. And in that case, he would be well advised to look more closely at his current girlfriend's behavior; he may be choosing a similar type of woman again. As discussed in chapter 2, people tend to waltz down a familiar path because of the ease of familiar behaviors—their own and their partners'.

"Barb" is another person who would do well not to forget the past. She and her husband experienced marital problems due to his indiscretion with other women. Just as she was hoping that they had moved beyond that crisis, she found an envelope containing a card in a book that her husband was reading. The handwriting on the envelope was distinctly feminine and she asked her husband about it. "Just a bookmark" was his response; but an hour later when Barb checked the book again, the envelope was gone. Barb admitted that she was ashamed for checking the book again; however, based on her husband's past behaviors as well as his present behavior her suspicion is well-founded. If it had just been an innocent note used as a bookmark, there would not have been any need to replace it with a blank sheet of paper. As Barb continues to observe her husband's behaviors, she might even get to know him within the context of his past and present behaviors.[19]

INFORMATION ABOUT THE PAST— WHO IS ENTITLED TO KNOW WHAT?

There are differences of opinion regarding how much individuals should disclose about their past and former relationships before making a serious commitment to another person. How much is the other person entitled to know in order to make a healthy decision? How much information does the other person want to know but is afraid to ask, perhaps not wanting to hurt the partner's feelings by opening old wounds or appearing to mistrust the person they are making the commitment to?

For instance, Julie, the young woman introduced in chapter 4, knew that her husband had been divorced before they met. Did she know the reasons for the divorce? No, she did not ask. Of course, if she had, that does not mean he would have told her the truth. However, another piece of information that was not pursued was the fact that Julie's future husband did not even introduce her to his parents under the pretext that they had not approved of his divorce. If Julie had insisted on at least contacting her future parents-in-law, would Matt have withheld their name and address from her? And if so, would she have been suspicious of the reasons for his resistance? What might Matt's parents have been able to tell Julie?

Similarly, Gina, the widowed registered nurse introduced in chapter 3, paid dearly by not looking into the reasons for her boyfriend's previous divorce. The topic of the possible impact of people's past is discussed in detail in chapter 3. The purpose of mentioning it here is to emphasize the notion that the past is not necessarily a closed chapter and that information about a partner's previous life is likely to be relevant to the present and the future of the relationship.

For instance, there has been some interest in the effects of early psychosocial stress (e.g., parental divorce, sexual abuse, etc.) on the incidence of divorce or separation and the number of lifetime sex partners. Focusing on this possible connection, a questionnaire study involving 326 women and 233 men showed no significant difference between women with high levels of early psychosocial stress and women with low levels of early psychosocial stress in the number of partners for duration lengths of ten years or less. However, men with high levels of early psychosocial stress had significantly more partners for each duration length lasting less than six years, compared to men with low levels of early psychosocial stress.[20]

It is conceivable that information regarding early stress experiences in a man's life could be of some interest to his female dating partner. Without the knowledge of this possible link, the young woman might develop sympathy for the man who endured such painful experiences, but she may not be aware that it could be a warning signal about the likely duration of this particular relationship. Of course, this does not mean that one should not feel sympathy for a person who had painful early life experiences; rather it would be beneficial for the satisfaction of future relationships to resolve—perhaps with the help of a therapist—the psychological impact of these early experiences before embarking on a long-lasting relationship.

ANOTHER SINGLE AGAIN GROUP MEETING

At the previous meeting the group leader had pointed out that most of the participants did not have an accurate knowledge of the characteristics and intentions of the partners they had been involved with. After group members had settled in their seats, the group leader asked about their experiences in thinking more about focusing their thoughts on themselves as they had been encouraged to do at the end of the previous meeting.

Michael, who had not been very active in the previous meeting, looked unhappy but was ready to speak. "I wished I had as much success as Timothy." His voice had a bitter tone to it. "I contacted Diana and tried to explain to her how I had felt and reacted to her tardiness, hoping that she would agree to meet and perhaps work on this issue with me."

Michael paused for a moment and Julie asked, "How did she respond?" Michael's face darkened as he answered, "Diana seemed just as offended with me as she was at the time of our divorce. When I mentioned how upset I had been on the many occasions that we were late, she said I should have told her right then and there how I felt instead of letting her go on with the behavior that was upsetting to me. She might not have liked it at first but she could have worked on it if she knew how I felt about it."

"Well, is she willing to work on it now?" was Ted's question.

"No, Diana said she had already made changes in that behavior because a friend had mentioned it to her. But the fact that I had remained quiet about it made her believe that she could not trust me. If I had been honest with her, she could have accepted that. In her opinion, honesty and trust are the most important things in a relationship. And then she added that not only had I not told her the truth, I had acted in a passive-aggressive way with my driving and she did not like that as a personality characteristic in a husband."

"Did Diana make any other comments?" the group leader wanted to know. "No, she hung up on me" was Michael's answer. Had Michael been aware of Diana's particular sense of honesty? the leader asked. Michael admitted that he never thought about it then; "she should have told me before it got so nasty." Michael sounded angry.

"It is sad how such a lack of communication can break a relationship that might otherwise have worked, given more time to explore each others' beliefs and attitudes," the leader responded, attempting to emphasize the importance of clear communication between partners.

"When can we be sure that we know ourselves well enough as well as knowing our partners to say it's all right to make a commitment?" was the question Dorothy asked, a question that had been on most participants' minds.

"That is a difficult question," the leader admitted. "Let's see if we can make sense of it by using one of our examples here. For instance Michael, he thought he could handle Diana's tardiness because he had known about it before their commitment. However, he did not know how it would affect him if he became part of the tardiness and could be judged by others on the basis of it."

"The fact that he did not discuss with Diana how he felt about being late says to me that Michael thought he had to handle everything by himself," Sally broke in; "he did not even give her a chance." "Isn't that what you did?" Michael responded. "From what you told us, it seems you never discussed your feelings with your ex-husband either." Sally looked shocked and turned her eyes to the group leader as if to ask if that was true. "That's part of our learning here. Apparently, both you and Michael acted on your thoughts and opinions—and even though you were aware of feeling anger at your partners—you refrained from discussing the issue in more detail with your partner," was the group leader's answer. "And since you did not confide in your partner, you'll never know how they might have responded at the time. This leaves you with less knowledge about your partner than you could have had."

"It sounds to me that Michael and Sally were condemning their spouses without giving them an opportunity for defense," Sue exclaimed. "If you can't discuss those issues with your spouse, how can you change anything for the better?"

"Perhaps that is the message of this workshop: if you don't know yourself to predict your responses to certain issues and you don't know your partner well enough that you can trust him or her to discuss the issues openly and honestly, then your marriage is doomed." Dorothy expressed her thoughts hesitatingly at first but with more confidence as members listened to her.

Ted, who had managed to sit next to Dorothy at this meeting, agreed, "I think you summarized the root of our problems. Most of us did not express our wishes and difficulties to our partners. We might even have tried to hide them in order to appear more competent or generous. I think I did, by acting as if I could keep everything in order for Arlene and me without interrupting her studies. And when she did not respond positively to my sexual desire I felt like I had been cheated even though I had not expressed my expectations clearly."

"Sometimes things happen too fast and you don't even know what you should discuss," Susan spoke up. "As you know, Jeff and I did not have much time before we had our son. At the time I did not exactly know what to expect from Jeff but I got much less help than I could ever believe."

"You have made some good discoveries in this discussion. If you hesitate to ask your partner questions or you hesitate to disclose what is on your mind, you are probably not ready to make a commitment because it indicates a lack of trust. Or, as in Sue's case, it is much too early for a commitment. That does not necessarily mean you should *distrust* the other person; it simply means you don't know each other well enough." The group leader responded to the members' comments. "We talk so much about intimacy in relationships and it seems that we mix up sexual intimacy with emotional and mental intimacy. Often we get to know the other person's body much better and earlier than his or her ideas, wishes, and feelings, including their feelings and thoughts about us."

Turning to Dorothy, the group leader said, "In a way you are answering your question from earlier today; when you don't feel right about disclosing your wishes, concerns, and questions to your partner, then you don't know enough about either one of you to make a commitment."

Attending to the rest of the group, the leader continued with the explanation that sometimes our own expectations and attitudes about a person prevent us from actually getting to know that person. As in Sally's case, she had let her disappointment and anger stand in the way of getting to know her husband during their cohabitation years. While she was obsessed with the idea that her husband did not love her enough to marry her without the need to legalize their situation because of their child, she might have missed some ways he expressed his loving feelings to her.

And Gregory's belief in chemistry kept him from exploring the women's personalities. He interpreted his sexual desire for them as a sign that the woman was the right one for him. Instead of knowing the woman, he concentrated on his reactions to what he thought she was. "It sounds complicated—and indeed it is"; the group leader ended the brief summary of what keeps people from knowing their partners.

"Even if you observe a few signs about your partner as I did with Matt's possessiveness and possibly even his tendency to physical violence, at the time one or two signs seem small when you consider the whole person and you think you can cope with it or the person will change, but we don't necessarily see the whole spectrum of the person's attitudes. So how many years do we have to wait to decide this is the person to commit to?" Julie, who had been quiet so far, spoke up.

"As you said, Julie, you observe some signs that disturb you, but then you make decisions about the severity or the durability of the observed behaviors and often wishful thinking has a voice in this, reducing in our mind the severity of what we have observed," the group leader agreed. "Could you be more specific about your concerns?"

Julie's facial expression reflected an internal struggle about answering the question that her comments had stirred up. Apparently she decided to disclose the basis for her comments, as she started to speak, hesitatingly at first. "There are some things I did not mention at the previous meeting. When I was very young, in my first semester at college, I fell in love with a sweet, sensitive guy, Ralph. His soft brown eyes were so full of feeling; it made me warm all over when he looked at me. He seemed to be a loner and didn't run around with a lot of the guys. We were sitting next to each other in English literature classes and met at the library to study together. He had such a deep understanding for some of the books we were reading. Walking from the library to our dormitories we sometimes held hands until we had to part to go to our buildings. Once Ralph kissed me; it was a gentle kiss."

Julie paused for a moment before continuing. "A couple of days later we made love as he sneaked me into his dormitory room. Again, it was gentle, not the passionate hungry type of lovemaking that some kids go through. I liked it. It was my first sexual experience. Ralph seemed surprised that I had still been a virgin. We tried to have sex a few more times although Ralph seemed to have some difficulties keeping an erection. The next thing I knew, Ralph was breaking up with me. In his gentle voice he explained to me that he realized that he was gay. He had thought so but then when he came to like me he hoped that he was 'normal' after all. But it didn't last; he had to admit to himself that his sexual preference was to be with another man, not a woman. Of course, I was devastated," Julie recalled.

But that was not all; a week or so later Julie realized that she was pregnant. She did not know what to do. Ralph was avoiding her. The following weekend she went home to confess to her mother and ask for advice. Julie's final decision was to have an abortion. After that she dropped out of college and moved back home. She found an office job in her hometown and later enrolled as a part-time student in a community college from which she transferred to another college a few years later. Julie's mother kept her daughter's secret, even from Julie's father who would have disapproved of Julie's decision and she advised Julie not to disclose it to anyone.

"I should have followed my mother's advice," Julie continued. "I never told anybody about the abortion when I was dating. But a few years into our marriage Matt was wondering why I did not get pregnant; he was in favor of starting a family. We tried having sex during my ovulation times but nothing happened. Finally I told him about the abortion, thinking that might be the reason for my being infertile. Matt flew into a rage; I should have told him before getting married. He added that abortions were a moral sin and later on he interpreted the abortion as an indication of being promiscuous. That's probably why he became so angry every time I worked overtime."

"Did you ever check out whether you could get pregnant or not? It could have been your ex-husband's problem," Marian asked.

"No, it didn't seem important at the time whom to blame. I just automatically assumed it was my fault. I will seek medical opinion before getting into another relationship—if I ever find another guy to trust," Julie answered.

"Or to trust yourself, as we are learning now," Michael brought up. "To observe carefully and to pay attention to signs and signals the other person may emit that would tell us more about the other person."

"That's well put, Michael," the group leader agreed without attending to the bit of sarcasm in Michael's voice.

"As you already know, I have always trusted others more than myself and I need to make a change with that." Dorothy sounded like she was thinking out loud. "Today's discussion is making that clear to me. At the previous meeting I had told you only part of my reason for leaving Robert. I knew he had been married before but I did not know the reason for his divorce. It was extremely painful for me to discover that Robert was addicted to pornography. It was a devastating blow to my already low self-confidence. I was not even a good enough lover to hold his interest."

"That must have been even more difficult when your divorce was followed by another disappointing relationship, as you told us last time," the group leader remembered.

"Yes, it was more than I thought I could handle, but here I am, trying to understand people's intentions and behaviors, to learn to distinguish and interpret the differences," Dorothy responded.

After a moment of silence, in a low voice the group leader said, "Dorothy, you just told us that you did not know the reason for your ex-husband's previous divorce," and hesitatingly as if just remembering continued, "Julie also mentioned that she did not have much knowledge about her husband's previous marriage and the reason he was estranged from his parents. Didn't you wonder about those situations?"

Dorothy blushed as she started to speak. "I hate to admit this. Robert appeared to be such a wonderful man, so much like my brother—although I realize now that my expectations made him appear more like Donald. When he mentioned that he was divorced I thought he must have been married to a mean woman who did not deserve someone as wonderful as Robert—or Donald would probably be more correct for me to say." Dorothy stuttered as she corrected herself.

Before anybody could respond, Julie came to Dorothy's aid. "I have to admit my reasons for not knowing more about my ex-husband are very similar to Dorothy's. I assumed that Matt's previous marriage had been a painful disappointment for him and the added hurt from his parents' disapproval of divorce made me believe it would be better not to make him go through all this again by telling me about it. I tried to respect his feelings and—much like Dorothy—I assumed that his ex-wife was to blame for the divorce. Besides, the past is the past."

"Dorothy and Julie, thank you both for your honesty." The group leader turned to them. "Because you wanted to believe that the men you selected for your husbands were wonderful individuals, you had to assign the blame for the failed marriages to your husbands' ex-wives, women very much like you. Women you did not know but believed to be bad because the men of your choice certainly could not be blameworthy."

"Of course, they would not believe their future husbands were not good men or they would not have wanted to marry them in the first place! Julie and Dorothy know they are nice people and they believed the same of the men of their choice," Michael tried to explain, challenging the group leader while acting as if defending the two young women.

"So it comes down to a fine line or a balance between believing in ourselves and trusting others," Sally chiming in, confronting Michael.

Sensing Michael's challenge as well as the tension that was developing between Sally and Michael, the group leader intervened. "It might be helpful to make the distinction here between believing and trusting," the group leader suggested. "Believing something can occur in the absence of supporting evidence that, indeed, a certain thing is true. On the other hand, we trust—and I am not talking about blind trust here—on the basis of some evidence. Evidence that is being collected through observation over time about a particular person, where one can almost make predictions of future behavior based on observations of the person's past actions. Or the evidence can be derived from our own logical conclusions in the past that have led to good decisions on our part. It increases our sense of competence and we can use that as a basis for trusting ourselves. But we need to be honest when examining our thinking patterns. If we make excuses about holes in our logic, we can't trust ourselves."

"Holes in our logic—that would apply to me when I told myself that Arlene would love me once she realized how devoted I was to her, right?" Ted asked.

"That's correct, Ted; your thinking sounded logical but it did have a hole in it because you assumed a cause-and-effect relationship between your actions and Arlene's feelings that did not exist. You can control your actions but you could not control Arlene's feelings, even if it might have been a good choice for her to have somebody as devoted as you were for her husband," confirmed the group leader.

"I kind of think that Ted would have deserved Arlene's love since he treated her so well," Dorothy said more to herself than to the group. "It certainly would have made me feel good to have that kind of encouragement and support."

Ted stretched out his hand. "Thank you for saying that, Dorothy; it helps me in getting over my disappointment and not becoming bitter." Dorothy took Ted's hand in response; for a moment they looked at each other and smiled.

"Yes, it would be great if our niceness would be rewarded with loving feelings from the recipient of the niceness," the group leader agreed with Dorothy and Ted, "but there are many people out there who do not respond in that way to niceness and many people telling themselves that they are in love with somebody who is not treating them well, either hoping for change or giving in because they believe they have no control over whom they love. Those are people that don't experience what you do here in our discussions. They are losing out on the knowledge you gain."

Marian had not participated much in the discussion lately but her face reflected some struggle perhaps between the urge to speak and the wish not to attract attention to herself. Apparently, the urge to speak won. "When you discussed the fact that we do not know enough about the past lives of our companions, do you mean we should ask questions and not let the past be the past? What kinds of questions should we ask?"

"I am so glad you picked up on that, Marian. I wondered about that myself since I had been so unsuccessful with my choices," Gregory exclaimed. "Do we have a right to ask people questions about their past?"

"Absolutely! If you consider entering into a close and lasting relationship with another person and that person seems interested in becoming part of this relationship, you have the right to ask all kinds of questions about the person's past."

Michael was ready to object. "How can you say that? If one wants to start a new life with a new person, it's the future that counts, not the past. People change; I'm not the same person I was ten, twenty years ago. I want to be loved and respected for the person I am now."

"Yes, people can change, Michael." The group leader agreed before continuing with the reasoning for the right to ask questions. "If you enter into an intimate and lasting relationship with another person, that person's past can easily become part of your future, just as your past can significantly influence your partner's present and future."

"If we pry into someone's past, that seems to be regarded by many as a disrespectful thing to do," Gregory said with a questioning tone in his voice. "For instance, if I meet another young woman that seems interesting to me, should I ask her how many relationships she had been involved in and why and how they ended?"

"Probably it might be offensive if you ask those questions early on after just meeting. However, if you are looking for a long-term involvement, you could carefully ask those questions if she has indicated a similar interest in you," the group leader responded.

"What if she says it's none of my business," Gregory asked again.

"Then it's none of your business," the group leader agreed, "because she might not be ready or willing to enter into a lasting relationship with you. Or it's none of your business because she is not the person to make a commitment to if she refuses to share her past with you."

Then turning to the other participants whose faces reflected various thoughts and questions, the group leader suggested that they give this topic more thought as it related to each of them and continue with the discussion at the next meeting.

· 7 ·

New Horizons—New Commitments

Love is an ideal thing, marriage a real thing;
A confusion of the real with the ideal never goes unpunished.

—Johann Wolfgang von Goethe

Are all marriages doomed then, and do all commitments inevitably lead to disappointment? Or are there solutions to the dilemma that can be applied with some success? Perhaps a first step would be to explore the word "love" as this emotion passes through several stages from the first passionate moments of meeting a wonderful new person—the stage of infatuation—to becoming more slowly introduced to some of the person's traits and qualities, to experiencing slight disappointments, to the more stable warmth of emotional closeness and mature love.

The first passionate stirrings for a particular person usually constitute the time of greatest excitement and in many cases this can be understood as infatuation rather than what we would describe as lasting love. What makes this first phase so exciting is the fact that we know very little about this particular person. But to round out our bits and pieces of information, we supply a generous amount of expectations of what we want the person to be. And with that as a main ingredient, the person becomes the greatest, most wonderful, most caring and considerate lover of all times. As pointed out in chapter 4, love grows best in an atmosphere of ignorance. The stage is set for Romeo and Juliet—to meet, to arouse passion in each other, and to die. They had to die to keep the myth of that passionate love alive.

Returning for a moment to Goethe's somewhat pessimistic proclamation, instead of *confusing* the ideal and the real, our challenge could be a *fusion* of the ideal and the real, where the fusion is understood as an ongoing process that combines the real and the ideal in different proportions. In other words, over time the ingredients change in their concentrations where at the outset the ideal portions may greatly outweigh the real ones, and with increasing knowledge, acceptance, and appreciation the real will eventually assume the larger part within the fusion. This later grade of fusion may be what some might call mature love and may well coexist with the institution of marriage.

EXPECTATIONS AND THEIR BLINDING FUNCTION

Much of the difficulty arises when two people commit to each other at the time when their feelings are at the passionate infatuation level, at a point where the fusion of the ideal and the real consists of a preponderance of the ideal. The basis for the ideal can be found in the particular individuals' expectations of what the other person is like and what life with that person will be—heaven, naturally! In the absence of knowledge of the real, expectations dominate the playing field. The space in the person's mind normally available to store information about the lover is mostly vacant at this early time and will easily accommodate the expanse of wishful thinking surrounding the thus-far-known favorable qualities of this wonderful person.

This can be seen in the example of a young woman who dated a man strongly resembling George Clooney, the movie star. Early in their dating period the woman had ample opportunity to supply the real man with the wonderful attributes that she had observed in the roles George Clooney portrayed in the movies she saw. If she observed slight discrepancies in her version of George Clooney compared to the movie role's behavior, she explained it away with statements like "He was probably too tired to realize that he was not as polite as he should have been," or "He did not realize that his remark hurt me because he was so busy thinking about other important things."[1]

The strong adherence to expectations receives support in part through our belief in certain traits that people have in common. We are eager to classify people into various categories to enhance our understanding of them. We can trace this trend to ancient Greece where we find the earliest literary descriptions of personality, such as in *Characters* written by Theophrastus, a pupil of Aristotle. These are outlines and descriptions of some common types of human beings that can be recognized by others as simplified but essentially correct images. Each one of the Characters has a brief definition of the dominant trait and typical examples of the operation of this trait.[2]

The field of psychology may have added strength to this notion by making the connection from traits to personality types, thus demonstrating a trend to categorizing people according to their lack or possession of certain characteristics. Whole theories of personality have been developed. People are categorized according to their characteristics by submitting them to tests and observations, giving them a diagnosis, a name. Personality tests, developed from those observations, can be encountered in certain training situations, job applications, medical treatment procedures, and so on.

Under the auspices of the American Psychiatric Association, the *Diagnostic and Statistical Manual of Mental Disorders* was formulated, which uses clusters of symptoms as diagnostic criteria for certain disorders. The designated clusters of symptoms in effect state that if symptoms A and B are observed, most likely others, such as C and D or E will also be evident if a given diagnosis can be expected to be relevant. Does that mean that a certain person embodies *all* the traits listed under that diagnostic category, or could he or she have some characteristics from a different category or some additional ones that are not found in any similar but perhaps an opposite category? For instance, can someone be friendly and sincere but not necessarily honest?[3]

This line of reasoning is not only relevant for illnesses or negative character patterns, it can also be applied to positive terms as well. If a person is observed to possess most of the characteristics that align with the Boys Scouts ethics, such as being trustworthy, loyal, helpful, friendly, courteous, kind, obedient, cheerful, thrifty, brave, clean, and reverent, does that mean he or she has them all? In other words, what is the likelihood that a friendly, courteous, kind, cheerful, and clean-appearing young man is also trustworthy? People's perceptions might automatically include particular traits in a person's personality makeup just because they expect them to be there, because they fit an overall pattern.

THE ROMANTIC DREAM WORLD VERSUS REALITY

During the early stages in their relationship lovers insist on living in the romantic dream of the always exciting, always loving, always harmonious world of two beautiful perfect people, always devoted and dedicated to each other. No outside interference will be strong enough to break through and disrupt the bliss and happiness. Little do they realize that if indeed they were isolated from the rest of the world, the state of bliss would not last as long; they would soon recognize each other for what they are and get tired of each other. In most cases, in order to survive the ideal union of two beautiful people becomes a part of and interacts with the larger world around them. The sustaining forces of the outside world may slow the process of recognition of the other while at the same time introducing interferences and temptations.

Within each relationship the fusion of the ideal and the real requires time and dedication to its maintenance as it becomes a process of shifting the balance from the dominance of the ideal to the expansion of the real. Often the process is delayed by one or both of the partners. It is difficult to give up the illusion of being loved by and in love with the most wonderful person. Who wants to approach acceptance of a less than perfect relationship? That may be good enough for others who have not experienced the heights of excitement that are part of the infatuation phase; for the perfect lovers it would be a letdown that they steadfastly resist.

Eventually, however, confrontation with reality will occur. That does not mean that the lovers are helpless; they can greatly influence the process and the outcome of the ideal-and-the-real fusion. The first step is, of course, to keep one's expectations in line with reality by refusing to blind oneself with an unrealistically hopeful outlook, denials, and excuses. Facing the reality of a prospective lover's character and behaviors and making an honest appraisal of the effect it will have on one's feelings can be a daunting task due to the likelihood of considerable disappointment. But it is better for the relationship and less painful for the persons involved than to wait for the rude awakening that will come on the heels of closing one's eyes for too long.

Once a decision has been made to accept and deal with the reality instead of the expectation or the dream of the other person, it is important to realize that it is not sufficient to just agree on the fusion of the ideal and the real and expect to live happily ever after. Accepting the reality is not enough; one has to learn to respond appropriately to reality by adapting to it in ways that will open the door to a happy and mutually satisfying coexistence for both partners.

Constant efforts in remembering the significance of the other person for our own happiness, assuring the other's presence by demonstrating behaviors that will make the significant other *want* to be with us, and gentle reminders to maintain the fusion are required. And all this will be occurring while in the outside world different rules apply, such that competitive behaviors often seem appropriate; but in the world of the two lovers competition will kill the love. Instead of competition, cooperation is the behavior sustaining the appropriate ideal-real fusion in the relationship. Encouraging and acknowledging the talents and achievements of the partner strengthens both individuals and their union.

"That is too much work. How can I ever relax? I would have to be constantly on my guard!" These complaints appear logical on the surface. On the other hand, we work hard in the outside world and we don't find it inappropriate to be on our guard at times. Wouldn't a lasting intimate relationship between two people deserve at least as much effort and attention? We need to be on guard to maintain the desirable ratio of the fusion. That does not mean that we have to live under constant fear and tension. We have opportunities to say, "I am sorry; I did not mean to hurt you," when we make a mistake. But we want to be careful about the frequency of saying "I am sorry" because apologies that are not accompanied by changed behaviors become meaningless.

The encouraging part is that loving behaviors—like most behaviors—with practice can become a natural part of our interactions. Although the responsibility for our behaviors falls upon us (the behaving person), in order to keep our loving feelings for the other intact, gentle reminders may be necessary when we perceive a disturbing change in the other's behavior. While we want to trust in the lasting love and caring of the significant other in our ideal world, we also want to trust ourselves to be competent guardians of the fusion of the ideal and the real in our relationship. This fusion requires carefully thought-out commitments that will function as the foundation for the fusion to occur.

There are as many types of commitments as people can think of; some are detailed and ironclad while others may be nebulous and open-ended. The types of commitments people make are often a reflection of their personality patterns as well as of their goals. Commitments can be time-limited or made for eternity. As already discussed to some degree in chapter 6, commitments have purposes and it is not necessarily certain that two people agreeing to a commitment have the same purpose or the same meaning in mind; in fact, they may not even know what purpose and goal the other person ascribes to a given commitment.

Most people entering marriage or other relationships of longer duration do not object to the notion or requirement of making commitments—it's just like entering an employment situation or deciding where to live for a while, one has to commit to something. But few people think about the purpose for the commitment, other than if they want to rent an apartment, they make a commitment to a lease covering a specified period of time because the landlord wants to be assured that his property will bring in money for the designated time period. The purpose of employment contracts is similar; the employer and the employee have a guaranteed time period of required work activity with an appropriate guaranteed amount of money in exchange.

COMMITMENTS BASED ON EXPECTATIONS

How many people make commitments for a significant portion of their lives without clearly specifying the terms of the commitment? The answer is not known but it can be scary to look at some of the life-determining promises individuals have uttered and listened to without knowing the full extent of the agreement. What does the "I do" of the wedding ceremony include? "Love, honor, cherish, and obey until death do us part?" Many of the participants might assume that sexual activities will be limited to the two spouses, but some of them may consider that as long as the other spouse does not know about extramarital involvement and is not hurt by it, it will still be a part of love, honor, and cherish. But usually they will not make a verbal addendum to that effect when they pronounce their I dos.

Some of the two partners' expectations have their roots in their families; in their parents' homes men provided the financial resources, took out the garbage, and performed the tasks in the garden while women took care of the children and did the grocery shopping, cooking, cleaning, and laundry. In this somewhat oversimplified version of common expectations, we do not see a need for further clarification because these expectations take on a normative value in people's minds.

In most cases individuals planning to get married tend to assume that the partner in this union adheres to the same or very similar values. Therefore, discussing these values or expectations in detail does not enter their minds because they assume it is not necessary. It is taken for granted that both partners have the same expectations and both partners act as if they knew the other's mind. They commit to their marriage believing that they are committing to the same rules, ideas, and criteria—but are they?

PURPOSE, GOALS, AND TERMS OF COMMITMENTS

What is the purpose of a marriage commitment? To share one's income, living expenses, housing, body, task completion, emotional and physical support, and so on with another specific person—all without squandering any of it on outsiders, who are not members of this specific union. Violations of this commitment may lead to dissolution of the marriage with varying kinds and degrees of penalties, although most marriage commitments do not specify what constitutes a violation and what the respective penalty would be.

What are the goals embedded in the commitment? They may not necessarily be the same for both partners. One goal in making commitments might well be the promise that their joint lifestyle will proceed as planned and agreed on prior to the commitment. For instance, did they agree on farm life or city life, two children or zero children, extensive travels or relaxing in a summer home and spending the rest of the year in their main residence, both following individual careers or one career, supported by the other, and so on. When two partners commit to particular lifestyles they usually desire the reassurance that there will be no major surprises and if changes are indicated that both partners discuss those and agree. That's the ideal version of a commitment.

In reality, terms of commitments get broken or changed, sometimes without knowledge to one of the parties. Depending on the situation, one of the partners might decide as conditions change to modify the terms of the commitment without communicating the modifications to the other; perhaps because it did not seem that important or perhaps it was easier not to let the partner know about the changing conditions. A case in point is the situation of a woman who became pregnant with her third child and confided to a friend that she purposely did not practice birth control but told her husband that the pregnancy was an "accident." Friends of the husband knew that the couple had wanted another child but both agreed that at the time it would not be a good choice financially. The husband added that he could not blame his wife for the pregnancy because—being an accident—it was not her fault.[4]

Not knowing the original commitment these two people made to each other, the situation could be seen as one of betrayal—first by disregarding the agreement of not having a third child, and second, by telling her friend how she had misled her husband, which demonstrated a lack of consideration for the husband's dignity. By transmitting more information about the couple's most intimate matters to an outsider than to her husband, one might think the wife violated the partner's trust in her loyalty. But most likely, any specific terms of what constitutes trust and violation thereof were not discussed in detail when the two partners first made the commitment to marriage.

"Lucky but Not Happy," a woman with two daughters from a previous marriage, has been married to Sam for seventeen years. They have a sixteen-year-old son. Lucky's goal for the marriage was to achieve stability, as she admitted. Sam provided that stability but now Lucky does not seem to like anything about Sam. She wants to return to the "real me"—enjoying concerts, dancing, travel, dinners out, and intellectual stimulation among other things. According to her description, Sam is overweight, diabetic, and impotent—a couch potato. Lucky sees herself as vulnerable if a better Mr. Right should come along. If he does, should she leave Sam?[5]

Although Lucky does not exactly spell out what qualities the "better Mr. Right" would have, it seems from her list of things she wants to do that he should be interested in dancing, concerts, travel, and intellectual stimulation to match the "real" her, but should that be instead of being stable or in addition to being stable? She does not specify that but one could guess that she became a bit bored with the stability that she first had been looking for now that the children are almost out of the house. And if a "better Mr. Right" came along, how would she explain her exit to her husband? "Your stability was great when I needed it for myself and my two daughters but now I want more excitement" could be her exit line.

However, a closer look at Lucky's thought process seems to indicate a certain degree of dependence on others. First she turned to Sam for the needed stability; now she is hoping for Mr. Right for the dancing, travel, concerts, and intellectual stimulation. If she really wanted to travel and attend concerts, she could do so on her own or with a group of friends. Similarly with the intellectual stimulation, she could read, listen to lectures, join discussion groups, or just simply have stimulating conversations with friends. Perhaps Sam would participate in discussing intellectual topics if she were to provide the stimulation for it. Even her desire for dancing could find some expression in groups where they accept single individuals for dance lessons.

Dependence on others for what one needs or desires when looking for a mate often reduces the range of options one can choose from. The priority ranking of the needed characteristics tends to overshadow the importance of those other desired aspects that can provide warmth, enjoyment, intimacy, and appreciation in a mutually satisfying relationship. In other words, those who are independent in providing for their own needs can afford to consider prospective partners from a larger volume of choices than those who feel driven to satisfy their more basic needs from the selection pool available to them. With needs as a basis of a relationship, much of it will be grounded in the dreary, mundane aspects of everyday life and the performance of the tasks necessary to maintain it.

On the other hand, one might wonder what could be the goal of a woman planning a wedding to a man who criticizes her before they even reach the "I do" stage. The young professional woman is planning her wedding with the knowledge that she will have to pay for it because her parents' limited financial resources will not allow such an expense. The young man's behaviors of urging her to ask her parents for money and comparing her parents' situation unfavorably to that of his parents' clearly indicate that he finds fault with his bride-to-be's attitude, yet he does not seem to offer financial assistance toward the wedding costs himself.[6]

Does the young woman really know what she is committing to, the wedding or the marriage? While she is involved in the immediate problem of the wedding, she is making a long-range commitment without paying attention to the signals the groom is emitting. He is criticizing her decision, judging her parents, and refraining from offering support or assistance. That should be enough information to raise at least a few questions, such as "Are those judgmental tendencies a part of the young man's personality and therefore can be expected to raise their ugly heads again later in the marriage?" or "Will he be more likely to criticize than to help in stressful situations?"

The relational dynamics between romantic or sexual partners involve an important but often neglected factor—the distribution of power in the relationship. This aspect, more or less visible, operates within the terms of a commitment. In relationships with an uneven distribution of power one of the partners may end up feeling exploited by the more powerful partner, the one with the greater resources who may also experience a lesser degree of commitment to the relationship. The commitment level realized regarding the relationship bestows differential levels of power to the involved partners, usually with the less committed partner enjoying a greater degree of power than the more strongly committed one. "Among other characteristics, the power differential is played out repeatedly in the sexual arena of life. The powerful partner can demand sex; the powerless one provides it."[7]

FOR BETTER OR WORSE

Sometimes individuals might be holding on to a commitment even though it is not in their best interest. In other words, they are committed to a commitment, whether it is of benefit to them or not, just for the commitment's sake. This was apparently the case with "Mrs. Miserable in California" who has been married for thirty-six years in a less than happy marriage that was interrupted by several separations. Apparently, husband Alvin had been unfaithful. Following the most recent affair, Mrs. Miserable—according to her own report—shamed her husband into returning home, only to finally realize that she cannot forgive him for the years of infidelity and that she does not love him anymore. Now she wishes he would leave, but apparently his guilt feelings prevent him from venturing out again.[8]

Feeling stuck, Mrs. Miserable has recognized that one needs to be careful about what one wishes for, or rather what one commits to. Perhaps at their wedding thirty-six years ago she committed to Alvin, expecting him to make her happy. Even though he apparently did not fulfill her expectations, she persisted in her commitment to him and the marriage. While she is waiting for the inspiration of the right words telling him to get out, Mrs. Miserable would do well to rethink the concept of commitment by modifying it to: making herself happy with or without the next husband.

What does it really mean to insist on believing that marriage is for better or worse, especially when one seems to be stuck in the "worse" part? Remaining for more than twenty-five years with a husband who had numerous affairs and abused drugs, one wonders what the woman committed to—her husband? A marriage? Unfortunately not to herself it seems. There is no money to pay the bills because he spends it on drugs and he blows up in anger if she nags him. The wife has no money, no car, and no job but is trying to find affordable housing for herself and her two daughters. The woman does not pretend to love her husband anymore. It would be high time for her to seriously consider the purpose and goals of the commitments she makes in the future.[9]

A similarly sad story is that of "Frustrated Christian," who during her three years of marriage discovered that her husband, Theo, had a drug addiction but has remained "clean" for the past two years. The surprising part of this relationship is that Frustrated Christian and Theo had lived together for about three years before marrying, yet she apparently did not recognize his drug problem. Another problem she seems to have overlooked for six years is Theo's inability to hold a job. Her own full-time job does not provide enough money to support her children and the household. The family's utilities have been turned off and they have a history of repossessed automobiles and evictions from their homes. After moving in with the woman's sister and her two children, Theo and Frustrated Christian still have difficulty paying their part of the rent.[10]

According to his wife, Theo's reason for remaining jobless is that he does not have a GED and can't get a job with a salary that he "deserves"—whatever that may be. In his opinion, he must deserve at least a supervisor's job because he tells his supervisor what to do, which results in Theo's being jobless after about two days of work. So far, marriage counseling and even the pastor's advice have not been helpful. Neither would the discussions in the previous chapter have made an impression on the advice seeker. After living with a person for three years, one would assume that a certain degree of knowledge about the person's functions and behaviors would be available to the observer. From the young woman's own statements, her commitment seemed to have been to marriage without a closer look at the other person in that marriage.

COMMITMENT FEARS

Some people are said to be commitment-shy, but that statement might require further clarification. It may be more the case that these people are not willing to agree to the particular commitments that are under consideration or have been suggested by others. In fact, they may be strongly committed not to agree to them.

Others change their commitments readily and easily—at the drop of a hat, one might say.

For instance, two years ago young "Torn" dated Anna, a wonderful woman. They lived together and shared a very special relationship. Then after about sixteen months Anna worried that they were actually moving apart and she proved it by leaving Torn, who, after recovering from the emotional problems caused by this relationship dissolution, discovered Zoey and entered into a relationship with her. But then Torn and Zoey had an argument that could easily be reconciled with an apology. In the meantime, however, Anna came back into the picture by contacting Torn and wanting to get together again. What should he do? he asked.[11]

The criteria most likely used by Torn when he made commitments were of the nature "for now, until something better comes along" or "until I change my mind" or more realistically, "until I grow up."

But Torn is not alone in his predicament. His older counterpart, a fifty-eight-year-old twice divorced man, appears to have similar commitment problems. With him it may not be so much a question of to whom to commit as whether to commit at all. With his fifty-year-old lady friend he has gone through a few periods of emotional closeness and anxious withdrawal without being willing to discuss what is going on. The man's description of himself as a "commitment-phobe" is supposed to be explanation enough for his behavior as he withdraws periodically from the woman he is dating. By diagnosing himself does he expect she will go along with his pattern of being intimate and withdrawing for as long as he wants to? Is he using her willingness to be in a relationship with him as license to dictate the terms of the relationship as he wishes?[12]

And consider the lady friend's position for a moment; how does she respond to the man's admission of being a commitment-phobe? Apparently, she is not accepting it as a fact of life but rather views it as a challenge, a contest that she is going to win—when winning may be impossible. So far reality has demonstrated that the man refuses to commit to her. He may have shown promising glimpses of something she wants, the emotional closeness, but he turns it off before she can really take a hold of it. Just because he is willing and able to demonstrate, at least at times, this desired entity, the emotional closeness, does that guarantee that he will be willing and able to give it to her permanently and indefinitely? Perhaps he is only able or willing to engage in emotional closeness when he knows that the relationship will not last forever. The knowledge that he can terminate the relationship at any time might just give him the sense of safety that enables him to be emotionally close to another person for brief periods of time. He does not have to worry about any consequences of having disclosed himself emotionally because he does not have to stick around long enough.

Another point of interest about her would be her lack of concern about this man having divorced two wives in the past, whom he apparently had made commitments to. How much of his behavior might have contributed to the divorces or was it solely the woman's fault every time? As she is focusing on her expectations that he could deliver what she wants, she might be blinding herself to some important signals that these divorces represent.

TO WHOM TO COMMIT?

While some people appear to be reluctant to commit themselves to another person, others have difficulty deciding who to commit to among several candidates, as the story of a man using the pseudonym "Drained" reflects. Having known his wife for seventeen years and being married to her for nine, he became complacent and lost interest in their relationship. They drifted apart, doing things separately, and then the wife found another man who made her feel good. Although—as she said—she still loved her husband, she wanted to spend more time with this other man and she encouraged the husband to go out and meet someone else.[13]

Drained went out for a few beers and met Nancy with whom he really hit it off. For the first time in years he felt alive. But when he told his wife about Nancy she didn't like it. She insisted that she still loved him and could not handle the thought of him being with another woman. Since then the spouses have done some soul searching and Drained feels it would be best to forget about Nancy but he can't stop thinking about her, which would make forgetting her indeed difficult. On the other hand, he believes the marriage will never be really good and it's not fair to any of them.

Drained does not even entertain the notion that he may not know the real Nancy, that he is in love with his version of her, the version that his expectations are painting for him—just as he probably experienced with his wife, acting on his expectations of her and their life together but then getting bored when the real wife slowly emerged and not doing anything to improve the situation by making himself more interesting to her. His wife in all likelihood went through a very similar process to get where she ended up being more excited by a stranger.

We usually think of committing to causes or people; rarely do we think of committing to ourselves, even though commitments to the self are the most important ones. If we don't consider ourselves important enough to make and keep commitments to, who else would want to do it for us? Starting with a commitment to oneself to be as happy as possible in a relationship would place the responsibility for our happiness on us—we have to make ourselves happy. In order to do this we would have to know what makes us happy; we would have to get to know ourselves. Most likely the requirements for our happiness will vary in significance. For instance, some elements we just have to have, whereas others may not be of the utmost importance to our happiness. Once this self-knowledge is achieved we can initiate the learning process about prospective partners—what are they really like and how will that match our specific criteria for our happiness? This learning process should be largely free of wishful thinking, excuses, blind beliefs, and other self-deceiving elements. Once a suitable partner has been selected, it would be a good investment to treat this person well to the point that this partner finds it extremely easy to demonstrate loving and caring behavior for us.

Some people hesitate to treat their partners lovingly because they are afraid that they will be taken for granted by them. In fact, they try hard to act in an indifferent manner, hoping to appear more valuable and less easy to capture in the eyes of those others. It is difficult to imagine how such reasoning could possibly lead to much happiness because the person who plays hard to get can never relax and has to remain almost unattainable; otherwise, the person might be taken for granted. An atmosphere where one has to be guarded all the time does not provide a basis for intimacy.

As was demonstrated by the study described in the first chapter, couples that remained happily married for more than fourteen years were the ones who had generated a warm emotional climate early in the marriage and maintained it. Emotionally warm and friendly climates that foster true intimacy are created by the individuals' personality traits of being even-tempered and warmhearted as well as possessing low levels of anxiety—not being guarded and suspicious. And without true intimacy a romantic relationship rarely bestows happiness upon the individuals involved in that relationship.

Furthermore, when the relationship disintegrates, as it most likely will without intimacy, individuals who have not devoted as much effort and caring to the partner and the relationship as they could have will never know if it would have worked out better had they invested more in their partners. Making it easy for our partner to demonstrate loving behavior toward us is usually a better investment than making it difficult to love us. The logical next step then would be to discover how we can induce in our partner those warm and loving feelings toward us that will make our relationship a truly intimate, lasting, and satisfying one.

Scholars and researchers have attempted to offer solutions. One of the many variables linked to partnership satisfaction has been the influence of different patterns in self and partner ratings. In general, individuals tend to view themselves more positively than they are perceived by others and this self-illusion seems to transfer into intimate relationships as these individuals believe that their relationship is better than those of friends and strangers around them. They also believe that their relationship is more likely to last. This self-illusion carries over to other aspects of the relationship, extending to ratings of their partners as being the same as or better than they are themselves or better than any others with whom they are not in a relationship. Such positive illusions are considered to be important for relationships because they help the partners to feel understood, to overlook one another's faults. There are different ways to compare ratings from partners in a relationship. An effective way for predicting couple outcomes is the comparison between how people rate themselves and how they rate their partners.[14]

Individuals tend to view their romantic partners in a positive light, either as capable and lovable as they perceive themselves to be or even slightly more so. Thus, the most influential type of self/partner comparison is the within-person perceived difference between how individuals see themselves as compared to how they view their partners. In order to identify how self ratings and partner ratings can facilitate the understanding about couple and individual relationship quality outcomes, a set of two independent studies using two samples of heterosexual couples collected the responses to a relationship evaluation questionnaire from more than five thousand participants.

The first study engaged a large cross-sectional quota sample to generate couple types based on how much participants enhanced their partners over themselves in terms of the personality trait of affability. The purpose of the second study was to obtain information about the possibility that enhancement scores for male and female partners might be linked to relationship stability over time. A longitudinal design was used assessing enhancement scores and affability scores at Time 1 and relationship stability at Time 2.[15]

The questionnaire tapped how partner- or self-enhancement patterns differentially influence relationship outcomes. Four outcome measures for different types of couples were identified, according to whether individuals rated the partner higher, the same, or lower than they rated themselves on the characteristic of affability. Couples in which one or both partners perceived themselves as more affable than the other showed poorer results on the relationship outcome measures and higher levels on negative communication and expectations for change than all other couples. Couples in which both individuals perceived the partner's personality as more affable than their own demonstrated more positive relationship outcomes. They had the highest relationship outcome scores in the large cross-sectional sample.

The investigators admit that these scores could be interpreted to mean that people are modest when rating themselves as compared to rating their partners; however, in their opinion, it is not the modesty effect that seems to be operating here but the idea that the partner becomes integrated into the view of self, such that the ratings of the partner reflect positively upon the self for the ability to choose well and to create positive qualities in others through caring behaviors. Over time people may even become more like those positive "illusions" held about them by their partners, which serves to increase the relationship satisfaction for both, making both feel better about themselves and the partner they love. In addition, the relationship structure in which the partner is considered equal to or above the self in capabilities may be conducive to resolving problems by encouraging individuals to take personal responsibility and action rather than blaming the partner and demanding changed behaviors from the partner.

A comparison of the different couple types on measures of expectation for change (how much the partner should change) and negative communication (criticizing partners, pointing out partner's faults, etc.) revealed that the self-enhancing couples were much worse than those in the other groups. It is very likely that without the structure of positive enhancement of the other, several important relationship elements, such as empathy, understanding, positive communication, and commitment, will be difficult to experience or sustain.

In general, one would expect newer, more infatuated relationships to be filled with a stronger positive emotional atmosphere than relationships of longer duration, but the influence of partner-enhancing patterns preserves the relationship satisfaction over time and is thereby linked to relationship duration. Furthermore, the benefits of partner-enhancement are operating regardless of the overall levels of affability. Levels of affability are important predictors of relationship satisfaction, but enhancement scores are the significant predictors of relationship stability. To be in a relationship with someone who is very affable compared to others would be very nice, but even if the person were less affable than another, it would still be beneficial if that person were perceived as more affable than the self. It seems that the reference point of the self is much more important than the reference points of other people.

Analysis of the data obtained in the studies indicates that enhancement is more powerful than affability in predicting which couples will change their status from premarried to married or which couples will break up. It is partner-enhancement, not affability, that influences relationship stability at Time 2 and with passing time partner-enhancement becomes increasingly more important for relationship durability.

Projecting stories such as Adam and Eve's in chapter 5 onto these research studies, it is not difficult to see why their relationship was doomed as soon as Eve decided to camouflage her sense of insecurity with criticism and complaints about Adam. Instead of enhancing and encouraging each other, their negative communications spiraled into hostility, burying their once loving union in the debris of their arguments and competition. Another example can be seen in beautiful Christine's story; she was so used to men's adoration that she demanded it when it was not offered automatically. Unfortunately, Christine never realized that expressing admiration is a two-way street and that the men in her life might have cared for some praise from her to feel satisfied within the relationship.

Similarly, the case of David and Lori, also described in chapter 5, demonstrates how David—in an effort to regain the view he held of himself—reduced the degree of enhancement bestowed onto his wife, Lori, and his feelings for Lori lost their previous glow. Their marriage did not dissolve at this point, but the beginning of the process of deterioration was set. With sufficient awareness on David's part about the experiences and changes that had occurred in himself, the negative emotional trend could still be stopped and turned around. The likelihood of David's awakening, however, is slim because it is so much easier to blame the other than see the mistake in oneself.

As discussed in chapter 1, some researchers believe that good marriages or good relationships require good people—people with stable personality traits, "good-hearted" people with low levels of anxiety. The solution seems easy enough: just choose a good person for your mate. But romantic love does not seem to follow a logical approach or lend itself to sensible considerations to partner selection; it is driven by pleasure and by pain. Although calculated marriages are not unheard of in our society, passionate love matches between "soul mates" are the preferred type of union.[16]

Other investigators downplay the significance of the soul mate notion, suggesting instead that the best predictor of long-term relationship satisfaction is the accuracy of one's perceptions of the partner's qualities. In a study of newlyweds married for up to half a year, despite the generally expected positive global view of their partners, differences in the ratings showed that couples with a realistic evaluation of their partners' attributes were more likely to experience high levels of marital satisfaction. If a partner has a negative (or positive) mind-set toward one's spouse, that mind-set colors the interpretation of behaviors and communication according to this predisposition.[17]

Comparing ratings of young men and women on the importance of love, faithfulness, and commitment for successful relationships, researchers using data from the National Longitudinal Study of Adolescent Health found that nearly all young adults adhere to major relationship values inherent in the romantic love ideology. However, as most theories of gender would suggest, women are more invested in the traditional relationship issues than men. The results of the study indicated that the romantic love myth is a pervasive cultural ideal still held by young adults. However, there were small but significant gender differences. Women value love, faithfulness, and lifelong commitment more than men but this applies only to heterosexual women. The general implication of this research seems to confirm that the romantic love myth remains highly influential as this new generation of young adults comes of age.[18]

Other studies of young, unmarried, heterosexual undergraduate students revealed that males were more likely than females to find casual sex with different partners acceptable. The young men also reported more intercourse partners than did the young women during the previous year. In addition, the young men expressed the wish for more sexual partners for the next five years. In connection with women strongly embracing the traditional romantic values of love, faithfulness, and commitment, an article in *Psychology Today* is of interest. In the magazine article a clinical psychologist discussed the observation of some women being attracted to "bad boys"—men who demonstrate a certain swagger in their behavior, indicative of boldness and bravado. Apparently, women find these men quite attractive for fleeting relationships. The scientific explanation for the phenomenon suggested that the women's choices were influenced by high-testosterone-fueled masculinity, which promises good-quality genes. Although these men may be excellent material for mating purposes, they usually don't stick around long enough to raise the offspring. Why would women want to take such risks? The psychologist's answer: "Secretly they harbor the fantasy of turning their genetically gifted cads into loving dads who stick around long-term, long enough to raise the kids."[19]

If he looks and acts like Casanova, chances are he *is* a Casanova-type male. Why bother with the challenge of changing a person when one can make a selection that already includes the desired characteristics? When attempting to change the cad into a dad, the swagger may be replaced by a drag in the transformation. With that change he may not be as attractive to the female as he once was. Furthermore, if he liked his previous personality style, it is highly unlikely that he will acknowledge the change in him induced by his female partner as an element of enhancement bestowed upon him by his partner. Most likely, he will resent his partner and the two of them will travel for a while on a path filled with negative emotions and negative communication until finally they'll part company for good—good-bye, happy ending!

THE SINGLE AGAIN GROUP

As the group members entered the room and selected a seat, they seemed to be eager to pick up where the previous session had ended. The issue of what one wants and needs to know about the past of the significant other in a relationship had stirred up questions as well as disagreements.

Dorothy was eager to start the meeting with a question. "I thought a lot about the discussion at our previous meeting. Trying to put myself into the situation, if I had asked Robert about the reasons for his divorce and he had told me that they were just not getting along—what would I have learned?"

"Probably not much, unless you had asked him for details. If he refused to be more specific, you could have let him know that it was important to you to learn more about him and what things might be upsetting to him. Of course, he could have lied and then you would have to weigh the likelihood of what he was telling you being the truth. Taking more time for the relationship to develop would be a good approach because it would give you more opportunities to observe. But if a person just absolutely refuses to disclose any details about his or her past, caution is indicated," was the group leader's advice.

"I tried to get some information from Matt about the breakup with his parents but he was evasive and I thought it was too painful for him to talk about it, so I did not press him for more. Besides, as you know, I had my own painful secret from the past. If he had asked me about that before we got married, I don't know if I would have told him. As I told you, there was my mother's advice; I believe now that it would be wrong for me to follow her advice," Julie told the group.

"Your concern about your mother's advice is justified, Julie. If Matt had very strong beliefs about abortion, one could think that he would be entitled to be told the truth. You probably did not discuss this topic before making the commitment because you did not think it would be that important. In general, though, it would be good practice to discuss topics that are so closely linked to people's values and beliefs before making marriage plans. Of course, we cannot force anybody to tell us the truth; however, as I said earlier, a refusal to disclose gives the inquiring person the right to say, 'This relationship is not for me.'" The group leader answered Julie's concerns.

"Even if you discuss and agree on certain issues before making a commitment that does not guarantee that both partners will be bound by the agreement." Michael could be relied on to come up with an objection. "A friend of mine discussed the issue of children with his future wife. He admitted that he would prefer not to have children; his wife seemed disappointed but said nothing. They got married and remained childless until her birth control system 'failed' after about a year and a half later. My friend, after suggesting an abortion, gave in to his crying wife, mumbling, 'All right, maybe one child.' Almost two years later the birth control method failed again and his wife was pregnant. My friend did not even suggest an abortion. By then he knew better than to even utter the word."

"Did your friend say that he would leave his wife if there were more children to come? You mentioned that he 'preferred' to be childless," Sue interrupted.

"No, he did not threaten to leave her. Anyway, his wife miscarried and my friend experienced a mixture of relief and guilt. He tried to console his wife as best he could." Michael continued, "A year later there was another birth control failure. This time his wife gave birth to twins. When he complained about her repeated pregnancies, his wife reminded him that he had told her at the first pregnancy that maybe one child would be all right. And she interpreted that to mean that maybe another one would be acceptable too. After that my friend lost all sexual interest in his wife. He had contemplated a secret vasectomy but dismissed the thought as being dishonest. Now he wished he had done that. What did he get for honestly discussing his views and wishes with his future wife?"

"From what you are telling us, your friend did not seem to be all that determined or clear about his wishes. It sounds a bit wishy-washy; it reminds me of Bertram." Marian expressed her opinion. "It would seem that after the miscarriage he would have done something to bring the situation to a decision rather than to just let it drift into the next pregnancy."

Gregory agreed, "Yeah, you would think he would go and have a vasectomy after his wife's miscarriage; instead he continued to have sex with her, knowing that her birth control method was unreliable."

"Maybe the husband does not really know what he wants, except that he has a reason to complain about his wife. Perhaps he doesn't really want to stay with her," Ted suggested.

"Although we don't know the whole story, from what Michael told us it appears that neither his friend nor the friend's wife had a clear communication about their wishes and expectations for the future." The group leader tried to summarize the situation. "As Marian said, the man was not adamant in what he stated as a preference and the woman apparently did not express clearly how important children were to her. According to Michael's report, she did not say much. And as Gregory pointed out, the husband continued to have sex with his wife, gambling whether or not she had swallowed her birth control pills or whatever method she used. This might lead to Ted's interpretation of the situation."

"So what's the point of discussing wishes and expectations when you don't know who is honest about it? You might as well jump into marriage with your eyes closed." Michael insisted on making his point.

"Your argument sounds logical on the surface, Michael. We cannot force anybody to tell us the truth, just as we cannot say everybody will be lying. That's why it is important to allow sufficient time to observe and get to know the other person. In cases of dishonesty, over time we may discover inconsistencies in the person's behavior and we can take that as a warning sign that might warrant further observation. In particular, there may be inconsistencies between the person's verbal and actual behavior. In other words, the person may say one thing but act on another. Marian has indicated that she observed such inconsistencies in Bertram's behavior." The group leader responded with a slight nod in Marian's direction.

Not willing to give up so easily, Michael spoke again. "In that case what do you believe—the verbal or the actual behavior?"

"That would be your choice, Michael," was the group leader's answer.

Timothy's face looked like he was ready to explode but his voice was surprisingly calm when he spoke. "Michael, in our first session here you were one of the group members encouraging me to make another attempt at talking to my wife and I thank you for that. As I mentioned earlier, she was more receptive and we have made progress in our relationship since we agreed to spend time together and openly discuss our feelings and expectations for the possibility of reconciling. Through what I learned here I see this as an opportunity to get to know my wife in a much deeper sense than when we first started out together. Actually, my wife has asked me to find out if she could join our group."

After a moment's thought Timothy continued, "What bothers me is that lately you seem to have objections to any of the subjects under discussion and you express your objections in a challenging way that take on the form of arguments." Looking at Timothy's face, one could see that it had been a struggle to express his feelings.

"Michael, when I joined this group I was angry at my husband, at myself, the whole world." Sally spoke. "During the first meeting you told me that I didn't have to move in with Kevin if I felt so strongly against cohabitation. That made me even angrier, but after some time I realized that you were right. It was not pleasant to face the fact that I had blown the opportunity for a good marriage."

"At the time I was only pointing out that your ex-husband had not forced you to live with him," Michael defended himself.

"When Kevin and I moved in together I tried to fulfill my part of the agreement but due to my disappointment that he did not propose marriage, I did not make the best of our time together. I did not treat him as lovingly as I would have had he married me. My disappointment overshadowed everything I felt and did. And with my lack of enthusiasm about our cohabitation I did not help to keep his excitement alive either. It wasn't just Kevin who killed our relationship. I have to deal with that as I go on and face our son." Then, looking straight at Michael's face, Sally ended in a soft tone of voice, "I wish you would let go of your anger, Michael."

It was absolutely quiet for a moment; nobody moved or even seemed to breathe. How would Michael respond?

"Diana got married again." He covered his face with his hands; the stillness in the room lingered until Michael spoke again: "Yes, I am angry and I was even angrier when I found out about Diana's wedding. But it seems almost that I am angrier about having made the mistake than having lost Diana. I don't quite understand that; it sounds so superficial but somehow it feels more profound." Michael's face reflected confusion rather than anger as he looked around the group for explanations, comfort, reassurance, sympathy—he was not quite sure what he was looking for.

Ted turned to him as he spoke in a low voice. "I don't want to pretend that I know your feelings, Michael, but it seems a lot like what I went through after making my mistakes with Arlene. And your relationship with Diana probably was a lot better than mine with Arlene—at least at the beginning of your marriage. Although I wanted Arlene for my wife and supported her goals, I never felt close to her. When she left me I did not miss any emotional intimacy because we never had that. I am just beginning to understand that now."

Michael's anger seemed to have subsided as he faced Ted: "Your experience sounds similar to what I meant. As much as I thought I loved Diana, this love had not become as meaningful a part of me as I believed."

The group leader addressed Michael and Ted, "You have made important observations. At the beginning of a relationship we act a lot on our expectations and we may not ask many questions. We are happy in the moment and we assume we know enough about the other person, just as we had discussed earlier. But this 'fake' knowledge often prevents us from searching deeper and investing realistically in this relationship."

"When you say 'investing' in a relationship," Sue asked, "do you mean the time we spend together or the financial resources we might pool together?"

"Those are certainly investments, Sue, and it would be beneficial for partners to discuss what their expectations in those areas are. But I am also thinking of another type of investment, the caring and good will toward our partners, the emotional support we are willing to give to make our partners feel good about us and about themselves."

Dorothy acted on the impulse of wanting to defend Ted when she spoke: "But isn't that what Ted did with Arlene? He fully supported her and her goals. That should have made her feel good about herself and about Ted."

Ted jumped in with his explanation: "That is what I tried to do, but there was another side to it. I could not let her see the real me. Because she did not love me I had to appear better than I thought I was in order to impress her. At the time I was not consciously aware of it, but I can see it now."

The group leader explained, "In our busy work lives we often forget to extend the same courtesy and consideration to our partners that we give to our boss because he signs our paycheck and hopefully may recommend us for a promotion. Too often we take our partners for granted and don't treat them like the valuable companions they are, or, as Ted just mentioned, we may not be as open and transparent to our partners to allow them to know us."

Looking at Timothy, the leader continued, "Remember what Timothy said in our first session about the wear and tear on relationships? 'We just wore down the good feelings between us.' I think that was telling the whole story in a sentence, a story without a happy ending. But to have the opportunity to contemplate and learn during a separation and then come back together again and be able to apply the learned lesson to life with the same partner is a chance few of us get or recognize."

Timothy admitted that without his participation in the group he would never have seized that opportunity because he hadn't even been aware of it.

Agreeing with Timothy about opportunities, Ted's voice was serious with a slight tremble betraying his hopes and concerns as he spoke: "This group experience has been an opportunity for me to learn about myself and to observe characteristics and attributes of others in this group. In our interactions I have found that I can disclose of myself without being laughed at or harshly criticized. In particular, I have had the opportunity to observe a person with very fine qualities, a person I would very much like to know better. Dorothy, it is not my intention to make you feel uncomfortable by expressing my appreciation of you in the presence of all of us here."

In the silence that followed, all eyes were on Dorothy, as could be expected. Her response was brief as she looked at him with a gentle smile on her face: "Thank you, Ted, I am very pleased and proud of what you just said," adding after taking a breath, "I have similar thoughts about you."

A round of applause and approving comments followed that interchange. Finally the group leader returned the conversation to the topic of investments in relationships by dispersing copies of a brief handout to the participants before closing the session.

HOW TO INVEST WISELY IN YOUR INTIMATE RELATIONSHIP

1. Despite the fact that many literary efforts and movies try to sell us on the notion of romantic love, in reality a more sensible approach might work better for most of us. Research in the field of marriage and relationships has demonstrated that those couples who evaluate their partners' characteristics and attributes realistically have a greater chance of experiencing high levels of relationship satisfaction. An evaluation that identifies your and the prospec-

tive partner's personality traits and how likely it is that they will combine well would be time well spent as an investment in the relationship's future.

2. When you have found that person, treat him or her well. Make your partners feel good about themselves and their connection with you. Remember, it's easier to love someone who praises you than one who criticizes you and that applies to your partner, too. Make being with you interesting and enjoyable rather than waiting for your partner to do that for you. That way you may end up taking turns doing the good work.

3. Protect your loving union from the deteriorating effects of time and outside influences by expressing pride in your partner's accomplishments. Such pride reflects back on you for having recognized your partner's attributes and talents. If you have chosen well, your partner will do the same for you.

EPILOGUE

A lasting relationship can be likened to a journey; it might be a journey on a long straight road with annoying billboards along the way or it could be traveling along a winding and hilly path, with each turn opening up to a surprising and intriguing view. It takes more energy and focused attention to travel along the winding path but the traveling time may seem shorter due to the many surprises or one may actually spend more time stopping at one of the inviting rest areas along this road. Traveling on the straight road for a longer time can be quite boring, so boring that some of the billboards' advertisements may be tempting to follow off the road—just to escape the boredom.

Many marriages appear to be traveling along the easy straight road, seemingly taken by surprise when they find themselves or their spouses in situations that apparently resulted from following the temptation offered by one of the billboards along the road. Travelers who out of boredom follow the seductions of the billboards may find themselves moving without ever reaching their goal, while those who stay on the winding path may not know where they are going but wherever it is they will be in the comforting company of their partners.

The Single Again group continued, with some participants leaving and others joining the group. What happened in the lives of those we met? Timothy's wife joined the group. They discovered new aspects in each other's personalities and found those interesting enough to get married again. Dorothy and Ted dated each other for about a year before they announced their engagement. Gregory embarked upon a path of self-exploration and Marian ended her ailing relationship with Bertram. Although feeling lonely, she is determined not to involve herself with a married man again. Julie took time to seriously reconsider her mother's advice about the abortion and decided not to keep it a secret from a man she was seriously interested in. She chose honesty as a basis for this new relationship. If the partners were not able to accept whatever darkness might have been in their pasts, then the relationship would not be strong enough to survive, was her reasoning.

Sue, although wanting to be in a lasting relationship, is hesitating to become involved with another man. She is not ready to trust any man. Her life has become more complicated; when she least expected it, Jeff, her ex-husband, found her and their son. He is trying to become a father and has made financial contributions for his son. Sue has allowed him to establish a relationship with their son but she is not ready to help Jeff grow into a husband, her husband.

That leaves Sally and Michael. During the group experience they recognized that they had several characteristics in common—beyond their angry feelings toward their previous spouses. And when Sally suggested Michael let go of his anger, instead of getting upset at her, he realized that it had not been a criticism—she understood him. They decided to get to know each other better and their developing relationship looks promising.

The paths of several of the participants have demonstrated that finding love that lasts is possible if people are willing to take seriously the importance of investing in their relationships and committing to themselves to create happiness with their partners.

Notes

CHAPTER 1: THE PATH OF THE REPEATEDLY SINGLE

1. *The State of Our Unions 2005*, Rutgers University's National Marriage Project, U.S. Census Bureau, and National Center for Health Statistics, "U.S. Divorce Statistics," at www.divorcemag.com/statistics/statsUS.shtml (accessed January 8, 2011); Cassandra Spratling, "Blended families can overcome daunting odds," *Burlington Free Press*, June 9, 2009, 9A; "First marriages ending in divorce," Census Bureau Reports, www.walb.com/.../census-bureau-news-embargo-of-marital-events-of-americans-2009-report.

2. Stephanie Coontz, "The world historical transformation of marriage," *Journal of Marriage and Family* 66 (2004): 974–79; Christopher Munsey, "Does marriage make us happy?" *Monitor on Psychology* 41 (2010): 20–21.

3. Barbara Dafoe Whitehead, *The Divorce Culture* (New York: Alfred Knopf, 1996), 3.

4. "Divorce and marriage rates 2009," CDC.gov, June 2, 2009 (accessed June 11, 2010); "The changing nature of marriage and divorce," National Bureau of Economic Research, at www.nber.org/digest/nov07/w12944.html (accessed January 7, 2011).

5. Statistics Canada, "Divorce," *The Daily*, December 2, 2002, 9–11; Zheng Wu and Christoph M. Schimmele, "Repartnering after first union disruption," *Journal of Marriage and Family* 67 (2005): 27–36.

6. Michael Joseph Gross, "A vast right-wing hypocrisy," *Vanity Fair*, February 2008, 102–8.

7. S. L. McGinnis, "Cohabiting, dating, and perceived costs of marriage: A model of marriage entry," *Journal of Marriage and Family* 65 (2003): 105–16.

8. Denise Previti and Paul R. Amato, "Why stay married? Rewards, barriers, and marital stability," *Journal of Marriage and Family* 65 (2003): 561–73.

9. L. M. Casper and P. N. Cohen, "How does POSSLQ measure up? Historical estimates of cohabitation," *Demography* 37 (2000): 237–45; U.S. Census Bureau,

Census 2000 Profile, Publication No. CB01-CN.67 (Washington, DC: Public Information Office, 2001).

10. Claire M. Kamp Dush, Catherine L. Cohan, and Paul R. Amato, "The relationship between cohabitation and marital quality and stability: Change across cohorts?" *Journal of Marriage and Family* 65, no. 3 (2003): 539–49.

11. Sharon Sassler and J. McNally, "Cohabiting couples' economic circumstances and union transition: A reexamination using multiple imputation techniques," *Social Science Research* 32 (2003): 553–78.

12. Vera Sonja Maass, *Lifestyle changes: A clinician's guide to common events, challenges, and options* (New York: Routledge/Taylor & Frances Group, 2008).

13. T. L. Huston and R. M. Houts, "The psychological infrastructure of courtship and marriage: The role of personality and compatibility in romantic relationships," in *The developmental course of marital dysfunction*, ed. Thomas N. Bradbury (New York: Cambridge University Press, 1998), 114–51; S. L. Murray, J. G. Holmes, and D. W. Griffin, "The self-fulfilling nature of positive illusions in romantic relationships: Love is not blind, but prescient," *Journal of Personality and Social Psychology* 71 (1996): 1155–80; J. M. Gottman, J. Coan, S. Carrère, and C. Swanson, "Predicting marital happiness and stability from newlywed interactions," *Journal of Marriage and the Family* 60 (1998): 5–22.

14. T. L. Huston, J. P. Caughlin, R. M. Houts, S. E. Smith, and L. J. George, "The connubial crucible: Newlywed years as predictors of marital delight, distress, and divorce," *Journal of Personality and Social Psychology* 80 (2001): 237–52.

15. Lawrence A. Kurdek, "Predicting the timing of separation and marital satisfaction: An eight-year prospective longitudinal study," *Journal of Marriage and Family* 64 (2002): 163–79.

16. Jean M. Twenge, W. Keith Campbell, and Craig A. Foster, "Parenthood and marital satisfaction: A meta-analytic review," *Journal of Marriage and Family* 65, no. 3 (2003): 574–83.

17. Maass, *Lifestyle changes*, 261–62.

18. Ellen Langer, *Mindfulness* (Reading, MA: Perseus Books, 1989), 51.

19. Whitehead, *The Divorce Culture*.

20. Richard D. McAnulty and Jocelyn M. Brineman, "Infidelity in dating relationships," *Annual Review of Sex Research* 18 (2007): 94–114.

21. Ariel Levy, *Female chauvinist pigs: Women and the rise of raunch culture* (New York: Free Press, 2005).

22. Aaron Ben-Zeév, "In the name of love," *Psychology Today* blog, October 31, 2008.

23. Luciano L'Abate, *Personality in intimate relationships: Socialization and psychopathology* (New York: Springer Science + Business Media, 2005).

24. Arthur Wassmer, *Making contact: A guide to overcoming shyness*, rev. ed. (New York: Henry Holt, 1978/1990), 48.

25. Munsey, "Does marriage make us happy?" 21.

26. D. Watson, E. C. Klohnen, A. Casillas, E. Simms, and J. Haig, "Match makers and deal breakers: Analyses of assortative mating in newlywed couples," *Journal of Personality* 72 (2004): 1029–68; L. T. Garcia and C. Markey, "Matching in sexual

experience for married, cohabiting, and dating couples," *Journal of Sex Research* 44 (2007): 250–55.

27. Vaughn Call, Susan Sprecher, and Pepper Schwartz, "The incidence and frequency of marital sex in a national sample," *Journal of Marriage and the Family* 57 (1995): 639–52; William Masters, Virginia Johnson, and Robert Kolodny, *Human sexuality* (New York: HarperCollins, 1992); Scott South and K. M. Lloyd, "Spousal alternatives and marital dissolution," *American Sociological Review* 60 (1995): 21–35.

28. Chien Liu, "A theory of marital sexual life," *Journal of Marriage and the Family* 62 (2000): 363–74.

29. V. S. Maass, *Facing the complexities of women's sexual desire* (New York: Springer Science + Business Media, 2007).

30. Sheila MacNeil and E. Sandra Byers, "Role of sexual self-disclosure in the sexual satisfaction of long-term heterosexual couples," *Journal of Sex Research* 46, no. 1 (2009): 3–14.

31. Ted L. Huston and Heidi Melz, "The case for (promoting) marriage: The devil is in the details," *Journal of Marriage and Family* 66 (November 2004): 943–58.

32. Huston and Melz, "The case for (promoting) marriage."

CHAPTER 2: JOURNEYS FOLLOWING OLD ROAD MAPS

1. Vera Sonja Maass and Margery A. Neely, *Counseling single parents: A cognitive-behavioral approach* (New York: Springer Publishing Company, 2000).

2. J. Brines and K. Joyner, "The ties that bind: Principles of cohesion in cohabitation and marriage," *American Sociological Review* 64 (1999): 333–55; Paul R. Amato, "Explaining the intergenerational transmission of divorce," *Journal of Marriage and the Family* 58 (1996): 628–40; Larry L. Bumpass, T. C. Martin, and J. A. Sweet, "The impact of family background and early marital factors on marital disruption," *Journal of Family Issues* 12 (1991): 22–42.

3. Susan E. Jacquet and Catherine A. Surra, "Parental divorce and premarital couples: Commitment and other relationship characteristics," *Journal of Marriage and Family* 63 (2001): 627–38.

4. For the "Early Years of Marriage" study, see Susan G. Timmer and Joseph Veroff, "Family ties and the discontinuity of divorce in Black and White newlywed couples," *Journal of Marriage and the Family* 62 (2000): 349–61.

5. P. R. Amato and D. D. DeBoer, "The transmission of marital instability across generations: Relationship skills or commitment to marriage?" *Journal of Marriage and Family* 63 (2001): 1038–51.

6. Gordon W. Allport, *Pattern and growth in personality* (New York: Holt, Rinehart, and Winston, 1961), 28.

7. Vera Sonja Maass, *Facing the complexities of women's sexual desire* (New York: Springer Science & Business Media, 2007).

8. G. L. Bouchard, Y. Lussier, and S. Sabourin, "Personality and marital adjustment: Utility of the five-factor model of personality," *Journal of Marriage and Family*

61 (1999): 651–60; Benjamin R. Karney and Thomas N. Bradbury, "The longitudinal course of marital quality and stability: A review of theory, method, and research," *Psychological Bulletin* 118 (1995): 3–34; Paul L. Hewitt and Gordon L. Flett, "Perfectionism in the self and social contexts: Conceptualization, assessment, and association with psychopathology," *Journal of Personality and Social Psychology* 60 (1991): 456–70.

9. Michelle Haring, Paul L. Hewitt, and Gordon L. Flett, "Perfectionism, coping, and quality of intimate relationships," *Journal of Marriage and Family* 65 (2003): 143–58.

10. Kathy Mitchell and Marcy Sugar, "Kids have left, but not the ex-wife," Annie's Mailbox, *Indianapolis Star*, September 6, 2010, E4.

11. Carolyn Hax, "Online chats only enable ex," *Indianapolis Star*, classifieds, July 31, 2009, C5; Mitchell and Sugar, "She was cheated on, now cheats on beau," *Indianapolis Star*, July 10, 2010, D10; Mitchell and Sugar, "Affair runs its course; let the boyfriend go," September 14, 2010, E4; Mitchell and Sugar, "Boyfriend isn't a cheater, he's spineless," October 9, 2010. [Hereafter, all columns by Mitchell and Sugar, C. Hax, and M. Howard appeared in the *Indianapolis Star*.]

12. John Bowlby, *A secure base* (New York: Basic Books, 1988).

13. J. Paris, "Does childhood trauma cause personality disorders in adults?" *Canadian Journal of Psychiatry* 43 (1998): 148–53; J. P. Paris, "Childhood trauma as an etiological factor in the personality disorders," *Journal of Personality Disorders* 11 (1997): 34–49; J. Bowlby, *Attachment and loss*, 3 vols. (New York: Basic Books, 1969–1980).

14. Paula R. Pietromonaco and Lisa Feldman Barrett, "The internal working models concept: What do we really know about the self in relation to others?" *Review of General Psychology* 4 (2000): 155–75.

15. K. Bartholomew, "Avoidance of intimacy: An attachment perspective," *Journal of Social and Personal Relationships* 7 (1990): 147–78.

16. A. Sherry, W. J. Lyddon, and R. K. Henson, "Adult attachment and developmental personality styles: An empirical study," *Journal of Counseling & Development* 85 (2007): 337–48; *Diagnostic and statistical manual of mental disorders*, 4th ed., text rev. (*DSM-IV-TR*) (Washington, DC: American Psychiatric Association, 2007).

17. Jude Cassidy, "Adult romantic attachments: A developmental perspective on individual differences," *Review of General Psychology* 4, no. 2 (2000): 111–31.

18. Mitchell and Sugar, "No fuddy-duddy women for him," September 1, 2010, E4.

19. Margo Howard, "Wife takes steps to go on without bully husband," Dear Margo, *Indianapolis Star*, classifieds, February 6, 2010, C10.

20. Deborah Tannen, *You just don't understand: Women and men in conversation* (New York: William Morrow, 1990).

21. Vera Sonja Maass, "Images of masculinity as predictors of men's romantic and sexual relationships," in *Men in relationships: A new look from a life course perspective*, ed. V. H. Bedford and B. F. Turner (New York: Springer, 2006), 51–78.

22. J. M. Gottman, J. Coan, S. Carrère, and C. Swanson, "Predicting marital happiness and stability from newlywed interactions," *Journal of Marriage and the Family* 60 (1998): 5–22; Karney and Bradbury, "The longitudinal course of marital quality and stability."

23. Vera Sonja Maass, *Lifestyle changes: A clinician's guide to common events, challenges, and options* (New York: Routledge/Taylor & Francis, 2008).

24. Mari L. Clements, Scott M. Stanley, and Howard J. Markman, "Before they said 'I do': Discriminating among marital outcomes over 13 years," *Journal of Marriage and Family* 66 (2004): 613–26.

25. H. J. Markman, S. M. Stanley, and S. L. Blumberg, *Fighting for your marriage*, new and revised (San Francisco: Jossey-Bass, 2001).

26. Maass, *Lifestyle changes*, 23.

27. The Emotional Interpretation gradient, R. L. Weiss, "Strategic behavioral marital therapy: Toward a model for assessment and intervention," in *Advances in family intervention, assessment, and theory*, vol. 1, ed. J. P. Vincent (Greenwich, CT: JAI Press, 1980), 229–71; M. W. Hawkins, S. Carrère, and J. M. Gottman, "Marital sentiment override: Does it influence couples' perceptions?" *Journal of Marriage and Family* 64 (2002): 193–201.

28. Maass, *Lifestyle changes*.

29. Maass, *Lifestyle changes*.

30. L. L. Bumpass and H.-H. Lu, "Trends in cohabitation and implications for children's contexts in the United States," *Population Studies* 54 (2000): 29–41.

31. Judith A. Seltzer, "Cohabitation in the United States and Britain: Demography, kinship, and the future," *Journal of Marriage and Family* 66 (November 2004): 921–28.

32. Laura Tach and Sarah Halpern-Meekin, "How does premarital cohabitation affect trajectories of marital quality?" *Journal of Marriage and Family* 71 (May 2009): 298–317.

33. Jay Teachman, "Premarital cohabitation and the risk of subsequent marital dissolution among women," *Journal of Marriage and Family* 65 (May 2003): 444–55.

34. Georgina Binstock and Arland Thornton, "Separations, reconciliations, and living apart in cohabiting and marital unions," *Journal of Marriage and Family* 65 (May 2003): 432–43.

35. Jaclyn Geller, *Here comes the bride: Women, weddings, and the marriage mystique* (New York: Four Walls Eight Windows, 2001), 214.

CHAPTER 3: IF HONESTY IS AN ISSUE

1. Dory Hollander, *101 lies men tell women and why women believe them* (New York: HarperCollins Publishers, 1995).

2. Mitchell and Sugar, "Are you better off with or without husband?" March 23, 2011, E2.

3. C. Hax, "Boyfriend's lie is a red flag," October 23, 2009, C5.

4. Mitchell and Sugar, "Forgiving takes time and effort," March 28, 2011, E2.

5. Mitchell and Sugar, "Third husband is in line to become the latest ex," November 18, 2010, E4.

6. Mitchell and Sugar, "Leave guilt behind and then move on," September 11, 2010, D9.

7. K. D. Vohs, R. F. Baumeister, and J. Chin, "Feeling duped: Emotional, motivational, and cognitive aspects of being exploited by others," *Review of General Psychology* 11 (2007): 127.

8. B. J. Sagarin, R. B. Cialdini, W. E. Rice, and S. B. Serma, "Dispelling the illusion of invulnerability: The motivations and mechanism of resistance to persuasion," *Journal of Personality and Social Psychology* 83 (2002): 526–41.

9. D. T. Miller, P. S. Visser, and B. D. Staub, "How surveillance begets perceptions of dishonesty: The case of the counterfactual sinner," *Journal of Personality and Social Psychology* 89 (2005): 117–28; Roy F. Baumeister, Ellen Bratlavsky, Catrin Finkenauer, and Kathleen D. Vohs, "Bad is stronger than good," *Review of General Psychology* 5 (2001): 323–70.

10. Mitchell and Sugar, "It's all good—except for her man's wife, kids," January 23, 2010, C10.

11. S. D. Boon and B. A. McLeod, "Deception in romantic relationships: Subjective estimates of success at deceiving and attitudes toward deception," *Journal of Social and Personal Relationships* 18 (2001): 463–76.

12. Paul Seager and Sandi Mann, *Would I lie to you?: Deception detection in relationships at work and in life* (London: Fusion, 2008), 127.

13. Mitchell and Sugar, "Wife fears husband might dump her just like he did ex," March 23, 2010, C5.

14. Brendan L. Smith, "Are Internet affairs different?" *Monitor on Psychology* 42, no. 3 (2011): 18–20.

CHAPTER 4: IN THE NAME OF LOVE

1. Nancy F. Cott, *Public vows: A history of marriage and the nation* (Cambridge, MA: Harvard University Press, 2000). Quoting sociologists Robert and Helen Lynd.

2. Susan Deitz, *Single file: How to live happily forever after with or without Prince Charming* (New York: St. Martin's Press, 1989).

3. C. Hax, "Face the truth about liar, your relationship," June 15, 2011, E2.

4. Jill Murray, *But I love him: Protecting your teen daughter from controlling, abusive dating* (New York: Regan Books, 2000).

5. Robert F. Bornstein, "The complex relationship between dependency and domestic violence: Converging psychological factors and social forces," *American Psychologist* 61 (2006): 595–606.

6. Ellen Burstyn, interviewed on the *Diane Rehm Show*, aired November 24, 2006.

7. Mitchell and Sugar, "Controlling boyfriend is a potential abuser," July 28, 2009, C5; C. Hax, "Woman's family sees signs of abusive boyfriend," October 2, 2009, C5; Mitchell and Sugar, "Dad's whining may signal other troubles," September 25, 2010, D10; Mitchell and Sugar, "Boyfriend's a potential abuser," March 11, 2011, E2.

8. Mitchell and Sugar, "Infatuation is no basis for a relationship," November 8, 2010, E4.

9. Vera Sonja Maass, *Facing the complexities of women's sexual desire* (New York: Springer Science & Business Media, 2007).

10. Mitchell and Sugar, "New husband isn't the man she thought he was," April 15, 2010, C8.
11. Mitchell and Sugar, "It hurts, but face it—he's interested in other woman," December 16, 2009, C14.
12. Mitchell and Sugar, "Domestic violence hotline can help," August 3, 2009, C5.
13. S. C. Clarke, *Advance report of final divorce statistics, 1998 and 1990* (Monthly Vital Statistics Report, vol. 43, no. 9, Supplement) (Hyattsville, MD: National Center for Health Statistics, 1995).
14. P. M. Bentler and M. D. Newcomb, "Longitudinal study of marital success and failure," *Journal of Consulting and Clinical Psychology* 46 (1978): 1053–70.
15. S. Ruggles, "The rise of divorce and separation in the United States, 1880–1990," *Demography* 34 (1997): 455–66.
16. Joseph Hopper, "The symbolic origins of conflict in divorce," *Journal of Marriage and Family* 63 (2001): 430–45.

CHAPTER 5: KNOW THYSELF

1. John P. Schuster, *The power of your past: The art of recalling, reclaiming, and recasting* (San Francisco: Berrett-Koehler Publishers, 2011), 10.
2. M. Howard, "Learn to appreciate boyfriend's qualities," December 5, 2009, C12.
3. M. Howard, "Marrying for money has its costs," September 5, 2009, C11.
4. Mitchell and Sugar, "Don't love him? Don't go back," January 27, 2011, E2.
5. Oliver C. Robinson and Jonathan A. Smith, "The stormy search for self in early adulthood: Developmental crisis and the dissolution of dysfunctional personae," *Humanistic Psychologist* 38 (2010): 120–45.
6. J. Sills, "When persona aces person," *Psychology Today* 5 (2007): 59–61. (Based on two essays on analytical psychology in Carl G. Jung, *The collected works of C. G. Jung* [London: Routledge, 1966].)
7. C. Booker, *The seven basic plots: Why we tell stories* (London: Continuum, 2005).
8. Cordelia Fine, *A mind of its own: How your brain distorts and deceives* (New York: W. W. Norton, 2006).
9. Carol Tavris and Elliot Aronson, *Mistakes were made (but not by me): Why we justify foolish beliefs, bad decisions, and hurtful acts* (New York: Harcourt, 2007), 13.
10. Tavris and Aronson, *Mistakes were made*, 159.
11. The Arbinger Institute, *Leadership and self-deception: Getting out of the box*, 2nd ed. (San Francisco: Berrett-Koehler Publishers, 2010).
12. Luciano L'Abate, *Personality in intimate relationships: Socialization and psychopathology* (New York: Springer Science + Business Media, 2005).
13. Arthur Wassmer, *Making contact: A guide to overcoming shyness*, rev. ed. (New York: Henry Holt, 1978/1990), 48.
14. Jon Kabat-Zinn, *Wherever you go; there you are: Mindfulness meditation in everyday life* (New York: Hyperion, 1994), 4.

15. M. Howard, "It's time to dump troublesome husband," October 9, 2010, D10.
16. Mitchell and Sugar, "Boyfriend's finances fall short," October 17, 2009, C11.
17. Mitchell and Sugar, "No fuddy-duddy women for him," September 1, 2010, E4.
18. Ronald E. Riggio, *The Charisma Quotient: What it is, how to get it, how to use it.* (New York: Dodd, Mead & Company, 1987).

CHAPTER 6: KNOW THE OTHER

1. C. Hax, "Finances sour relationship," January 28, 2011, E2.
2. Ellen Fein and Sherrie Schneider, *All the rules: Time-tested secrets for capturing the heart of Mr. Right* (New York: Grand Central Publishing, 2007); first compilation edition of *The Rules* and *Rules II.*
3. Neil Strauss, *The game: Penetrating the secret society of pick-up artists* (New York: HarperCollins, 2005), 48.
4. Mitchell and Sugar, "New husband isn't the man she thought he was," April 15, 2010, C8.
5. Mitchell and Sugar, "Baby daddy needs the boot," April 15, 2011, E2.
6. Cindy Chupack, interview by Bruce Grierson, "Weathering the storm," *Psychology Today* 42, May/June 2009, 68.
7. Mitchell and Sugar, "Girlfriend is gone with no word about the baby," May 25, 2010, C5.
8. M. Howard, "Hubby's actions filled with hurt," October 17, 2009, C11.
9. Mitchell and Sugar, "Wife's criticisms nearing critical mass," January 3, 2011, E4.
10. Mitchell and Sugar, "Husband's vacation leaves wife behind," March 25, 2010, C8.
11. Mitchell and Sugar, "Runaway common-law wife may not be ready to return," August 27, 2009, C8.
12. Mitchell and Sugar, "Something's wrong: Husband can't see it, and wife won't tell," January 19, 2010, C5.
13. Mitchell and Sugar, "Tired of waiting for a commitment," August 5, 2010, E4.
14. Mitchell and Sugar, "'Mr. H' may be hiding something," July 19, 2010, E4.
15. Mitchell and Sugar, "It's a sweet deal—but only for him," April 7, 2010, C13.
16. M. Howard, "No use telling off sleazy guy dating your sister," January 23, 2010, C10.
17. C. Hax, "Cohabitation is no solution," May 20, 2011, E2.
18. C. Hax, "His past haunts their future," April 15, 2011, E2.
19. Mitchell and Sugar, "Bookmark? Read between lines," April 22, 2011, E2.
20. Nicole Koehler and James S. Chisholm, "Early psychosocial stress affects men's relationship length," *Journal of Sex Research* 46, no. 4 (2009): 366–74.

CHAPTER 7: NEW HORIZONS—NEW COMMITMENTS

1. V. S. Maass, *Coping with control and manipulation* (Santa Barbara, CA: Praeger, 2010).

2. *Theophrastus: Characters* (Cambridge Classical Texts and Commentaries), translated by James Diggle (Cambridge: Cambridge University Press, 2007).

3. *Diagnostic and statistical manual of mental disorders*, 4th ed. (Washington, DC: American Psychiatric Association, 1994).

4. Mitchell and Sugar, Annie's Mailbox, *Sunday Star*, April 17, 2011, Indy Living, G2.

5. Mitchell and Sugar, "Saving marriage is worth effort," March 6, 2011, E2.

6. C. Hax, "Call a halt to this wedding," February 18, 2011, E2.

7. V. S. Maass, *The Cinderella test: Would you really want the shoe to fit?* (Santa Barbara, CA: Praeger, 2009), 98.

8. Mitchell and Sugar, "Adult son puts mom on edge," April 2, 2011, E2.

9. Mitchell and Sugar, "She needs help to move on," May 3, 2011, E2.

10. Mitchell and Sugar, "Husband may be depressed," May 10, 2011, E2.

11. Mitchell and Sugar, "Motherhood changes relationships," November 22, 2010, E4.

12. C. Hax, "Confront boyfriend and his frequent exits," November 12, 2010, E5.

13. Mitchell and Sugar, "Counseling might help muddled marriage," August 30, 2010, E4.

14. S. L. Murray, J. G. Holmes, and D. W. Griffin, "Reflections on the self-fulfilling effects of positive illusions," *Psychological Inquiry* 14 (2003): 289–95; B. J. Fowers, E. M. Lyons, K. H. Montel, and N. Shaked, "Positive illusions of marriage among married and single individuals," *Journal of Family Psychology* 15 (2001): 95–109; C. Miller and R. C. Bailey, "Dating commitment and within-personal perceptual congruency," *Social Behavior and Personality* 30 (2002): 383–90; S. L. Murray, J. G. Holmes, G. Bellavia, D. W. Griffin, and D. Dolderman, "Kindred spirits? The benefits of egocentrism in close relationships," *Journal of Personality and Social Psychology* 82, no. 4 (2002): 563–81; Dean M. Busby and B. C. Gardner, "How do I analyze thee? Let me count the ways: Considering empathy in couple relationships using self and partner ratings," *Family Process* 47 (2008): 229–42.

15. Dean M. Busby, Thomas B. Holman, and Sylvia Niehuis, "The association between partner enhancement and self-enhancement and relationship quality outcomes," *Journal of Marriage and Family* 71 (August 2009): 449–64.

16. Carolyn E. Cutrona, "A psychological perspective: Marriage and the social provisions of relationships," *Journal of Marriage and Family* 66 (November 2004): 992–99.

17. Marita P. McCabe, "Satisfaction in marriage and committed heterosexual relationships: Past, present, and future," *Annual Review of Sex Research* 17 (2006): 39–58.

18. Ann Meier, Kathleen E. Hull, and Timothy A. Ortyl, "Young adult relationship values at the intersection of gender and sexuality," *Journal of Marriage and Family* 71 (August 2009): 510–25.

19. Nando Pelusi, "The appeal of the bad boy," *Psychology Today* 42 (2009): 59.

Bibliography

Allport, Gordon W. *Pattern and growth in personality*. New York: Holt, Rinehart, & Winston, 1961.
Amato, Paul R. "Explaining the intergenerational transmission of divorce." *Journal of Marriage and the Family* 58 (1996): 628–40.
Amato, Paul R., and D. D. DeBoer. "The transmission of marital instability across generations: Relationship skills or commitment to marriage?" *Journal of Marriage and Family* 63 (2001): 1038–51.
Arbinger Institute. *Leadership and self-deception: Getting out of the box*, 2nd ed. San Francisco: Berrett-Koehler, 2010.
Bartholomew, K. "Avoidance of intimacy: An attachment perspective." *Journal of Social and Personal Relationships* 7 (1990): 147–78.
Baumeister, Roy F., Ellen Bratlavsky, Catrin Finkenauer, and Kathleen D. Vohs. "Bad is stronger than good." *Review of General Psychology* 5 (2001): 323–70.
Bentler, P. M., and M. D. Newcomb. "Longitudinal study of marital success and failure." *Journal of Consulting and Clinical Psychology* 46 (1978): 1053–70.
Ben-Zeév, Aaron. "In the name of love." *Psychology Today* blog, October 31, 2008.
Binstock, Georgina, and Arland Thornton. "Separations, reconciliations, and living apart in cohabiting and marital unions." *Journal of Marriage and Family* 65 (May 2003): 432–43.
Booker, C. *The seven basic plots: Why we tell stories*. London: Continuum, 2005.
Boon, S. D., and B. A. McLeod. "Deception in romantic relationships: Subjective estimates of success at deceiving and attitudes toward deception." *Journal of Social and Personal Relationships* 18 (2001): 463–76.
Bornstein, Robert F. "The complex relationship between dependency and domestic violence: Converging psychological factors and social forces." *American Psychologist* 61 (2006): 595–606.
Bouchard, G. L., Y. Lussier, and S. Sabourin. "Personality and marital adjustment: Utility of the five-factor model of personality." *Journal of Marriage and Family* 61 (1999): 651–60.

Bowlby, John. *Attachment and loss.* 3 vols. New York: Basic Books, 1969–1980.
———. *A secure base.* New York: Basic Books, 1988.
Brines, J., and K. Joyner. "The ties that bind: Principles of cohesion in cohabitation and marriage." *American Sociological Review* 64 (1999): 333–55.
Bumpass, Larry L., and H.-H. Lu. "Trends in cohabitation and implications for children's contexts in the United States." *Population Studies* 54 (2000): 29–41.
Bumpass, Larry L., T. C. Martin, and J. A. Sweet. "The impact of family background and early marital factors on marital disruption." *Journal of Family Issues* 12 (1991): 22–42.
Busby, Dean M., and B. C. Gardner. "How do I analyze thee? Let me count the ways: Considering empathy in couple relationships using self and partner ratings." *Family Process* 47 (2008): 229–42.
Busby, Dean M., Thomas B. Holman, and Sylvia Niehuis. "The association between partner enhancement and self-enhancement and relationship quality outcomes." *Journal of Marriage and Family* 71 (August 2009): 449–64.
Call, Vaughn, Susan Sprecher, and Pepper Schwartz. "The incidence and frequency of marital sex in a national sample." *Journal of Marriage and the Family* 57 (1995): 639–52.
Casper, L. M., and P. N. Cohen. "How does POSSLQ measure up? Historical estimates of cohabitation." *Demography* 37 (2000): 237–45.
Cassidy, Jude. "Adult romantic attachments: A developmental perspective on individual differences." *Review of General Psychology* 4, no. 2 (2000): 111–31.
Clarke, S. C. *Advance report of final divorce statistics, 1998 and 1990* (Monthly Vital Statistics Report, vol. 43, no. 9, Supplement). Hyattsville, MD: National Center for Health Statistics, 1995.
Clements, Mari L., Scott M. Stanley, and Howard J. Markman. "Before they said 'I do': Discriminating among marital outcomes over 13 years." *Journal of Marriage and Family* 66 (2004): 613–26.
Coontz, Stephanie. "The world historical transformation of marriage." *Journal of Marriage and Family* 66 (2004): 974–79.
Cott, Nancy F. *Public vows: A history of marriage and the nation.* Cambridge, MA: Harvard University Press, 2000. Quoting sociologists Robert and Helen Lynd.
Cutrona, Carolyn E. "A psychological perspective: Marriage and the social provisions of relationships." *Journal of Marriage and Family* 66 (November 2004): 992–99.
Deitz, Susan. *Single file: How to live happily forever after with or without Prince Charming.* New York: St. Martin's Press, 1989.
Diagnostic and statistical manual of mental disorders, 4th ed. Washington, DC: American Psychiatric Association, 1994.
Diagnostic and statistical manual of mental disorders, 4th ed., text rev. (*DSM-IV-TR*). Washington, DC: APA, 2007.
Fein, Ellen, and Sherrie Schneider. *All the rules: Time-tested secrets for capturing the heart of Mr. Right.* New York: Grand Central Publishing, 2007; first compilation edition of *The Rules* and *Rules II.*
Fine, Cordelia. *A mind of its own: How your brain distorts and deceives.* New York: W. W. Norton, 2006.

Fowers, Blaine J., E. M. Lyons, K. H. Montel, and N. Shaked. "Positive illusions of marriage among married and single individuals." *Journal of Family Psychology* 15 (2001): 95–109.

Garcia, L. T., and Charlotte N. Markey. "Matching in sexual experience for married, cohabiting, and dating couples." *Journal of Sex Research* 44 (2007): 250–55.

Geller, Jaclyn. *Here comes the bride: Women, weddings, and the marriage mystique*, 214. New York: Four Walls Eight Windows, 2001.

Gottman, John M., James A. Coan, Sybil Carrère, and C. Swanson. "Predicting marital happiness and stability from newlywed interactions." *Journal of Marriage and the Family* 60 (1998): 5–22.

Grierson, Bruce. "Weathering the storm." *Psychology Today* 42 (May/June 2009): 68.

Gross, Michael Joseph. "A vast right-wing hypocrisy." *Vanity Fair* (February 2008): 102–8.

Haring, Michelle, Paul L. Hewitt, and Gordon L. Flett. "Perfectionism, coping, and quality of intimate relationships." *Journal of Marriage and Family* 65 (2003): 143–58.

Hawkins, M. W., Sybil Carrère, and John M. Gottman. "Marital sentiment override: Does it influence couples' perceptions?" *Journal of Marriage and Family* 64 (2002): 193–201.

Hewitt, Paul L., and Gordon L. Flett. "Perfectionism in the self and social contexts: Conceptualization, assessment, and association with psychopathology." *Journal of Personality and Social Psychology* 60 (1991): 456–70.

Hollander, Dory. *101 lies men tell women and why women believe them*. New York: HarperCollins, 1995.

Hopper, Joseph. "The symbolic origins of conflict in divorce." *Journal of Marriage and Family* 63 (2001): 430–45.

Huston, Ted L., J. P. Caughlin, R. M. Houts, S. E. Smith, and L. J. George. "The connubial crucible: Newlywed years as predictors of marital delight, distress, and divorce." *Journal of Personality and Social Psychology* 80 (2001): 237–52.

Huston, Ted L., and R. M. Houts. "The psychological infrastructure of courtship and marriage: The role of personality and compatibility in romantic relationships." In *The developmental course of marital dysfunction*, edited by Thomas N. Bradbury, 114–51. New York: Cambridge University Press, 1998.

Huston, Ted L., and Heidi Melz. "The case for (promoting) marriage: The devil is in the details." *Journal of Marriage and Family* 66 (November 2004): 943–58.

Jacquet, Susan E., and Catherine A. Surra. "Parental divorce and premarital couples: Commitment and other relationship characteristics." *Journal of Marriage and Family* 63 (2001): 627–38.

Jung, Carl G. *The collected works of C. G. Jung—two essays on analytical psychology*. London: Routledge, 1966.

Kabat-Zinn, Jon. *Wherever you go; there you are: Mindfulness meditation in everyday life*, 4. New York: Hyperion, 1994.

Kamp Dush, Claire M., Catherine L. Cohan, and Paul R. Amato. "The relationship between cohabitation and marital quality and stability: Change across cohorts?" *Journal of Marriage and Family* 65, no. 3 (2003): 539–49.

Karney, Benjamin R., and Thomas N. Bradbury. "The longitudinal course of marital quality and stability: A review of theory, method, and research." *Psychological Bulletin* 118 (1995): 3–34.

Koehler, Nicole, and James S. Chisholm. "Early psychosocial stress affects men's relationship length." *Journal of Sex Research* 46, no. 4 (2009): 366–74.

Kurdek, Lawrence A. "Predicting the timing of separation and marital satisfaction: An eight-year prospective longitudinal study." *Journal of Marriage and Family* 64 (2002): 163–79.

L'Abate, Luciano. *Personality in intimate relationships: Socialization and psychopathology*. New York: Springer Science + Business Media, 2005.

Langer, Ellen. *Mindfulness*. Reading, MA: Perseus Books, 1989.

Levy, Ariel. *Female chauvinist pigs: Women and the rise of raunch culture*. New York: Free Press, 2005.

Liu, Chien. "A theory of marital sexual life." *Journal of Marriage and the Family* 62 (2000): 363–74.

Maass, Vera Sonja. *The Cinderella test: Would you really want the shoe to fit?* Santa Barbara, CA: Praeger, 2009.

———. *Coping with control and manipulation*. Santa Barbara, CA: Praeger, 2010.

———. *Facing the complexities of women's sexual desire*. New York: Springer Science + Business Media, 2007.

———. "Images of masculinity as predictors of men's romantic and sexual relationships." In *Men in relationships: A new look from a life course perspective*, edited by V. H. Bedford and B. F. Turner, 51–78. New York: Springer, 2006.

———. *Lifestyle changes: A clinician's guide to common events, challenges, and options*. New York: Routledge/Taylor & Frances, 2008.

Maass, Vera Sonja, and Margery A. Neely. *Counseling single parents: A cognitive-behavioral approach*. New York: Springer, 2000.

MacNeil, Sheila, and E. Sandra Byers. "Role of sexual self-disclosure in the sexual satisfaction of long-term heterosexual couples." *Journal of Sex Research* 46 (2009): 3–14.

Markman, Howard J., Scott M. Stanley, and S. L. Blumberg. *Fighting for your marriage*, new and revised. San Francisco: Jossey-Bass, 2001.

Masters, William, Virginia Johnson, and Robert Kolodny. *Human sexuality*. New York: HarperCollins, 1992.

McAnulty, Richard D., and Jocelyn M. Brineman. "Infidelity in dating relationships." *Annual Review of Sex Research* 18 (2007): 94–114.

McCabe, Marita P. "Satisfaction in marriage and committed heterosexual relationships: Past, present, and future." *Annual Review of Sex Research* 17 (2006): 39–58.

McGinnis, Sandra L. "Cohabiting, dating, and perceived costs of marriage: A model of marriage entry." *Journal of Marriage and Family* 65 (2003): 105–16.

Meier, Ann, Kathleen E. Hull, and Timothy A. Ortyl. "Young adult relationship values at the intersection of gender and sexuality." *Journal of Marriage and Family* 71 (August 2009): 510–25.

Miller, C., and R. C. Bailey. "Dating commitment and within-personal perceptual congruency." *Social Behavior and Personality* 30 (2002): 383–90.

Miller, D. T., P. S. Visser, and B. D. Staub. "How surveillance begets perceptions of dishonesty: The case of the counterfactual sinner." *Journal of Personality and Social Psychology* 89 (2005): 117–28.

Munsey, Christopher. "Does marriage make us happy?" *Monitor on Psychology* 41 (2010): 20–21.

Murray, Jill. *But I love him: Protecting your teen daughter from controlling, abusive dating.* New York: Regan Books, 2000.

Murray, S. L., J. G. Holmes, G. Bellavia, D. W. Griffin, and D. Dolderman. "Kindred spirits? The benefits of egocentrism in close relationships." *Journal of Personality and Social Psychology* 82, no. 4 (2002): 563–81.

Murray, S. L., J. G. Holmes, and D. W. Griffin. "Reflections on the self-fulfilling effects of positive illusions." *Psychological Inquiry* 14 (2003): 289–95.

———. "The self-fulfilling nature of positive illusions in romantic relationships: Love is not blind, but prescient." *Journal of Personality and Social Psychology* 71 (1996): 1155–80.

Paris, J. P. "Childhood trauma as an etiological factor in the personality disorders." *Journal of Personality Disorders* 11 (1997): 34–39.

———. "Does childhood trauma cause personality disorders in adults?" *Canadian Journal of Psychiatry* 43 (1998): 148–53.

Pelusi, Nando. "The appeal of the bad boy." *Psychology Today* 42 (2009): 58–59.

Pietromonaco, Paula R., and Lisa Feldman Barrett. "The internal working models concept: What do we really know about the self in relation to others?" *Review of General Psychology* 4 (2000): 155–75.

Previti, Denise, and Paul R. Amato. "Why stay married? Rewards, barriers, and marital stability." *Journal of Marriage and Family* 65 (2003): 561–73.

Riggio, Ronald E. *The Charisma Quotient: What it is, how to get it, how to use it.* New York: Dodd, Mead & Company, 1987.

Robinson, Oliver C., and Jonathan A. Smith. "The stormy search for self in early adulthood: Developmental crisis and the dissolution of dysfunctional personae." *Humanistic Psychologist* 38, no. 2 (2010): 120–45.

Ruggles, S. "The rise of divorce and separation in the United States, 1880–1990." *Demography* 34 (1997): 455–66.

Sagarin, Brad J., Robert B. Cialdini, W. E. Rice, and S. B. Serma. "Dispelling the illusion of invulnerability: The motivations and mechanism of resistance to persuasion." *Journal of Personality and Social Psychology* 83 (2002): 526–41.

Sassler, Sharon, and J. McNally. "Cohabiting couples' economic circumstances and union transition: A reexamination using multiple imputation techniques." *Social Science Research* 32 (2003): 553–78.

Schuster, John P. *The power of your past: The art of recalling, reclaiming, and recasting.* San Francisco: Berrett-Koehler Publishers, 2011.

Seager, Paul, and Sandi Mann. *Would I lie to you? Deception detection in relationships at work and in life.* London: Fusion, 2008.

Seltzer, Judith A. "Cohabitation in the United States and Britain: Demography, kinship, and the future." *Journal of Marriage and Family* 66 (November 2004): 921–28.

Sherry, A., W. J. Lyddon, and R. K. Henson. "Adult attachment and developmental personality styles: An empirical study." *Journal of Counseling & Development* 85 (2007): 337–48.

Sills, J. "When persona aces person." *Psychology Today* 5 (2007): 59–61.

Smith, Brendan L. "Are Internet affairs different?" *Monitor on Psychology* 42, no. 3 (2011): 18–20.

South, Scott, and K. M. Lloyd. "Spousal alternatives and marital dissolution." *American Sociological Review* 60 (1995): 21–35.

Spratling, Cassandra. "Blended families can overcome daunting odds." *Burlington Free Press*, June 9, 2009, 9A.

Statistics Canada. "Divorce." *The Daily*, December 2, 2002, 9–11.

Strauss, Neil. *The game: Penetrating the secret society of pick-up artists*, 48. New York: HarperCollins, 2005.

Tach, Laura, and Sarah Halpern-Meekin. "How does premarital cohabitation affect trajectories of marital quality?" *Journal of Marriage and Family* 71 (May 2009): 298–317.

Tannen, Deborah. *You just don't understand: Women and men in conversation*. New York: William Morrow, 1990.

Tavris, Carol, and Elliot Aronson. *Mistakes were made (but not by me): Why we justify foolish beliefs, bad decisions, and hurtful acts*. New York: Harcourt, 2007.

Teachman, Jay. "Premarital cohabitation and the risk of subsequent marital dissolution among women." *Journal of Marriage and Family* 65 (May 2003): 444–55.

Timmer, Susan G., and Joseph Veroff. "Family ties and the discontinuity of divorce in Black and White newlywed couples." *Journal of Marriage and the Family* 62 (2000): 349–61.

Twenge, Jean M., W. Keith Campbell, and Craig A. Foster. "Parenthood and marital satisfaction: A meta-analytic review." *Journal of Marriage and Family* 65 (2003): 574–83.

U.S. Census Bureau. *Census 2000 Profile*. (Publication No. CB01-CN.67). Washington, DC: Public Information Office, 2001.

Vohs, Kathleen D., Roy F. Baumeister, and Jason Chin. "Feeling duped: Emotional, motivational, and cognitive aspects of being exploited by others." *Review of General Psychology* 11 (2007): 127–41.

Wassmer, Arthur. *Making contact: A guide to overcoming shyness*, rev. ed. New York: Henry Holt, 1978/1990.

Watson, D., E. C. Klohnen, A. Casillas, E. Simms, and J. Haig. "Match makers and deal breakers: Analyses of assortative mating in newlywed couples." *Journal of Personality* 72 (2004): 1029–68.

Weiss, R. L. "Strategic behavioral marital therapy: Toward a model for assessment and intervention." In *Advances in family intervention, assessment, and theory*, vol. 1, edited by J. P. Vincent, 229–71. Greenwich, CT: JAI Press. 1980.

Whitehead, Barbara Dafoe. *The divorce culture*. New York: Alfred Knopf, 1996.

Wu, Zheng, and Christoph M. Schimmele. "Repartnering after first union disruption." *Journal of Marriage and Family* 67 (2005): 27–36.

Index

101 lies men tell women and why women believe them, 55
abandonment: fear of, 19, 39–40; minimizing possibility of, 79; of self, 109
abuse: in relationships, 79, 94, 130; as a way of life, 81
anger: control of, 81; in the grip of, 13; intermittent eruptions of, 77; in relationships, 130, 134, 139, 143–44; toward self, 109
attachment: dimensions, predictive of personality styles, 42; emotional, importance to women, 21; insecure, link to infidelity, 15; pattern, 41; theory, 41–42

Bartholomew's attachment style theory, 42
battered women: return to abuser, 79; shelters for, 79
behavior: as communication, 45, 116; language of one's, 118; purpose of, 133–34; verbal vs. action, 134–35, 170
behavioral observations, taking time for, 128
behaviors, main ingredients of people's interactions, 36

believing vs. trusting, 147
Bowlby, John, 40, 41
Burstyn, Ellen, 81

casual sex, gender differences in acceptance of, 167
chemistry, in relationships, 11–12, 88, 96–97, 144
children, effects on marriage, 8–9, 34
Chupack, Cindy, 129
cognitive dissonance, 15, 102
cohabitation: and divorce rate, 2; vs. marriage, differences, 50–51, 77–78, 170; prelude to marriage or alternative lifestyle, 48–50; premarital, and marriage stability, 6; reasons for, 6
comfort, based on familiarity, 27–28
commitments: for commitment's sake, 126, 159; cost and benefits comparison, 13; based on expectations, 155–56; fears of, 160; hasty, 22; to inequality, 132; marital, 34; purposes, goals, and terms of, 155–57, 159, 160; reluctance to make, 133, 135; types of, 155, 161; to whom or what, 127, 160, 162
communication: lack of clear, 33–34, 143, 169; levels of, 117; negative, 164–67;

online, 38, 58; vehicle for expressing wishes, 45; willingness, important factor in sexual relationships, 22

communication styles: automatic responses to stimuli, 46; expression of personalities, 46; gender linked, 45

compliance, silent, cost of, 107, 109

courtship: categories, 24–25; phase, 7, 9; relationship, model of, 5; styles, impact on relationship, 23–24

criticism, camouflaging as false sense of security, 106–107, 131, 165

cybersex, 15, 72, 73

dead-end affairs, 106

deception, detection ability, 66; self-, 68, 101

Denver Family Development Project, 46

dependence on others, 158

dependent personality disorder, 79

destiny, belief in, 83

developmental personality styles, 42

Diagnostic and Statistical Manual of Mental Disorders, 153

dishonesty: focus on the other's, 54; insult to recipient, 61; Internet as vehicle for, 73; justification of, 58; lasting effects of, 69; partial, 63; path to, 57–58, 68; protection from, 67; tolerating it, 55; victims of partner's, 66

divorce: determinants of, 6; frequently cited reason, extramarital sex, 21; initiators of, characteristics, 86; opportunity for make-over, 14; parental, impact of, 33–34; predictive factors, 8; primary risk period for, 46; rude awakening, 125; statistics, 1–2; timing of, 7

The Divorce Culture, 2

Don Juan syndrome, 14, 16, 82

double standards, celebrities and general population, 3–4

early psychosocial stress, effects on relationships, 141–42

early signals, acknowledging them, 129–30, 136

Early Years of Marriage study, 34

emotional dependency, need for belonging, 79. *See also* dependent personality disorder

emotional interpretation gradient, gendered effects, 47

epilogue, 173–74

expectations: and their blinding function, 152, 162; as basis for commitments, 155; as main ingredients of infatuation, 151; of others, 42, 101, 122; aligning with reality, 154; overshadowing reality, 84, 97, 144; unexpressed, 7, 144; unrealistic, of self, 36

extramarital affairs, and their secrecy, 74

familiar behaviors, ease of, 30–31

fantasy, and online affairs, 73

financial inequality, in marriage. *See* commitment to inequality

fusion, of the real and the ideal, 151–52, 154

global sentiment, as a marriage bond, 47

guilt, a companion of betrayal, 58–60

high testosterone-fueled masculinity, attractiveness to women, 167

hurt feelings: in intimate relationships, 18; swallowing and regurgitating of, 107–108

infidelity, predictors of, 15

jealousy, 79, 80; equals love, 79

judgment, errors in, 63

Jung, Carl, 101

Kabat-Zinn, Jon, 110

Kennedy, John F., 119

knowledge of the other, 125–28

Langer, Ellen, 13

lies: ability to detect, 61, 65–66; effects on receiver's self-esteem, 61, 62; and empty promises, 53–54; meaning and concept of, 55–57; whose interest do they serve?, 57, 67–68
lies and broken promises, signs of, 65–66
love: at first sight, 82, 83; and ignorance, 84–85; as justification, 75, 77; misuse of the concept, 79; stages of, 151

marital: disintegration, early signs of, 24; roles, changes in, 34; satisfaction, communication pattern as predictor of, 45; stability, intergenerational transmission, 34; tension, contributing factors, 86
marriage: as buffer against illness, 1–2; conceptual models, 7; Sleeping Beauty pattern of, 9–10; world view of basis for, 75
marriages and divorce, statistics, 1
mindfulness, 13, 110
Mindfulness, 13

National Longitudinal Study of Adolescent Health, 166
National Marriage Project, 1

Ostrich Syndrome, 66

parents' examples, models to follow or not, 31–32
partner-enhancement and relationship stability, 165
past histories: lessons from, 140; right to know, 141–42, 146, 148–49, 168
perfectionism, 36–37
personal insecurities, effects on relationships, 113–14
personality: development, precursors of, 41; early descriptions of, 152
personality traits: effects on relationship quality and marital adjustment, 34, 36, 130; and marriage stability, 25

pornography, 72–74; addiction to, 83, 146; effects on marriage, 83
possessiveness, 79, 144
power, distribution in relationships, 159
"power law," 119
previous relationships, unresolved issues from, 37–38
promises, empty, 93, 106
protection vs. possession, 136
Psychology Today, 167

reality: confrontation with, 154; denial of, 104–106
relationship: breakup, gaining self-knowledge from, 27; dissolution, contributing factors, 6–9
relationship stability, intergenerational transmission of, 33, 34; linked to couples' courtship styles, 23
relationships: costs and rewards, 12–13; goals within, 126–28; investment in, 171, 172–73
repetition compulsion, 35
romantic dreams vs. reality, 153
romantic love myth, influence of, 167
rude awakenings, 130–32; at relationship terminations, 99
The Rules, 126

secrets, from the past, 137–40, 146, 147
self-abandonment, harm of, 109–10
self-awareness, about one's personality characteristics, 13
self-deception, reduction of, 101
self-exploration, purpose of, 118
self-illusion, 164
self-justification, as world view, distorting effects, 104
self-justifying behaviors, 102–104
self-knowledge: lack of, 110–12; process of achieving it, 99–101
sentiment override. *See* global sentiment
serial monogamy, 17
Sex and the City, 129

sexual: activities, frequency in marriage, 21; choices, based on similarities, 20–21; incompatibility, 19–20; satisfaction, 22; self-disclosure, in relationships, 22
shattered dreams, 93–94
shyness, effect on intimacy, 18
signs and signals: people emit, 12, 70, 80, 88, 129, 136, 158; reading one's own, 115–18
Single—Again group, 76, 87
Single—Again group meeting, 89–98, 119–23, 142–49, 167–73
Single—Again group, process description, 88–89

Theophrastus, 152
toxic relationships, legacy of, 43–44
trust, 8; based on evidence, 147; impact of parents' divorce on, 33–34; in one's judgment, 19; lack of, 39–40, 41–42, 56, 57, 89, 142; sacredness of, 66–67; in self, 33, 146; violating one's, 157; wanting to, 155

Whitehead, Barbara Defoe, 2
wishful thinking, 17, 62, 95, 128, 132, 152, 163; clouding one's view, 12; and half-truths, 63, 65; overshadowing reality, 145; power of, 63

About the Author

Vera Sonja Maass, PhD, is a licensed clinical psychologist, counselor, and marriage and family therapist in private practice. Dr. Maass has enjoyed adjunct faculty status at local colleges and universities and has conducted several personal growth groups addressing popular psychological topics of interest to the community. She is the author of several books, including *The Cinderella Test: Would You Really Want the Shoe to Fit? Subtle Ways Women Are Seduced and Socialized into Servitude and Stereotypes* and *Lifestyle Changes: A Clinician's Guide to Common Events, Challenges, and Options*.